E

MATTHEW ARNOLD was born at Laleham-on-Thames on Christmas Eve 1822, the eldest son and second of the nine surviving children of the Revd Thomas Arnold and Mary Penrose Arnold. He was educated at Winchester; at Rugby School, where his father was headmaster; and at Oxford. In 1845 he was elected to a fellowship at Oriel College, Oxford, and in 1846–7 spent an extended period of time in France. He started to publish his poetry in the late 1840s and early 1850s. In 1847 he became personal secretary to Lord Lansdowne, a leading Whig politician, through whose influence he was appointed inspector of schools in 1851, which gave him a secure enough position to marry Frances Lucy Wightman. It was a close marriage, and they had six children (three of whom died young), to whom Arnold was devoted. Most of Arnold's poetry was written in the first half of his life, on themes of love, faith and doubt, stoicism and aesthetic pleasure. From the mid-1860s his role as a critic came into prominence. Whilst continuing his job as a school inspector, he published reports on education on the Continent, and began to write regularly for the periodical press. He wrote about the place of literature—and of criticism—in modern society, especially drawing on classical and European writers to highlight qualities which he felt were lacking in contemporary English culture. As Professor of Poetry at Oxford (1857–67) he also delivered four lectures on the study of Celtic literature. His practical and theoretical work on education led him to a wider social criticism, which bore fruit in *Culture and Anarchy*. His lifelong reflection on his own religious experience, on the religious life of the nation, and on the ideas of his father, was to develop from this point into writing on explicitly religious themes. In the later 1870s and 1880s he returned to writing about poetry, and also went on two lecture tours to the United States. In April 1888 he died suddenly of a heart attack in Liverpool.

JANE GARNETT is Fellow and Tutor in Modern History at Wadham College, Oxford. She is a founder member of the editorial board of the *Journal of Victorian Culture*, and from 1994 to 2004 acted as Consultant Editor for Women on the *Oxford Dictionary of National Biography*.

D1149041

C015143487

OXFORD WORLD'S CLASSICS

For over 100 years Oxford World's Classics have brought
readers closer to the world's great literature. Now with over 700
titles—from the 4,000-year-old myths of Mesopotamia to the
twentieth century's greatest novels—the series makes available
lesser-known as well as celebrated writing.

The pocket-sized hardbacks of the early years contained
introductions by Virginia Woolf, T. S. Eliot, Graham Greene,
and other literary figures which enriched the experience of reading.
Today the series is recognized for its fine scholarship and
reliability in texts that span world literature, drama and poetry,
religion, philosophy and politics. Each edition includes perceptive
commentary and essential background information to meet the
changing needs of readers.

OXFORD WORLD'S CLASSICS

MATTHEW ARNOLD

Culture and Anarchy

Edited with an Introduction and Notes by
JANE GARNETT

OXFORD
UNIVERSITY PRESS

OXFORD
UNIVERSITY PRESS

Great Clarendon Street, Oxford OX2 6DP

Oxford University Press is a department of the University of Oxford.
It furthers the University's objective of excellence in research, scholarship,
and education by publishing worldwide in

Oxford New York

Auckland Cape Town Dar es Salaam Hong Kong Karachi
Kuala Lumpur Madrid Melbourne Mexico City Nairobi
New Delhi Shanghai Taipei Toronto

With offices in

Argentina Austria Brazil Chile Czech Republic France Greece
Guatemala Hungary Italy Japan South Korea Poland Portugal
Singapore Switzerland Thailand Turkey Ukraine Vietnam

Oxford is a registered trade mark of Oxford University Press
in the UK and in certain other countries

Published in the United States
by Oxford University Press Inc., New York

Editorial material © Jane Garnett 2006

The moral rights of the author have been asserted
Database right Oxford University Press (maker)

First published as an Oxford World's Classics paperback 2006
Reissued 2009

All rights reserved. No part of this publication may be reproduced,
stored in a retrieval system, or transmitted, in any form or by any means,
without the prior permission in writing of Oxford University Press,
or as expressly permitted by law, or under terms agreed with the appropriate
reprographics rights organization. Enquiries concerning reproduction
outside the scope of the above should be sent to the Rights Department,
Oxford University Press, at the address above

You must not circulate this book in any other binding or cover
and you must impose this same condition on any acquirer

British Library Cataloguing in Publication Data

Data available

Library of Congress Cataloging in Publication Data

Data available

ISBN 978-0-19-953874-4

3

Typeset in Ehrhardt
by RefineCatch Limited, Bungay, Suffolk
Printed in Great Britain by
Clays Ltd, St Ives plc

CONTENTS

CULTURE AND ANARCHY

ABBREVIATIONS

INTRODUCTION

Where there is no vision, the people perish

Proverbs 29: 18

Always place a definite purpose before you

Thomas à Kempis, *The Imitation of Christ*

THESE quotations were copied by Arnold into his notebook for 1867, alongside many of the references used in the essays which became *Culture and Anarchy*.[1] The project of writing the essays was a very serious one for Arnold, who wanted to establish his credibility as a cultural critic of society as a whole, to ensure that his ideas made an impact, and to dispel accusations of dilettantism. He wanted to defend his role as a thinker, rather than a doer (in the political sense), but, in so doing, to promote the idea of culture as an active principle, an approach to life—as the engaged thought without which action was futile. In Arnold's view, people *needed* to think more, and in a more disciplined way. The ideas of *Culture and Anarchy* made an immediate mark—negatively as well as positively—and the terms which Arnold used entered the vocabulary of later Victorian cultural debate. But it was in the twentieth century that the book acquired the status of a classic. The image of Arnold presented by Max Beerbohm in his famous 1904 cartoon is on the face of it a rather different one from that captured in the notebook entries and fits better the notion of him as an intellectual dandy: Arnold stands in a debonair pose, leaning with one leg folded over the other, an elbow on the mantelpiece, a wide grin on his face, whilst a small pigtailed girl looks up at him and says: 'Why, Uncle Matthew, oh why, will not you be always wholly serious?' The girl is his niece, Mary, by this point the famous novelist Mrs Humphry Ward, who had a reputation for lacking a sense of humour. The irony of Beerbohm's cartoon has multiple layers: as well as making play with Mary Ward, it suggests Arnold's reputation for poking fun, whilst in fact the joke at Mary Ward's expense is funnier if one sees Arnold as fundamentally serious. For Beerbohm, reacting against High Victorian earnestness,

---

[1] *Note-Books*: Proverbs text: 43 (1867) and 66 (1868); *Imitation* text: almost every year between 1858 and 1870.

Arnold was in fact a sympathetic figure: it was because he was so highly serious that one enjoyed the outbursts of fun.[2] Whereas to many of Arnold's contemporaries, the tone of his writing was often problematic (as Sir Michael Sadler put it in 1923, he had a 'suppressed impishness which came out as impertinence'[3]), for the post-Victorians this tone either did not matter, or was a positive recommendation by comparison with that of other Victorian critics. T. S. Eliot, writing in 1930, whilst critical of Arnold, thought that the form of his satire made _Culture and Anarchy_ still approachable in a way in which the writing of Thomas Carlyle or John Ruskin (and, indeed, much of the rest of Arnold's own writing) was not.[4]

Eliot was right that the status of _Culture and Anarchy_ as a classic, whilst obviously being due to the continued relevance of the themes which he addressed, was also due to the fact that Arnold was indeed more playful and less 'puritanical' than many of the Victorian critics who tackled the same issues. The unsystematic nature of his thought—the accumulation of vivid dialectical images rather than rigorous argument—made it stimulating and suggestive over a wide range. Meanwhile—ironically—his tendency to associate materialistic narrowness with Nonconformity both echoed and served to reinforce metropolitan and university prejudices to this day. Arnold's essential optimism about the potential for educational progress and his positive view of the role of the State came to resonate in Britain with Welfare State idealism. The first substantive new twentieth-century edition of the text was published in 1932, edited by J. Dover Wilson, Professor of Education at King's College London—an edition which had been reprinted twelve times by 1963, when it was described on the back cover as 'a _living_ classic . . . addressed to the flexible and the disinterested'. In the late twentieth century, in a Western cultural environment which was much less cohesive, Arnold's cultural project was reassessed in the context of

---

[2] _Letters of Max Beerbohm 1892–1956_, ed. R. Hart-Davis (Oxford, 1989), 139–40.

[3] M. Sadler, 'Matthew Arnold', _Nineteenth Century and After_, 93/552 (Feb. and Mar. 1923), 199–207 and 366–77, at 204. Arnold himself used the word 'impertinence' when writing to Gladstone (26 Mar. 1869) about the Preface to _Culture and Anarchy_: 'one or two impertinences about the Liberal policy towards the Irish Church' (_Letters_, iii. 328).

[4] T. S. Eliot, 'Arnold and Pater' [1930], _Selected Essays_ (2nd edn., London, 1934), 393–405, at 394–5. A review of _Culture and Anarchy_ in the _Spectator_ for 6 Mar. 1869 already described Carlyle as a prophet of a rugged sort, and Arnold as more modern and milder (p. 243).

multiculturalism, of postmodern challenges to concepts of tradition, and of radically different views of the State. There were two new popular editions of *Culture and Anarchy* in the 1990s, which reflected on these challenges.[5] Even in the relatively short time since then, however, the interpretative context for the reader of these essays has in some respects shifted again.

Although Arnold was developing trains of thought already established in his writings on education, on the role of criticism, and on the study of Celtic literature, the *Culture and Anarchy* essays also marked the beginning of something new. They initiated a series of substantive engagements in the 1860s and 1870s with the inter-relationship between religion and culture, and between individual and social purpose in this context: *Culture and Anarchy* was followed by *St Paul and Protestantism* (1870) and by *Literature and Dogma* (1873). Many of the questions which Arnold posed in these three major works have had an ongoing resonance with critics confronting analogous tensions between pluralism and integration. In the nineteenth century, debate about religious purpose was fundamental to the moral definition of society and the State in ways in which it is not in the early twenty-first century. Yet in the most recent decade religion has come back to the heart of the political and cultural agenda in both global and national contexts. Competing religious visions of the world and of the individual's role in it have a renewed significance. New questions are being raised about religious education, about the relationship of religious identity to a sense of citizenship, about the relationship between multiculturalism and liberalism, about the challenges of cross-cultural understanding. All these were issues with which Arnold (and others) wrestled a century and a half ago—in terms which, of course, were particular to the time. The Book of Proverbs and the *Imitation of Christ* were read in particular ways, and this introduction elaborates the contemporary context in which Arnold developed his ideas, and the controversy which he aroused. In doing so, and in giving some sense of the vibrancy of debate at the time, it also hopes to demonstrate that *Culture and Anarchy* is no less 'living' a text than it was in the

---

[5] M. Arnold, *Culture and Anarchy and Other Writings*, ed. S. Collini (Cambridge, 1993), in a series of texts in political thought; *Culture and Anarchy*, ed. S. Lipman (Yale, 1994), with essays by Maurice Cowling, Gerald Graff, Samuel Lipman, and Steven Marcus, in a series called 'Re-Thinking the Western Tradition'.

1960s (or the 1860s)—that it has the flexibility to speak to a new set of preoccupations.

Arnold's Life as a Critic

Arnold began his creative life as a poet, and, whilst the poetic inspiration had left him by the mid-1860s, he never lost a poet's way of reading and reflecting. He was stimulated by felicitous language, by the epigrammatic, by lines of poetry which connected different ideas, or a few sentences of a book or article, rather than by the whole of an argument. Although he was anxious about his reading, wrote lists of books which he intended to read carefully, and disciplined himself by reading the New Testament in Greek, this was always in tension with a more impulsive intellect. The poet in him yearned for unity and universality, yet as a poet, even as a critic, he had focused on the forces which pulled in different directions—doubt and faith, renunciation and self-indulgence, loss and reconciliation. He recognized that he was living in a period where old certainties were under attack—the Sea of Faith was withdrawing, as he famously put it in his poem 'Dover Beach'—and he addressed the ways in which his contemporaries needed to sharpen up both their intellectual and their imaginative apprehension of the competing tensions which needed to be harmonized. Although in many ways the trajectory of Arnold's early life—his rather idle time as an undergraduate at Oxford, his stay in Paris in 1846–7 going to the theatre and meeting George Sand, the writing of romantic poetry—made him seem a rebellious son of Thomas Arnold, the headmaster of Rugby School, so renowned for his religious high-mindedness, in fact he remained very much the son of his father. The seriousness of religion, and the importance of finding new ways of talking about it in an age of scientific and philosophical challenges to its credibility, were fundamental stimuli to Arnold's thought and writing. His exposure at Oxford in the early 1840s to the conflict between parties within the Anglican Church reinforced in him a lifelong conviction inherited from his father of the destructiveness of privileging doctrinal differences over fundamental unities. At the same time he could see the attraction of the spiritual and devotional revival represented by the Oxford Movement led by his godfather, John Keble, by John Henry Newman and Edward Bouverie Pusey, and he recognized the force of its opposition to philosophical and religious liberalism in ways which his father could not acknowledge. He also began to read more eclectically in religious writings from different traditions—Catholic, Jewish, Hindu, and Buddhist. From 1851, when he started his career as a school inspector, inspecting Nonconformist schools around the country, his own life became an exercise in creative tension—as he divided his time between his job (and his reflections on what it taught him) and his critical writing which gave him a wider canvas on which to draw. Oscillation between these two poles heightened the contrasts which he was increasingly to point between different ways of understanding and living religious experience—the narrow and the more expansive—and shaped his own social philosophy.

The 1860s presented a range of challenges to Arnold. He was increasingly preoccupied with his own mortality (from the late 1840s he knew that he had inherited the heart defect which had killed his father at the age of 47): his notebooks are full of texts (over a range from the Bible to George Sand to Tao to Confucius) relating to the proper use of time, to self-renunciation and self-control, to the need to establish a purpose and to achieve it. He worried about the time spent on mundane tasks as a school inspector, about his literary work, and about how best to make a mark and have a tangible social and moral influence. When he was not appointed as one of the commissioners on the education commission which was to prepare for the 1870 Education Bill, he justified it to himself by arguing that it was better for him 'to act upon the public mind till it is willing to employ the means that are really required, rather than to labour at doing what can be done with the imperfect means it is at present prepared to concede'.[6] In 1867 he copied in his notebook Wordsworth's hope that his poems would 'co-operate with the benign tendencies in human nature and society, and . . . in their degree, be efficacious in making men wiser, better and happier'. This was shortly followed by a passage which found its way (in a modified form) into *Culture and Anarchy*:

It cannot but weigh heavily on a tender conscience to be accused in a practical nation like ours, of keeping aloof from the life and work of so many care-threatened men, and of merely toying with poetry and literature. So it is with no little satisfaction that I find myself in the

[6] *Letters*, iii. 352 (18 June 1869).

position of one who has made a contribution in and of the practical
necessities of our times. The great thing, it will be observed, is to find our
best self.[7]

This search for an intellectual role was already the context in which
he had framed his essay on 'The Function of Criticism at the Present
Time' (1864). There he had set out the need for disinterested criticism—the free play of mind on all subjects. Only if this were
achieved could the English be shaken out of their self-satisfaction,
and be guided towards perfection.[8]

Contemporary English society offered Arnold much evidence of
the need for criticism, and he emulated Thomas Carlyle in identifying the 'signs of the times'.[9] Britain in the 1860s was at the height of
its industrial and commercial pre-eminence, and the middle-class
political community which had been enfranchised by the 1832
Reform Act (which itself had followed the political emancipation of
Protestant Nonconformists and Roman Catholics in 1828 and 1829)
was comfortably established. There was abundant scope for carrying
self-confidence to the point of smugness, and Arnold was not the
only critic to identify in middle-class complacency and hypocrisy
about values the chief problem of modern society. His concept of
Philistinism, borrowed from the German critic Heine, captured this
double sense of complacency and hypocrisy. Because the pursuit
of wealth on free trade principles in Britain had been ratified by
religious and moral language, and Britain's Protestantism was
widely held to be intrinsic to her economic success, it seemed the
more difficult to spot the potential contradictions and confusions
about the relationship between means and ends. Social and spiritual anarchy could go hand in hand, as the language of radical individualism—of 'doing as one likes'—spread promiscuously through
economic, political, and religious debate. Arnold's plea for a general,
rather than specialized, cultural criticism was in part to heighten
people's consciousness to such seepages of language. Carlyle and
Matthew's father Thomas Arnold had identified the same tendencies

---

[7] *Note-Books*, 63–4.
[8] 'The Function of Criticism at the Present Time' [*National Review*, Nov. 1864],
Essays in Criticism, First Series, Super, iii. 270–1.
[9] Thomas Carlyle wrote his famous essay, 'Signs of the Times', in 1829 (*Edinburgh
Review* 49; repr. in *Critical and Miscellaneous Essays*, 5 vols. (1899 edn.), ii. 56–82).

in the 1820s and 1830s,[10] and they seemed all the more entrenched by the 1860s.

To Arnold the problems were more fundamental than those recognized by suffrage and other institutional reformers: they lay with the very meaning of citizenship and civil society, and hence with the religious basis for that society. Like many other mid-Victorian liberal thinkers at the time of debates over parliamentary reform in 1866–7, Arnold was concerned about arguments for the extension of the franchise on the basis of abstract theories of rights and liberties, which paid insufficient attention to the duties and obligations of citizenship; and also about the potential incompatibilities between the demands of wealth, intellectual capacity, and force of numbers. Moreover, an inadequate conception of the State was evidenced for Arnold in the lack of government response to the civil disobedience of the Hyde Park reform demonstrators in 1866: to him the State did not have confidence in its capacity to embody the corporate will of the nation. Debates about the degree to which the State could constitute a centre of moral authority were sharpened by the tension between the continued privileges of the Anglican Establishment and the strength of Nonconformity, especially in areas of commercial and industrial expansion. The resistance of Nonconformists to extension of State control over education was one symptom of this, which caused Arnold particular frustration. Here Arnold thought comparatively about England in relation to France, Germany, and America, and reflected on what he saw as excessive suspicion of the State (related to a woefully narrow conception of it) in England, held in conjunction with an excessive devotion to the principles of laissez-faire political economy. America, which seemed in many respects a more developed case of rampant individualism, remained for Arnold a negative point of reference. He also thought about the constituents of national spirit, and here the relationship between England, Wales, Scotland, and Ireland within a British culture came into play. This process of reflection was sharpened by contemporary events: the impact of the famine in Ireland in the 1840s and ongoing debate about English attitudes to Ireland; the rise of more militant Irish nationalism; and the Liberal Prime Minister

[10] Carlyle, *Past and Present* (1843); Thomas Arnold set up *The Englishman's Register* in 1831 as a vehicle for Christianizing feelings on political and economic matters; cf. his *Letters to the Hertford Reformer* (1839–41).

Gladstone's promotion of the disestablishment of the Church of Ireland in 1868–9. Arnold used the example of Ireland to expose the inconsistencies of English liberal nostrums, which on the one hand were held to apply to the English and not to the Irish, and which by the same token might, in his view, be less beneficial than they were assumed to be to the English (e.g. *Culture and Anarchy*, p. 59).

Having identified the current potential for both social and spiritual anarchy, Arnold raised questions about social and moral integration and the development of a good community. The problems were those of the integration of plural cultures—of preventing these cultures being introverted and exclusive, whilst enabling their positive energy to contribute to the common good. The critical categories which he developed were dialectical: the tension between the ordinary self and the best self; strictness of conscience versus spontaneity of consciousness; right acting versus right thinking. These were aspects of the overarching critical opposition which he developed in *Culture and Anarchy*: that between Hebraism and Hellenism. These terms carried different connotations at different parts of the argument; each tendency in theory carried the same aim of perfection, and, if held in a proper balance, they would contribute together to that ultimate goal. Yet, insofar as Hebraism incorporated the tendency to sacrifice all other sides of our nature to the religious side (which for Arnold could—and did—have the effect of producing a narrowed and distorted conception of religion itself), whereas Hellenism suggested the application of the clear light of the critical and expansive intellect, the balance of desirability was loaded in favour of Hellenism. Arnold's response to criticism that he underplayed the positive social contribution of 'Hebraistic' religious energy was to say that there was no danger in the Britain of his day that this would be underestimated: all the dangers were on the other side. The challenge which Arnold set himself in *Culture and Anarchy* was to see to what extent this opposition, with its sub-forms, could provide general critical principles or explanatory frameworks. Could it offer suggestive ways of thinking about other contemporary critical oppositions, where the balance of esteem seemed equally overloaded in one direction, threatening a more profound and culturally satisfactory unity? Could it be mapped on to the dialectical relationships between Saxon and Celt, English and European, Anglican and Nonconformist, Protestant and Catholic, political economist and cultural critic, and suggest any scope for achieving a higher degree of harmony?

Culture and Anarchy

'Culture and its Enemies'—the last of Arnold's lectures as Professor of Poetry in Oxford (delivered on 7 June 1867)—was intended to define culture as an active principle of engagement, in opposition to the refined literary escapism with which he had been taxed by critics of his earlier writings.[11] He picked up on themes which he had developed in his lecture 'On the Function of Criticism at the Present Time' (1864), where he had accused his countrymen of being too practical, too disinclined to the theoretical, too ready to apply their critical faculties solely in sectarian disputes, assertions which had brought down on him the criticism of being detached and fastidious. However, much of the criticism to which the lecture was intended to respond was repeated when it was published as an article in the *Cornhill Magazine* in July 1867, and it was the ongoing reflection on the debate caused which led to Arnold's writing of the subsequent essays over 1867–8.[12] 'Culture and its Enemies', which became the first chapter of *Culture and Anarchy* when it was published in book form in 1869, was the most ambitious and the most slippery of the articles. Subsequent articles addressed particular aspects of the themes set up, and tried to ground them in relation to the most significant critiques. Arnold reverted frequently to the need to demonstrate the essential practicality of his concept of culture, particularly at the beginning of chapters (especially Chs. 1, 3, and 6), where he emphasized that his critical flexibility, far from being detached, was fundamental to making culture a practical force. Culture was defined first as an internal condition, but was developed as a principle of action which should inform an enhanced conception of the State (Ch. 2). The concept of the best self which was the fruit of cultivation was intended always to stand as an ideal, a critical tool with which to transcend the pull of class or sectional interest (Chs. 3,

[11] Esp. Fitzjames Stephen, 'Matthew Arnold and his Countrymen', *Saturday Review* (3 Dec. 1864), 683–5.

[12] e.g. F. Harrison, 'Culture; A Dialogue', *Fortnightly Review*, 11 (Nov. 1867), 603–14; H. Sidgwick, 'The Prophet of Culture', *Macmillan's Magazine*, 16 (1867), 271–80. Sidgwick's full article is reprinted in the Appendix to this edition, pp. 157–72; for a full list of responses, see S. Coulling, *Matthew Arnold and his Critics: A Study of Arnold's Controversies* (Athens, Ohio, 1974).

5, and 6). The complex interplay between references to positions taken up in unfolding political debate and references to scriptural or other religious (as well as classical) texts represents Arnold's attempt to confound both critics of his detachment from present concerns and those who attacked his religious credentials. At the same time, he could use the juxtapositions to suggest the superficiality of much political debate, and the need for a richer cultural ideal to live by.

Arnold began to write the Preface to *Culture and Anarchy* on the Sunday which was the last day of his son Tommy's life (22 November 1868). 'I remember turning round from the table where I was writing to look at him dozing . . . I have not touched the preface since— there was some persiflage in what I had written and I could not go on in that strain; now I must see how the thing is to be turned.' On the day of Tommy's death he wrote a text from the devotional works of the eighteenth-century Bishop Wilson in his diary, and the following day found a complementary text from the *Imitation of Christ*. On 24 December (his own birthday, when he was within one year of the age at which his father had died), he wrote to his mother. He told her that the biblical chapter for the day of Tommy's death was the first chapter of Isaiah; the first Sunday after was Advent Sunday 'with its glorious collect', and in its epistle the passage which converted St Augustine: as he put it, 'All these things point to a new beginning.'[13] In this context, the immediate focus at the beginning of the Preface to *Culture and Anarchy* on Bishop Wilson by comparison with the *Imitation of Christ* takes on a particular significance. Arnold emphasized both that Wilson should be widely read, 'with a direct aim at practice', and that, whilst the type of religion exhibited was a high ideal to be aimed at, 'being English, it [was] possible and attainable' for English readers (p. 5). Arnold's own devotional reading of Wilson was to provide key structural elements of *Culture and Anarchy*, and the priority given to devotional reading set up a model for the right relationship between reading, reflection, and practice.

Bishop Wilson's motto 'To make reason and the will of God prevail!' forms the centrepiece of 'Culture and its Enemies', and was intended to provide a principle of coherence, but the precise relationship between right reason and the will of God remained suggestive and ambiguous. In rooting culture in the study of perfection—the

---

[13] *Letters*, iii. 303, 293–94, 305.

moral and social passion for doing good—Arnold emphasized that it
required effort first to work out what was God's will and then to
produce the sustained commitment to making it prevail. Arnold cut
(whether before or after the lecture was given is not clear) a long
passage developing the pertinence to his idea of culture of Wilson's
discussion of curiosity, an important contested term in establishing
the moral force of culture. Wilson had defined appropriate and
necessary curiosity, warning against the pursuit of light for the
wrong ends—for idle curiosity or vanity—but also arguing against
the neglect of knowledge and instruction. Religion must not lose
sight of the thought and reason which are necessary in order to guide
emotion and affection and to give them their true object. For Arnold
this conception of religion and of the role of curiosity in the proper
pursuit of its goals had a fundamental significance: this was an ideal
of religion which was open and critical, as opposed to the view of
religion as a narrow self-justifying system—religion as it was 'generally conceived by us' (p. 36). By cutting his elaboration of Wilson's
point, Arnold improved the flow of the lecture, but left more ambiguity in his conception of the relationship between an ideal religion
and an ideal culture. Arnold also recast two passages dealing with the
relationship between religion and culture, one of which came close
to anticipating *Literature and Dogma* in identifying the highest form
of religion with poetry.[14] He was left with some revealingly con-
voluted sentences in which he was trying to relate (essentially
by association) religion, morality, history, philosophy, and poetry
(pp. 35–6). The initial emphasis in the lecture was on culture—
sometimes by analogy with, sometimes in necessary conjunction
with, the right sort of religion—as an active and reflective *process*:
'Not a having and a resting, but a growing and a becoming' (p. 36).[15]
This provided a dynamic which was general, and not just individual.
In fact the individual, starting from within, needed to work towards
a perfection which was collective. Drawing heavily on Carlyle,
Arnold drew out the role of this conception of culture in confronting
the narrowness, inflexibility, and individualism of modern mechanical civilization. By distinguishing between means and ends, and
challenging conventional materialistic criteria of progress, culture

[14] 'Culture and its Enemies', MS Balliol College, Oxford; S. Coulling, 'The
Manuscript of "Culture and its Enemies"', *Nineteenth-Century Prose*, 21 (1994), 11.
[15] This point was picked up by Frederic Harrison in 'Culture; A Dialogue', 607–8.

established a route towards perfection. However, when he introduced the phrase 'sweetness and light', representing beauty and intelligence, to gloss his concept of perfection, Arnold shifted his ground towards the Greek ideal of religion and poetry as a common force. He opposed this concept of culture to the 'Puritan' religion, which he held to underpin a more general middle-class Philistinism. This opposition thus anticipated the opposition later developed between Hellenism and Hebraism, and signalled that the critical terms were already loaded in favour of Hellenism, and that religion, which was meant to embrace elements of each approach, risked being relegated entirely to Hebraism, as some critics felt that Arnold was doing.

For Henry Sidgwick, a philosopher himself grappling with the relationship between religious belief and the moral basis of society, Arnold's argument was unsatisfactory because it was overambitious, and at the same time vague and perverse. In the most perceptive and compelling of the critiques of Arnold's lecture,[16] Sidgwick criticized Arnold's imprecision in the definition of terms. He argued that Arnold was unclear about whether he was discussing culture as something actual or ideal, and that he did not confront what Sidgwick took to be an essential (and potentially creative) tension between self-development, which was the characteristic of culture, and self-sacrifice, which characterized religion. Associating Arnold with Hegel (whose philosophy was based on the synthesis of dialectical oppositions), Sidgwick wondered whether he intended to point to the reconciliation of antagonisms, but observed that they would need each to be probed to a much more profound depth for this to be achieved. Sidgwick's own dialectical opposition between culture and religion became that between 'sweetness and light' and 'fire and strength'. To Sidgwick the present world needed all the self-sacrifice which fire and strength could inspire (and religious energy could not be borrowed), whilst ultimately the two qualities stood as two sides of a magical shield[17]—each leading to perfection of results, but shining with different principles. Sidgwick argued for culture—for sweetness and light—as a breadth of sympathetic understanding, and on this criterion found Arnold's conception both of religion and of culture limited by his scorn for Philistinism and the 'dissidence of

---

[16] See above, n. 14.

[17] It is not clear whether Sidgwick had in mind the shield of Achilles or of Aeneas, Perseus' shield of wisdom, or an amalgam of classical and Christian allusions.

Dissent'. By the very title of his essay—'The Prophet of Culture'—and his reference to the critic James Macdonell's description of Arnold as an 'elegant Jeremiah',[18] Sidgwick reinforced the impression that Arnoldian culture was excessively detached. By appearing to deprecate enthusiasm, it risked a Kantian disinterestedness of aesthetic response, which would undermine the active, life-changing role for culture which Arnold himself envisaged. Arnold's own model of disinterestedness was in fact intended to be a much wider social and moral principle.

Sidgwick's exposure of the unexamined tensions in Arnold's lecture still resonates: the confrontation between self-development and self-sacrifice remains a central ethical problem. In 1871 Arnold's friend the Scottish literary critic J. C. Shairp was also to pick up on the different senses in which Arnold used the term 'religion', and to state that religion was either an end in itself or it was not. It could not serve its function of inspiring self-sacrifice if simply used instrumentally.[19] Arnold had recognized the force of this, and indeed in places in the later articles or in the Preface he had made a point of recognizing the significance of the different histories which different religious groups had experienced in giving energy to their convictions, and of acknowledging the important contribution of Hebraism. His main retaliation to Sidgwick was to refer to the Zeitgeist: that different periods presented different cultural challenges, and that England in the second half of the nineteenth century needed sweetness and light more than it needed fire and strength. Referring to Sidgwick's critique in a letter to his mother in August 1867, and comparing his own project to his father's, Arnold used telling words: that an enlargement of the idea of religion, and a 'bringing into it of a number of other things which the old narrow religionists thought had nothing to do with it—is the great want of our spiritual intellectual life in England at present'.[20] To Arnold's eye, religion itself needed sweetness and light, otherwise it would lose its force—its capacity for fire and strength.

Arnold caused offence to Nonconformists because he associated them with narrow religion and an impoverished cultural outlook, and the tone in the Preface with which he introduced the notion of

---

[18] [J. Macdonell] in the *Daily Telegraph*, 8 Sept. 1866, 4–5.
[19] J. C. Shairp, *Culture and Religion* (London, 1871), 276.
[20] *Letters*, iii. 166.

doing them good and leading them to perfection through incorporation into a core culture was extremely patronizing. He retained a blind spot about Nonconformity which nothing would shift; indeed he claimed superior knowledge because of his job inspecting Nonconformist elementary schools. Multiple ironies resulted. The manual of Buddhism from which he noted definitions of karma in his notebooks had been written by a Wesleyan missionary.[21] His identification of the MP Thomas Bazley with the mean of the middle-class Philistine was unfair and at odds both with Bazley's Anglicanism and with his commitment to a wide range of cultural and educational projects in Manchester.[22] When Arnold pointed to the growth of commercial immorality and suggested the ease with which this could sit alongside 'Puritan' professions of faith (p. 117), he ignored the complex self-critical literature of Christian economic ethics which both Nonconformists and Anglicans were producing to confront pressing issues of moral and social responsibility in the commercial communities in which they were concentrated.[23] He complained about the sectarianism of journals leading to cultural atomism, whilst it was evident, not least from their engagement with his own writing, that Nonconformists *were* integrated into periodical debate, if not into other aspects of institutional culture still dominated by Anglicans. Most fundamentally of all, in using their political campaigns to suggest that Nonconformists were privileging matters of unimportant machinery over wider intellectual and spiritual goals, he underestimated the degree to which things look very different to those coming from a position of cultural marginalization. As the Congregationalist Henry Allon observed tartly in his review of *Culture and Anarchy* and *St Paul and Protestantism*, of course Nonconformists were lacking in Arnold's particular version of sweetness and light: they had been excluded from Oxford and Cambridge.[24] In this respect Arnold's blindness to his own lack of disinterestedness, and his easy assumption of cultural superiority are object lessons which remain for any proponents of hegemonic culture. Sidgwick's

[21] R. Spence Hardy, *A Manual of Buddhism* (London, 1860).

[22] For Bazley, see Explanatory Notes: note to p. 67.

[23] See e.g. J. Garnett, 'Nonconformists, Economic Ethics and the Consumer Society in Mid-Victorian Britain', in J. Shaw and A. Kreider (eds.), *Culture and the Nonconformist Tradition* (Cardiff, 1999), 95–116.

[24] [H. Allon], 'Mr Matthew Arnold and Puritanism', *British Quarterly Review*, 52/103 (1870), 170–99, at 194.

plea for sympathy to understand what drives different groups in society and to take them seriously retains its force.

Matthew Arnold increasingly saw himself as developing his father's work (and this not just when writing to his mother). Thomas Arnold's ideal type of an inclusive Church and State functioning like the Athenian polis in cultivating a committed citizenship serving the common good lies behind *Culture and Anarchy*. So, too, does Coleridge's conviction that civilization needed to be grounded in cultivation, and his articulation of the role of the clerisy (a religious and intellectual elite) in developing that cultivation within the nation (which inspired Matthew Arnold's idea of the 'aliens' who are led to transcend their class and sectional interests through the love of human perfection).[25] Both Thomas Arnold and Coleridge were writing in the early 1830s to provide rationales for the role of the Anglican Church in a religious and political environment which was newly pluralistic. Both wanted to do so on terms which were neither utilitarian nor rooted in an appeal to ecclesiastical authority (or vested interest). Both produced ideal types rather than defences of the Anglican status quo. In all these respects Matthew Arnold was their heir. The second chapter of *Culture and Anarchy* focused on this aspect of the argument, and, by distinguishing between the ordinary self and the best self, provided an ideal conception of the State transcending class and reinforcing the idea of the whole community. The idea remained vague, but the central focus on the cultural role of the State and of a creative relationship between its historical and its ideal reality contributed to the tradition of Liberal Anglican political thought which extended well into the twentieth century and inspired theorists of the Welfare State such as William Temple.[26]

Matthew Arnold also absorbed from Thomas Arnold and Coleridge a wider intellectual approach—a reaction against utilitarianism, and against reason defined in terms of narrow rationalism. In these respects, *Culture and Anarchy* was infused with a religious breadth of outlook, which was developed into *St Paul and Protestantism* and *Literature and Dogma*. Coleridge had developed a radical

---

[25] S. T. Coleridge, *On the Constitution of the Church and State* (1830; London, 1972 edn.); T. Arnold, *Principles of Church Reform* (1833; London, 1962 edn.).

[26] M. Grimley, *Citizenship, Community, and the Church of England: Liberal Anglican Theories of the State between the Wars* (Oxford, 2004).

approach to reading the Bible in a non-literal way: arguing that its discursive nature enabled it to live through symbols and poetry which resonated historically through generations of readers, each of which brought their own understanding to it.[27] Thomas Arnold had discussed history in ways which prefigured his son's approach to the Bible: that knowledge of the past was vital but should not be confined to the past. He set composition exercises which took the form of conversations between people of different epochs—for example, the medieval theologian Thomas Aquinas, the hero of the Industrial Revolution James Watt, and the historical novelist Walter Scott. He argued that ancient writers should not be described as ancient, because in fact they were virtually our contemporaries and our countrymen, with the advantage enjoyed by the intelligent traveller of being able to point out through our reading of them what we could not otherwise see for ourselves.[28] Matthew Arnold asserted this as a literary principle, and developed it into the proposition that nobody who did not know more than the Bible could really even know the Bible (*Culture and Anarchy*, pp. 113, 107). He commended his father for his European outlook, and stressed the importance of reflection on foreign thought as a check on a parochialism and narrowness to which the English were particularly prone.[29] Here culture, in the sense of knowing the best that has been thought and known in the world, became also a way of reading—of reading with a purpose. Reading the Bible 'with right tact and justness of judgement' was the ultimate test of this reading with a purpose, and underpinned the fundamental link between culture and conduct.[30] The Zeitgeist again came into play: intellectual challenges to traditional grounds of belief demanded a recasting of religion and the development of a new justification for reading the Bible: 'at the present moment two things about the Christian religion must surely be clear to anyone with eyes in his head. One is that men cannot do without it; the

---

[27] M. J. Lloyd, 'The Historical Thought of S. T. Coleridge: The Later Prose Works', unpublished University of Oxford D.Phil., 1998, 197.

[28] J. Fitch, *Thomas and Matthew Arnold and their Influence on English Education* (London, 1897), 37–8; D. Forbes, *The Liberal Anglican Idea of History* (Cambridge, 1952), 87.

[29] *Letters*, iii. 317: 'owing to his historical sense, [Thomas Arnold] was so wonderfully, for his nation time and profession, *European*, and thus so got himself out of the narrow medium in which after all, his English friends lived'; M. Arnold, 'The Function of Criticism at the Present Time', Super, iii. 258–85, at 284–5.

[30] M. Arnold, *Literature and Dogma*, Super, vi. 152–3, 162.

other, that they cannot do with it as it is'.[31] This necessitated, for Arnold, the abandonment of the transcendental and miraculous, and the reliance on the experiential and poetic nature of the biblical tradition. This move was to give him a place in the development of Liberal Protestantism in the twentieth century, when his approach to the Bible seemed illuminating in constructing new Christian apologetics.[32]

Arnold's dialectic between an expansive incorporative Hellenism and a rigorous Hebraism could both capture a suggestive ideal, and at the same time threaten, in its actual form and practice, to cause a rift between right thought and right action—to become a distinction between abstract critical reflection and grounded sectarian fetishism. In the same way the poetic understanding of the Bible could threaten to become relativistic or purely aesthetic.[33] Arnold's rather breezily expressed assertion that the fundamental thing for Christians was not the miracle of the incarnation but the imitation of Christ posed a real theological challenge.[34] The Catholic modernist theologian George Tyrrell felt the dilemma sharply. He was troubled by Arnold's abandonment of dogma, feeling that 'what [Arnold] hoped for was, roughly speaking, the preservation of the ancient and beautiful husk after the kernel had been withered up and discarded'.[35] At the same time, he recognized the creative potential of Arnold's concept of culture in turning a 'stream of fresh and free thought' upon stock notions and habits in the Catholic Church of Tyrrell's day. The tension between these two positions—which relates back to the questions posed by Sidgwick—was and is a profound one, and it sits at the heart of Arnold's conception of culture. Arnold was well aware that unity should not imply uniformity, but at times his concern with redressing overemphases on one side of the equation did

[31] *God and the Bible*, Super, vii. 378.

[32] J. C. Livingston, *Matthew Arnold and Christianity: His Religious Prose Writings* (Columbia, SC, 1986).

[33] L. Stephen, 'Mr Matthew Arnold and the Church of England', *Fraser's Magazine* N.S. 2 (1870); F. H. Bradley, *Ethical Studies* (London, 1876); C. C. J. Webb, 'Morality and Religion', *A Century of Anglican Theology and Other Lectures* (Oxford, 1923), 55–101.

[34] M. Arnold, Preface to Popular Edition of *Literature and Dogma* (1883), Super, vi. 146.

[35] G. Tyrrell, 'Coventry Patmore', *The Month*, 96 (Dec. 1900), 561–73, at p. 573, cited in N. Sagovsky, *Between Two Worlds: George Tyrrell's Relationship to the Thought of Matthew Arnold* (Cambridge, 1983), 25–6.

lay him open to Tyrrell's and Sidgwick's criticism. Moreover, the
stances which he took were not consistent. But it is partly in this
inconsistency, and in the gaps between the parallels which he draws,
that creative thought is inspired. In reading him now, there is a
stimulus in reflecting on the ways in which he sets out analogous
dialectics which pivot around this axis of pluralism and integration.

Arnold did have great confidence in the capacity of his critical
principle to be creative and sustaining, and not to have a corrosive
effect on traditions. Rather than moving to a pluralistic or relativistic
position, his goal was always to maintain a principle of unity. At the
same time he wanted to distinguish his position from latitudinarianism (*Culture and Anarchy*, p. 18). He wanted to acknowledge cultural
diversity and to harness its critical power, but always within a cultural whole. When discussing Celtic literature, he said: 'I don't want
to find myself everywhere.'[36] But in fact the way in which he read,
identifying common themes across cultures which could reinforce
the validity of his own cultural and religious tradition, risked his
doing just that. Complex critical manoeuvres were involved in drawing on the best which has been known and thought in the world. He
himself was very attracted by Catholic spirituality, and by the idea of
Catholicism as a cosmopolitan, European, and imaginative religious
tradition, by contrast with the provincial and prosaic nature of
Protestantism. This was part of what attracted him to John Henry
Newman. He thought that if the Catholic Church could be liberal-
ized, whilst retaining its old usages, it would then long outlast
Protestantism.[37] Yet he adhered to his father's conviction that
Catholics could not be a part of the ideal type of the nation, in part
because of that very cosmopolitanism and allegiance to a non-
English establishment.[38] Celtic influences, on the other hand, should
be brought into the nation, but in a strictly literary form: the Welsh
could not resist the Saxon in the world of fact and brute force, and
for business the Welsh needed to learn English, but an appreciation
of the Welsh language as a historical form would provide an injection
of spiritual—indeed, 'Greek'—power into English culture.[39] This
incorporative strategy, which sought to preserve a historical culture

---

[36] M. Arnold, *On the Study of Celtic Literature*, Super, iii. 297–8.
[37] *Letters*, iv. 162–4; 199.
[38] M. Arnold, 'Puritanism and the Church of England', Super, vi. 107.
[39] M. Arnold, *On the Study of Celtic Literature*, Super, iii. 296–7; 328, 344.

within and on the terms of the hegemonic English whole, was none the less rooted in a real sympathy for Welsh culture, and a sense that it had maintained a creative continuity with the past which the Saxons had lost. The proposition that it could not deal with the world of modern business of course in one sense consigned it to a romantic remnant—a beautiful husk—but as a critical principle moved it to the fore in the role of confronting the impoverished values which underpinned capitalist modernity. Arnold's broader reflections on Indo-Germanic cultures, in relation to Semitic culture, also picked up on this theme. In this comparison, England owed more of its cultural force to the 'delicate and apprehensive genius of the Indo-Germanic [i.e. 'Hellenic'] race', although real strength had come also from the Hebrew inheritance. Arnold saw as Indo-European the English power of imaginatively acknowledging 'the multiform aspects of the problem of life, and of thus getting itself unfixed from its own over-certainty, of smiling at its own over-tenacity' (*Culture and Anarchy*, p. 105). In reinforcing his own role as cultural critic, engaging with the over-certainties of a hegemonic laissez-faire political economy, he put himself in this cosmopolitan mainstream. The fact that this was counter-cultural to dominant English values which were usually gendered masculine, and that the approbatory terms which he used carried feminine connotations by contrast to the 'muscularity' of Hebraism, in part accounts for the criticism which saw his culture as effete and over-refined (*Culture and Anarchy*, pp. 54, 127). Social criticism in the Victorian period was often gendered, and here Arnold's attraction to the Catholic and to the Celt, as well as to the Indo-European and the Hellenic, drew him cumulatively to highlight the cultural importance of qualities gendered feminine. It is striking that he reverts to the charge of effeminacy in the penultimate sentence of his conclusion, only to turn it on its head and argue for the power of the '[d]ocile echoes of the eternal voice' (p. 155).

Late Victorian culture was complex and self-reflexive. Those who read Arnold came from different critical vantage points, especially in relation to the boundaries between core and periphery and to the relative merits of ideals of unity and ideals of pluralism. Yet there was an overarching concern to find cultural coherence and to reaffirm principles of order. For some these could only be drawn from a reinforcement of dogmatic authority, whether religious or political. For others the answer lay in a more flexible accommodation of

difference. Arnold's cultural criticism fell in both camps: it had its
cultural dogmatisms, although it rejected the rigidity of systems. His
style was intended to challenge from different angles. As he said in
December 1867,

I see more and more what an effective weapon, in a confused, loud-
talking, clap-trappy country like this, where every writer and speaker to
the public tends to say rather more than he means, is *irony*, or according to
the strict meaning of the original Greek word, the saying rather less than
one means. The main effect I have had on the mass of noisy claptrap and
inert prejudice which chokes us has been, I can see, by the use of this
weapon; and now, when people's minds are getting widely disturbed and
they are beginning to ask themselves whether they have not a great deal
that is new to learn, to increase this feeling in them irony is more useful
than ever.[40]

Irony fixed on areas of contemporary over-certainty for its targets,
and in this sense there were inevitable imbalances of emphasis.
Believing that English resistance to enhancing the authority of the
State was so strong that there was no danger of a lurch the other
way, he laid himself open to the charge of giving the State too great
(and open-ended) a cultural role. But he was speaking to a cultural
world which still did have a great deal of common ground and common assumptions. The debate which was sparked off by Sir John
Lubbock's address to the Working Men's College in 1886 giving a
list of a hundred best books for working men to read, whilst producing a variety of comments and alternative choices, resonated with
Arnold's own reading practice and ideas about the importance of the
discipline of reading seriously.[41]

In a New Year's Day letter to his sister in 1882, Arnold described
reading the best that had been written as living in the best company,
and reflected gloomily on whether it was doomed as a practice: 'if I
live to be 80 I shall probably be the only person left in England who
reads anything but newspapers and scientific publications'.[42] In the
early twenty-first century we live in a cultural world on the one
hand highly specialized and professionalized (a culture of 'scientific'

---

[40] *Letters*, iii. 196.

[41] *The Best Hundred Books: Containing an Article on the Choice of Books by Mr John
Ruskin, a Hitherto Unpublished Letter by Thomas Carlyle and Contributions by Many
Others* (London, Pall Mall Gazette Office, 1886).

[42] *Note-Books*, pp. x–xi; cf. *Letters*, v. 182.

publications in Arnold's terms), on the other bombarded with trivia
and anecdote in newspapers and other ephemeral media. The notion
of the 'best' is relativized, there are fewer centres of authority, and
yet the terminology of principles of action and of criteria of merit is
still used. Arnold's thought finds new relevance here.

Culture and Anarchy *in the Twenty-First Century*

In beginning to read Arnold in the early twenty-first century it may
be illuminating to look at a work of the early twentieth century
which was entirely framed by *Culture and Anarchy*, although the
book was in fact never mentioned (a telling sign of the continuance
of a culture in which the allusions would be recognized), and
which reached a very different conclusion from Arnold's own.
R. H. Tawney's *The Acquisitive Society* (1921) started by outlining
the English lack of curiosity about theory, their taking of funda-
mentals for granted: they were 'more interested in the state of the
roads than their place on the map'. In his view the nation needed
urgently to reflect, to 'travel beyond the philosophy momentarily in
favour with the proprietors of its newspapers', and to 'refer to some
standard more stable than the momentary exigencies of industry or
social life'. Tawney's specific call was for a focus on social purpose
and the common good. The only alternative was a bleak one—war
and the destruction of civilization: 'The havoc which the assertion of
the right to unlimited economic expansion has made of the world of
States needs no emphasis.'[43] Tawney's absorption of Arnold's view
of Nonconformity led him to underplay the degree to which different religious groups had in fact anticipated this call in the nineteenth
century: he saw the churches as having sold out to the gospel of
economic success. His arguments for the recognition of the role of
religion in the twentieth century followed Arnold's diagnosis, whilst
adapting the means of impact to a very different Zeitgeist. Rather
than dreaming of universal Christian norms, and a Christian society,
and in opposition to Arnold's idealization of Constantine's conception of an integrated Church and State (*Culture and Anarchy*, p. 22),
he saw the role of Christians as analogous to that of the Christians
in the Roman Empire before Constantine—as a small but sincere
sect in a pagan society. Such a sect would challenge and make

[43] R. H. Tawney, *The Acquisitive Society* (London, 1921), 1–3, 223–4.

uncomfortable those who wished 'to dwell at ease in Zion'. It could not assume a wholesale conversion to its particular ends, but it could suggest the need for reflection on ends. A complex combination of unity and diversity was only possible in a society which subordinated its activities to the *principle* of purpose.[44]

Tawney was speaking the same language as Arnold, but was confronting a cultural reality which in some ways approximates much more closely to our own, in which Christianity stands as one of a number of sources of value. His argument shows one way in which Arnold's questions and critical approaches can be translated into different contexts. Arnold believed that one could not *argue* anyone to a position of faith: the means of persuasion had to be imaginative and sympathetic.[45] The same applied to the development of a sense of social purpose. His own critical tools were sometimes unpersuasive because, despite his ideals, he did not really engage profoundly enough with cultural perspectives which he did not share. In many respects, to read him now is to appreciate more deeply the foreignness of the Victorian past. Such an understanding can give a creative point of reference. Or one may discern in him elements of both the 'ancient' and the 'modern'—and may be able to develop transhistorical and cross-cultural conversations of the sort which Thomas Arnold prescribed. The principles of critical engagement which Matthew Arnold outlined remain fundamental: the embracing of disciplined curiosity; the commitment to transformation rather than affirmation; the development of a 'sensibility for perfection'; the setting of a purpose and being obstinate in its pursuit.[46]

[44] Ibid. 240. My italics.

[45] M. Arnold, 'Bishop Butler and the Zeit-Geist', Super, viii. 11–62, at pp. 28–9.

[46] Bishop Thomas Wilson: 'He can never be good that is not *obstinate* in doing what he knows he ought to do', *Note-Books*, 43 (1867), 66 (1868).

NOTE ON THE TEXT

THE text reproduced here is that of the first book edition of *Culture and Anarchy* of 1869. The first chapter began life as the last lecture which Arnold gave as Professor of Poetry at Oxford on 7 June 1867, under the title 'Culture and its Enemies'. It was published in the *Cornhill Magazine* in July 1867. Even as Arnold returned the proofs, he told the editor that he wanted to follow it up with another essay, to be called 'Anarchy and Authority', in the August number. However, as critiques of 'Culture and its Enemies' started to appear, he decided to delay, so that he could respond to them all. He wrote to his mother on 16 November that 'I have to do a sort of pendant to Culture and its Enemies to be called Anarchy & Authority and to appear in the Christmas Cornhill. It will amuse me to do it, as I have many things to say and Harrison, Sidgwick, and others, who have replied to my first paper, have given me golden opportunities' (*Letters*, iii. 191). In fact, in the end one article extended to five, which were published in the *Cornhill* in January, February, June, July, and August 1868. In this sequence of essays Arnold responded both to the criticism of the first article and to that of the subsequent ones as they came out, and also to contemporary events as they unfolded.

As early as May 1868 Arnold started to contemplate putting the articles together to make a book—initially thinking of including his essay, 'My Countrymen', and his 'Arminius' letters (which later became part of *Friendship's Garland*). By October he seems to have decided to confine the volume to the six essays which form the chapters of *Culture and Anarchy*, reprinted with minor alterations from the articles as they were published. The Preface to the book, together with a brief introduction and conclusion, were of course written last, and the book was published on 25 January 1869.

Three more editions were produced in Arnold's lifetime—a second edition in 1875, and a third in 1882; in 1883 *Culture and Anarchy* was combined with *Friendship's Garland* for an American edition. For the second edition Arnold provided chapter headings (which are noted for information in this edition at the beginning of the notes to each chapter, since they have become famous). He also omitted many of the personal names and topical references, as well as correcting some errors.

Arnold's essays grew out of long-standing preoccupations, but the form which they took was to a considerable extent shaped by current circumstances—events and speeches reported in the press, articles engaging with his own work, books which had just come out. To read the 1869 edition is to recapture something of the immediacy of the debate. The disjointedness of the text, the repetitions and overlaps, and the almost conversational way in which several of the chapters open are characteristic of the challenges of Victorian reading. Many works of criticism were first published in serial form, and journal articles would assume a level of awareness of other critical essays on the same theme coming out in different periodicals. None the less, the text of *Culture and Anarchy* is a particularly complex one, and the range of intertextual references and allusions which one requires to read it is striking. The Explanatory Notes in this edition are intended to provide in some respects a parallel narrative of the ways in which Arnold's mind was working and the stimuli to which he was responding. They also pursue in more detail themes set up in the Introduction.

Footnotes are by Matthew Arnold; editorial notes are marked with an asterisk and can be found at the back of the book.

SELECT BIBLIOGRAPHY

Editions of Arnold's writings

The principal scholarly point of reference for Arnold's prose works is R. H. Super's magisterial *Complete Prose Works of Matthew Arnold* (Ann Arbor, 1960–77), an edition in eleven volumes with extensive notes and details of all textual variants. The edition of *Culture and Anarchy* which he printed was that of the 1883 American edition, which he placed between parts of *Friendship's Garland*, in order to maintain the chronological order of publication of the original parts. Following the same logic, he printed the Preface to *Culture and Anarchy* at the end of the six chapters. Of the popular twentieth-century editions of *Culture and Anarchy*, the first substantive new one was that edited by J. Dover Wilson and published by Cambridge University Press in 1932, with nine more hardback reprintings, followed by a paperback edition in 1960, itself reprinted. The text is a hybrid one: Dover Wilson broadly reproduced the first edition, but incorporated several of the changes from both the 1875 and 1882 editions. He included the chapter headings. Of later twentieth-century editions, the two most readily available are that edited by Stefan Collini—*Culture and Anarchy and Other Writings* (Cambridge, 1993)—which used Super's 1883 text, and that edited by Samuel Lipman (New Haven, 1994), which reproduced the 1869 text (with the later chapter headings in parenthesis). The standard edition of Arnold's poetry is *The Poems of Matthew Arnold*, ed. K. Allott (2nd edn. rev. M. Allott, London, 1979). Arnold's letters have been published in six volumes edited by Cecil Y. Lang: *The Letters of Matthew Arnold* (Charlottesville, Va., and London, 1996–2001). His notebooks (*The Note-Books of Matthew Arnold*) were published by Oxford University Press in 1952, edited by H. F. Lowry, K. Young, and W. H. Dunn.

Biography

Park Honan's *Matthew Arnold: A Life* (London, 1981) is the most comprehensive biographical study. Also useful is N. Murray, *A Life of Matthew Arnold* (London, 1996). Stefan Collini wrote the life of Arnold in the *Oxford Dictionary of National Biography* (2004), which is also a fundamental resource for biographical material on all the British figures mentioned by Arnold. The *ODNB* is available online at *http://www.oxforddnb.com*.

Critical Studies

The volume in the Critical Heritage series dealing with reviews of Arnold's prose writings is very valuable: *Matthew Arnold: Prose Writings*, ed. C. Dawson and J. Pfordresher (London, 1979). Also extremely helpful for getting a sense of the way in which Arnold developed his ideas in relation to criticism is S. Coulling, *Matthew Arnold and his Critics: A Study of Arnold's Controversies* (Athens, Ohio, 1974). Other critical studies of Arnold, which especially bear on the themes raised by *Culture and Anarchy*, are S. Collini, *Matthew Arnold: A Critical Portrait* (Oxford, 1994); J. Livingston, *Matthew Arnold and Christianity: His Religious Prose Writings* (Columbia, SC, 1986); Ruth apRoberts, *Arnold and God* (Berkeley and Los Angeles, 1983); C. Machann and F. D. Burt (eds.), *Matthew Arnold in his Time and Ours: Centenary Essays* (Charlottesville, Va., 1988); J. P. Farrell, *Revolution as Tragedy: The Dilemma of the Moderate from Scott to Arnold* (Ithaca, NY, 1980); W. Robbins, *The Ethical Idealism of Matthew Arnold: A Study of the Nature and Sources of His Moral and Religious Ideas* (Toronto, 1959). Clinton J. Machann's *The Essential Matthew Arnold: An Annotated Bibliography of Major Modern Studies* (New York, 1993) gives an overview of the vast modern secondary literature on Arnold up to that point; see also his more recent *Matthew Arnold: A Literary Life* (Basingstoke, 1996). F. G. Walcott, *The Origins of Culture and Anarchy: Matthew Arnold and Popular Education in England* (London, 1970), is dated, but historiographically interesting; even more so is the older, classic interpretation of Arnold by Lionel Trilling, *Matthew Arnold* (New York, 1939).

Further Reading in Oxford World's Classics

Bagehot, Walter, *The English Constitution*, ed. Miles Taylor.

Engels, Friedrich, *The Condition of the Working Class in England*, ed. David McLellan.

Ruskin, John, *Selected Writings*, ed. Dinah Birch.

CHRONOLOGY

	Life	*Historical & Cultural Background*
1822	Born (24 December) at Laleham-on-Thames as the eldest son of the Reverend Thomas Arnold and Mary Penrose Arnold.	
1828	The family move to Rugby on Dr Arnold's appointment as Headmaster of Rugby School.	Repeal of the Test and Corporation Acts.
1829		Catholic Emancipation Act.
1830		S. T. Coleridge, *Of the Constitution of the Church and State* Auguste Comte, *Cours de philosophie positive* (to 1842)
1832		First Reform Act.
1833		John Keble's *Assize Sermon* starts the Oxford Movement.
1834	Fox How, near Ambleside, completed and from now on becomes the holiday home of the Arnolds in the Lakes. Wordsworth is a neighbour and frequent visitor.	Thomas Arnold, *Principles of Church Reform*
1836	Arnold's first attempts at writing verse, including 'The First Sight of Italy' and 'Lines written on the seashore at Eaglehurst'. With his brother Tom enters Winchester College as a Commoner.	
1837	Arnold wins a school verse-speaking prize with a speech from Byron's *Marino Faliero* and makes his first visit to France; leaves Winchester and enters the Fifth Form at Rugby.	Thomas Carlyle, *The French Revolution*
1838		Formation of Anti-Corn Law Association in Manchester.

	Life	Historical & Cultural Background
1839		Formation of Anti-Corn Law League in London; first Chartist petition. Carlyle's *Chartism*
1840	Arnold wins school prize for English essay and English verse, and his prize poem, 'Alaric at Rome', printed at Rugby; gains open scholarship to Balliol College, Oxford.	
1841	Arnold shares school prizes for Latin essay and Latin verse. He goes into residence at Oxford, when his close friendship with Arthur Hugh Clough begins. He deeply admires Newman's preaching at St Mary's but is not drawn into the Oxford Movement.	Thomas Arnold appointed Regius Professor of Modern History in Oxford. Carlyle's *On Heroes, Hero-Worship and the Heroic in History*
1842	Arnold *proxime accessit* for Hertford Latin Scholarship. Sudden death of his father of heart disease (12 June).	
1842–5	Arnold reads and is influenced by Carlyle, Emerson, George Sand, Goethe, and Spinoza. Member of the 'Decade' undergraduate society.	
1843	Arnold's Newdigate prize poem *Cromwell* printed.	J. S. Mill, *A System of Logic* Carlyle, *Past and Present*
1844	Arnold obtains BA Second Class in Literae Humaniores.	British Anti-State Church Association (from 1853 Liberation Society).
1845	Arnold appointed temporary assistant master at Rugby (Feb.–Apr.) and elected Fellow of Oriel College, Oxford.	Irish famine begins.
1846	Arnold visits France; meets George Sand at Nohant and sees Rachel act in Paris, where he stays until February 1847. Probably begins his close reading of Senancour and Sainte-Beuve at this time.	Repeal of the Corn Laws.

Life	Historical & Cultural Background
1847	Arnold becomes Private Secretary to Lord Lansdowne, Lord President of the Council and Whig elder statesman.	Tennyson, *The Princess*
1848	Arnold visits Switzerland and meets 'Marguerite' at Thun.	Revolutions in Europe. J. S. Mill, *Principles of Political Economy*
1849	Arnold publishes his first volume, *The Strayed Reveller, and Other Poems*. He visits Switzerland and meets 'Marguerite' for the second and last time.	
1850		Tennyson, *In Memoriam*; made Poet Laureate.
1851	Arnold appointed Inspector of Schools, marries Frances Lucy, daughter of Sir William Wightman, Justice of the Queen's Bench, at Hampton, and goes on a delayed honeymoon journey in France, Italy, and Switzerland, during which he visits the Grande Chartreuse. Begins work as a school inspector, and from now on is committed to a heavy programme of work and constant travelling as an inspector and, for some years, marshal to his father-in-law on circuit.	
1852	Arnold publishes *Empedocles on Etna, and Other Poems*.	
1853	Arnold publishes *Poems. A New Edition*, a selection of his poems, excluding 'Empedocles on Etna' and including among new poems 'Sohrab and Rustum' and 'The Scholar-Gipsy'.	

	Life	Historical & Cultural Background
1854	Arnold publishes *Poems. Second Series*, a further selection from his two earlier volumes, with 'Balder Dead' as the single important new poem. (Title page dated 1855.)	Oxford University Act.
1855	'Stanzas from the Grande Chartreuse' and 'Haworth Churchyard' published in *Fraser's Magazine* (April, May).	
1856		J. A. Froude, *History of England from the Fall of Wolsey to the Defeat of the Spanish Armada* (to 1870)
1857	Arnold elected Professor of Poetry at Oxford and delivers his Inaugural Lecture 'On the Modern Element in Literature' (14 Nov.); creates a precedent by lecturing in English instead of Latin; re-elected (1862) at the end of his first term of five years; publishes *Merope*.	H. W. Buckle, *History of Civilization in England* (to 1861)
1858	Arnold settles in London at 2 Chester Square.	W. P. Frith's painting *Derby Day* Thomas Hughes, *Tom Brown's Schooldays*
1859	Arnold visits France, Holland, and Switzerland as Foreign Assistant Commissioner to the Newcastle Commission on Elementary Education.	Charles Darwin, *On the Origin of Species* J. S. Mill, *On Liberty*
1860		Cobden Free Trade Treaty with France. *Cornhill Magazine* started. *Essays and Reviews*
1861	Arnold publishes *On Translating Homer* and *The Popular Education of France* with the introductory essay 'Democracy'.	Spurgeon's Metropolitan Tabernacle built.

Life	Historical & Cultural Background
1862 Arnold risks official hostility by publishing in *Fraser's Magazine* 'The Twice-Revised Code', attacking Robert Lowe's 'Payment by Results' as a method of distributing government grants for education; also publishes *On Translating Homer: Last Words*. Publication of Clough's *Collected Poems* with memoir by Palgrave.	Robert Lowe's 'revised code' implemented. John Ruskin, *Unto this Last*
1864 Arnold publishes *A French Eton*. From now on most of his work appears in periodicals before being published in book form.	John Henry Newman, *Apologia Pro Vita Sua*
1864–7	Schools Inquiry (Taunton) Commission.
1865 Arnold publishes *Essays in Criticism: First Series*; visits France, Italy, Germany, and Switzerland as Foreign Assistant Commissioner to the Taunton Commission (Schools Inquiry).	W. S. Jevons, *The Coal Question* Walter Bagehot, *The English Constitution* published serially (to 1867)
1866 Arnold applies unsuccessfully for the post of Charity Commissioner; publishes 'Thyrsis', his elegy on Clough, in *Macmillan's Magazine*.	Russell/Gladstone Reform Bill defeated; minority Conservative Government under Derby; Hyde Park riots; Real Estate Intestacy Bill defeated.
1867 Arnold applies unsuccessfully for the Librarianship of the House of Commons. Publishes *Celtic Literature, New Poems* (restoring 'Empedocles on Etna' at Browning's request). From now on writes little verse, and is increasingly known for his controversial social and religious writings.	Second Reform Act; William Murphy's anti-Catholic lectures in Birmingham. William Hepworth Dixon, *New America*

	Life	Historical & Cultural Background
1868	Arnold loses two of his sons, his infant son Basil (Jan.) and his eldest son Thomas, aged 16 and a Harrow schoolboy (Nov.). Moves to Byron House, Harrow.	Disraeli succeeds Derby as prime minister; Gladstone's first government; Compulsory Church-Rate Abolition Act. W. H. Dixon, *Spiritual Wives*
1869	Arnold publishes *Culture and Anarchy*, his major work of social criticism, the first collected edition of his *Poems*; his essay on 'Obermann' in the *Academy* (Oct.), and, after the death of Sainte-Beuve, his commemorative essay also in the *Academy* (Nov.). Applies unsuccessfully for appointment as one of the three commissioners under the Endowed Schools Act.	Disestablishment of the Irish Church; Endowed Schools' Act; Marriage with a Deceased Wife's Sister Bill brought in and then withdrawn.
1870	Arnold publishes *St Paul and Protestantism*, receives the Honorary Degree of DCL at Oxford, and is promoted Senior Inspector of Schools.	Elementary Education Act.
1871	Arnold publishes *Friendship's Garland*.	University Tests Act.
1872	Arnold loses a third son, Trevenen William, aged 18 (Feb.).	
1873	Arnold publishes *Literature and Dogma*. Moves to Pains Hill Cottage, Cobham, Surrey. His mother dies at Fox How (Sept.).	
1874		Disraeli's second government; Public Worship Regulation Act.
1875	Arnold publishes *God and the Bible*, reviewing objections to *Literature and Dogma*.	

Life	*Historical & Cultural Background*
1877	Arnold declines renomination for the Professorship of Poetry at Oxford and nomination for the Lord Rectorship of St Andrews University. He publishes *Last Essays on Church and Religion* and 'George Sand' in the *Fortnightly Review* (June). W. H. Mallock portrays Arnold as 'Mr Luke' in his *The New Republic*.	
1878	*Selected Poems of Matthew Arnold* (Golden Treasury Series) published.	
1879	Arnold publishes *Mixed Essays* and his selected *Poems of Wordsworth*.	
1880	Arnold attends the reception in London given in honour of Cardinal Newman by the Duke of Norfolk 'because I wanted to have spoken once in my life to Newman' (12 May). He contributes three essays to T. H. Ward's *The English Poets*: Introduction (later called 'On the Study of Poetry'), 'Thomas Gray', and 'John Keats'.	Gladstone's second government; elementary education compulsory in England and Wales; foundation of Mason's College, Birmingham.
1881	Arnold publishes his selected *Poetry of Byron*.	
1882	Arnold publishes 'Westminster Abbey', his elegy on Stanley, in the *Nineteenth Century* (Jan.), and *Irish Essays*.	
1883	Arnold accepts Civil List Pension of £250 a year 'in public recognition of service to the poetry and literature of England'. Begins his lecture tour of the USA which ends in March 1884.	
1884	Arnold becomes Chief Inspector of Schools.	Third Reform Act.

	Life	*Historical & Cultural Background*
1885	Arnold publishes *Discourses in America* and his three–volume collected edition of poems. He again declines renomination for the Professorship of Poetry in spite of a memorial from Oxford heads of colleges and another from four hundred undergraduates. Visits Germany for the Education Department.	Gladstone's government resigns; Salisbury's first government.
1886	Arnold abroad again in France, Switzerland, and Germany for the Education Department. He retires from Inspectorship of Schools and makes his second visit to USA.	Gladstone's third government; second Salisbury government.
1888	Arnold dies suddenly of heart failure at Liverpool while awaiting the arrival of his married daughter from America (15 Apr.). His *Essays in Criticism. Second Series* published posthumously.	Mrs Humphry Ward, *Robert Elsmere*

CULTURE AND ANARCHY

An Essay in Political and Social Criticism

PREFACE

My foremost design in writing this Preface is to address a word of exhortation to the Society for Promoting Christian Knowledge.* In the essay which follows, the reader will often find Bishop Wilson* quoted. To me and to the members of the Society for Promoting Christian Knowledge his name and writings are still, no doubt, familiar; but the world is fast going away from old-fashioned people of his sort, and I learnt with consternation lately from a brilliant and distinguished votary of the natural sciences,* that he had never so much as heard of Bishop Wilson, and that he imagined me to have invented him. At a moment when the Courts of Law have just taken off the embargo from the recreative religion* furnished on Sundays by my gifted acquaintance and others, and when St Martin's Hall and the Alhambra will soon be beginning again to resound with their pulpit-eloquence, it distresses one to think that the new lights should not only have, in general, a very low opinion of the preachers of the old religion, but that they should have it without knowing the best that these preachers can do. And that they are in this case is owing in part, certainly, to the negligence of the Christian Knowledge Society. In old times they used to print and spread abroad Bishop Wilson's *Maxims of Piety and Christianity*; the copy of this work which I use is one of their publications, bearing their imprint, and bound in the well-known brown calf which they made familiar to our childhood; but the date of my copy is 1812. I know of no copy besides, and I believe the work is no longer one of those printed and circulated by the Society. Hence the error, flattering, I own, to me personally, yet in itself to be regretted, of the distinguished physicist already mentioned.

But Bishop Wilson's *Maxims* deserve to be circulated as a religious book, not only by comparison with the cartloads of rubbish circulated at present under this designation, but for their own sake, and even by comparison with the other works of the same author. Over the far better known *Sacra Privata* they have this advantage, that they were prepared by him for his own private use, while the *Sacra Privata* were prepared by him for the use of the public. The *Maxims* were never meant to be printed, and have on that account, like a work of, doubtless, far deeper emotion and power, the *Meditations* of Marcus Aurelius,* something peculiarly sincere and first-hand about them. Some of the best things from the *Maxims* have passed into the *Sacra Privata*; still, in the *Maxims*, we have them as they first arose; and whereas, too, in the *Sacra Privata* the writer speaks very often as one of the clergy, and as addressing the clergy, in the *Maxims* he almost always speaks solely as a man. I am not saying a word against the *Sacra Privata*, for which I have the highest respect; only the *Maxims* seem to me a better and a more edifying book still. They should be read, as Joubert* says Nicole* should be read, with a direct aim at practice. The reader will leave on one side things which, from the change of time and from the changed point of view which the change of time inevitably brings with it, no longer suit him; enough will remain to serve as a sample of the very best, perhaps, which our nation and race can do in the way of religious writing. Monsieur Michelet* makes it a reproach to us that, in all the doubt as to the real author of the *Imitation*,* no one has ever dreamed of ascribing that work to an Englishman. It is true, the *Imitation* could not well have been written by an Englishman; the religious delicacy and the profound asceticism of that admirable book are hardly in our nature. This would be more of a reproach to us if in poetry, which requires, no less than religion, a true delicacy of spiritual perception, our race had not done such great things; and if the *Imitation*, exquisite as it is, did not, as I have elsewhere remarked, belong to a class of works in which the perfect balance of human nature is lost, and which have therefore, as spiritual productions, in their contents something excessive and morbid, in their form something not thoroughly sound. On a lower range than the *Imitation*, and awakening in our nature chords less poetical and delicate, the *Maxims* of Bishop Wilson are, as a religious work, far more solid. To the most sincere ardour and unction, Bishop Wilson unites, in these *Maxims*, that downright honesty and plain good sense which our English race has so powerfully applied to the divine impossibilities of religion; by which it has brought religion so much into practical life, and has done its allotted part in promoting upon earth the kingdom of God. But with ardour and unction religion, as we all know, may still be fanatical; with honesty and good sense, it may still be prosaic; and the fruit of honesty and good sense united with ardour and unction is often only a prosaic religion held fanatically. Bishop Wilson's excellence lies in a balance of the four qualities, and in a fulness and perfection of them, which makes this untoward result impossible; his unction is so perfect, and in such happy alliance with his good sense, that it becomes tenderness and fervent charity; his good sense is so perfect and in such happy alliance with his unction, that it becomes moderation and insight. While, therefore, the type of religion exhibited in his *Maxims* is English, it is yet a type of a far higher kind than is in general reached by Bishop Wilson's countrymen; and yet, being English, it is possible and attainable for them. And so I conclude as I began, by saying that a work of this sort is one which the Society for Promoting Christian Knowledge should not suffer to remain out of print or out of currency.

To pass now to the matters canvassed in the following essay. The whole scope of the essay is to recommend culture as the great help out of our present difficulties; culture being a pursuit of our total perfection by means of getting to know, on all the matters which most concern us, the best which has been thought and said in the world, and, through this knowledge, turning a stream of fresh and free thought upon our stock notions and habits, which we now follow staunchly but mechanically, vainly imagining that there is a virtue in following them staunchly which makes up for the mischief of following them mechanically. This, and this alone, is the scope of the following essay. I say again here, what I have said in the pages which follow, that from the faults and weaknesses of bookmen a notion of something bookish, pedantic, and futile has got itself more or less connected with the word culture, and that it is a pity we cannot use a word more perfectly free from all shadow of reproach. And yet, futile as are many bookmen, and helpless as books and reading often prove for bringing nearer to perfection those who use them, one must, I think, be struck more and more, the longer one lives, to find how much, in our present society, a man's life of each day depends for its solidity and value on whether he reads during that day, and, far more still, on what he reads during it. More and more he who examines himself will find the difference it makes to him, at the end of any given day, whether or no he has pursued his avocations throughout it without reading at all; and whether or no, having read something, he has read the newspapers only.* This, however, is a matter for each man's private conscience and experience. If a man without books or reading, or reading nothing but his letters and the newspapers, gets nevertheless a fresh and free play of the best thoughts upon his stock notions and habits, he has got culture. He has got that for which we prize and recommend culture; he has got that which at the present moment we seek culture that it may give us. This inward operation is the very life and essence of culture, as we conceive it.

Nevertheless, it is not easy so to frame one's discourse concerning the operation of culture, as to avoid giving frequent occasion to a misunderstanding whereby the essential inwardness of the operation is lost sight of. We are supposed, when we criticise by the help of culture some imperfect doing or other, to have in our eye some well-known rival plan of doing, which we want to serve and recommend. Thus, for instance, because I have freely pointed out the dangers and inconveniences to which our literature is exposed in the absence of any centre of taste and authority like the French Academy, it is constantly said that I want to introduce here in England an institution like the French Academy.* I have indeed expressly declared that I wanted no such thing; but let us notice how it is just our worship of machinery, and of external doing, which leads to this charge being brought; and how the inwardness of culture makes us seize, for watching and cure, the faults to which our want of an Academy inclines us, and yet prevents us from trusting to an arm of flesh,* as the Puritans say,—from blindly flying to this outward machinery of an Academy, in order to help ourselves. For the very same culture and free inward play of thought which shows us how the Corinthian style, or the whimsies about the One Primeval Language* are generated and strengthened in the absence of an Academy, shows us, too, how little any Academy, such as we should be likely to get, would cure them. Every one who knows the characteristics of our national life, and the tendencies so fully discussed in the following pages, knows exactly what an English Academy would be like. One can see the happy family in one's mind's eye as distinctly as if it was already constituted. Lord Stanhope,* the Bishop of Oxford,* Mr Gladstone,* the Dean of Westminster,* Mr Froude,* Mr Henry Reeve,*—everything which is influential, accomplished, and distinguished; and then, some fine morning, a dissatisfaction of the public mind with this brilliant and select coterie, a flight of Corinthian leading articles, and an irruption of Mr G. A. Sala.* Clearly, this is not what will do us good. The very same faults,—the want of sensitiveness of intellectual conscience,* the disbelief in right reason, the dislike of authority,—which have hindered our having an Academy and have worked injuriously in our literature, would also hinder us from making our Academy, if we established it, one which would really correct them. And culture, which shows us truly the faults, shows us this also just as truly.

It is by a like sort of misunderstanding, again, that Mr Oscar Browning,* one of the assistant-masters at Eton, takes up in the *Quarterly Review* the cudgels for Eton, as if I had attacked Eton, because I have said, in a book about foreign schools, that a man may well prefer to teach his three or four hours a day without keeping a boarding-house; and that there are great dangers in cramming little boys of eight or ten and making them compete for an object of great value to their parents; and, again, that the manufacture and supply of school-books, in England, much needs regulation by some competent authority. Mr Oscar Browning gives us to understand that at Eton he and others, with perfect satisfaction to themselves and the public, combine the functions of teaching and of keeping a boarding-house; that he knows excellent men (and, indeed, well he may, for a brother of his own, I am told, is one of the best of them,) engaged in preparing little boys for competitive examinations, and that the result, as tested at Eton, gives perfect satisfaction. And as to school-books he adds, finally, that Dr William Smith,* the learned and distinguished editor of the *Quarterly Review*, is, as we all know, the compiler of school-books meritorious and many. This is what Mr Oscar Browning gives us to understand in the *Quarterly Review*, and it is impossible not to read with pleasure what he says. For what can give a finer example of that frankness and manly self-confidence which our great public schools, and none of them so much as Eton, are supposed to inspire, of that buoyant ease in holding up one's head, speaking out what is in one's mind, and flinging off all sheepishness and awkwardness, than to see an Eton assistant-master offering in fact himself as evidence that to combine boarding-house-keeping with teaching is a good thing, and his brother as evidence that to train and race little boys for competitive examinations is a good thing? Nay, and one sees that this frank-hearted Eton self-confidence is contagious; for has not Mr Oscar Browning managed to fire Dr William Smith (himself, no doubt, the modestest man alive, and never trained at Eton) with the same spirit, and made him insert in his own *Review* a puff, so to speak, of his own school-books, declaring that they are (as they are) meritorious and many? Nevertheless, Mr Oscar Browning is wrong in thinking that I wished to run down Eton; and his repetition on behalf of Eton, with this idea in his head, of the strains of his heroic ancestor, Malvina's Oscar,* as they are recorded by the family poet, Ossian, is unnecessary. 'The wild boar rushes over their tombs, but he does not disturb their repose. They still love the sport of their youth, and mount the wind with joy.' All I meant to say was, that there were unpleasantnesses in uniting the keeping a boarding-house with teaching, and dangers in cramming and racing little boys for competitive examinations, and charlatanism and extravagance in the manufacture and supply of our school-books. But when Mr Oscar Browning tells us that all these have been happily got rid of in his case, and his brother's case, and Dr William Smith's case, then I say that this is just what I wish, and I hope other people will follow their good example. All I seek is that such blemishes should not through any negligence, self-love, or want of due self-examination, be suffered to continue.

Natural, as we have said, the sort of misunderstanding just noticed is; yet our usefulness depends upon our being able to clear it away, and to convince those who mechanically serve some stock notion or operation, and thereby go astray, that it is not culture's work or aim to give the victory to some rival fetish, but simply to turn a free and fresh stream of thought upon the whole matter in question. In a thing of more immediate interest, just now, than either of the two we have mentioned, the like misunderstanding prevails; and until it is dissipated, culture can do no good work in the matter. When we criticise the present operation of disestablishing the Irish Church,* not by the power of reason and justice, but by the power of the antipathy of the Protestant Nonconformists,* English and Scotch, to establishments, we are charged with being dreamers of dreams, which the national will has rudely shattered, for endowing the religious sects all round; or we are called enemies of the Nonconformists, blind partisans of the Anglican Establishment. More than a few words we must give to showing how erroneous are these charges; because if they were true, we should be actually subverting our own design, and playing false to that culture which it is our very purpose to recommend.

Certainly we are no enemies of the Nonconformists; for, on the contrary, what we aim at is their perfection. Culture, which is the study of perfection, leads us, as we in the following pages have shown, to conceive of true human perfection as a *harmonious* perfection, developing all sides of our humanity; and as a *general* perfection, developing all parts of our society. For if one member suffer, the other members must suffer with it; and the fewer there are that follow the true way of salvation the harder that way is to find. And while the Nonconformists, the successors and representatives of the Puritans,* and like them staunchly walking by the best light they have,* make a large part of what is strongest and most serious in this nation and therefore attract our respect and interest, yet all that, in what follows, is said about Hebraism and Hellenism,* has for its main result to show how our Puritans, ancient and modern, have not enough added to their care for walking staunchly by the best light they have, a care that that light be not darkness; how they have developed one side of their humanity at the expense of all others, and have become incomplete and mutilated men in consequence. Thus falling short of harmonious perfection, they fail to follow the true way of salvation. Therefore that way is made the harder for others to find, general perfection is put further off out of our reach, and the confusion and perplexity in which our society now labours is increased by the Nonconformists rather than diminished by them. So while we praise and esteem the zeal of the Nonconformists in walking staunchly by the best light they have, and desire to take no whit from it, we seek to add to this what we call sweetness and light,* and develope their full humanity more perfectly; and to seek this is certainly not to be the enemy of the Nonconformists.

But now, with these ideas in our head, we come across the present operation for disestablishing the Irish Church by the power of the Nonconformists' antipathy to religious establishments and endowments. And we see Liberal statesmen, for whose purpose this antipathy happens to be convenient, flattering it all they can; saying that though they have no intention of laying hands on an Establishment which is efficient and popular, like the Anglican Establishment here in England, yet it is in the abstract a fine and good thing that religion should be left to the voluntary support of its promoters, and should thus gain in energy and independence; and Mr Gladstone has no words strong enough to express his admiration of the refusal of State-aid by the Irish Roman Catholics, who have never yet been

seriously asked to accept it, but who would a good deal embarrass
him if they demanded it. And we see philosophical politicians, with a
turn for swimming with the stream, like Mr Baxter* or Mr Charles
Buxton,* and philosophical divines with the same turn, like the Dean
of Canterbury,* seeking to give a sort of grand stamp of generality
and solemnity to this antipathy of the Nonconformists, and to dress
it out as a law of human progress in the future. Now, nothing can be
pleasanter than swimming with the stream; and we might gladly,
if we could, try in our unsystematic way to help Mr Baxter, and
Mr Charles Buxton, and the Dean of Canterbury, in their labours at
once philosophical and popular. But we have got fixed in our minds
that a more full and harmonious development of their humanity
is what the Nonconformists most want, that narrowness, one-
sidedness, and incompleteness is what they most suffer from; in a
word, that in what we call *provinciality* they abound, but in what we
may call *totality* they fall short.

And they fall short more than the members of Establishments.
The great works by which, not only in literature, art, and science
generally, but in religion itself, the human spirit has manifested its
approaches to totality, and a full, harmonious perfection, and by
which it stimulates and helps forward the world's general perfection,
come, not from Nonconformists, but from men who either belong to
Establishments or have been trained in them. A Nonconformist minister, the Rev. Edward White,* who has lately written a temperate and
well-reasoned pamphlet against Church Establishments, says that
'the unendowed and unestablished communities of England exert
full as much moral and ennobling influence upon the conduct of
statesmen as that Church which is both established and endowed.'
That depends upon what one means by moral and ennobling influence. The believer in machinery may think that to get a Government
to abolish Church-rates* or to legalise marriage with a deceased
wife's sister* is to exert a moral and ennobling influence upon
Government. But a lover of perfection, who looks to inward ripeness
for the true springs of conduct, will surely think that as Shakespeare
has done more for the inward ripeness of our statesmen than
Dr Watts,* and has, therefore, done more to moralise and ennoble
them, so an Establishment which has produced Hooker,* Barrow,*
Butler,* has done more to moralise and ennoble English statesmen
and their conduct than communities which have produced the

Nonconformist divines. The fruitful men of English Puritanism and Nonconformity are men who were trained within the pale of the Establishment, —Milton,* Baxter,* Wesley.* A generation or two outside the Establishment, and Puritanism produces men of national mark no more. With the same doctrine and discipline, men of national mark are produced in Scotland; but in an Establishment.* With the same doctrine and discipline, men of national and even European mark are produced in Germany, Switzerland, France; but in Establishments. Only two religious disciplines seem exempted, or comparatively exempted, from the operation of the law which seems to forbid the rearing, outside of national establishments, of men of the highest spiritual significance. These two are the Roman Catholic and the Jewish. And these, both of them, rest on Establishments, which, though not indeed national, are cosmopolitan; and perhaps here, what the individual man does not lose by these conditions of his rearing, the citizen, and the State of which he is a citizen, loses.

What, now, can be the reason of this undeniable provincialism of the English Puritans and Protestant Nonconformists, a provincialism which has two main types,—a bitter type and a smug type,—but which in both its types is vulgarising, and thwarts the full perfection of our humanity? Men of genius and character are born and reared in this medium as in any other. From the faults of the mass such men will always be comparatively free, and they will always excite our interest; yet in this medium they seem to have a special difficulty in breaking through what bounds them, and in developing their totality. Surely the reason is, that the Nonconformist is not in contact with the main current of national life, like the member of an Establishment. In a matter of such deep and vital concern as religion, this separation from the main current of the national life has peculiar importance. In the following essay we have discussed at length the tendency in us to *Hebraise*,* as we call it; that is, to sacrifice all other sides of our being to the religious side. This tendency has its cause in the divine beauty and grandeur of religion, and bears affecting testimony to them; but we have seen that it has dangers for us, we have seen that it leads to a narrow and twisted growth of our religious side itself, and to a failure in perfection. But if we tend to Hebraise even in an Establishment, with the main current of national life flowing round us, and reminding us in all ways of the variety and fulness of human existence,—by a Church which is historical as the State itself is historical,* and whose order, ceremonies, and monuments reach, like those of the State, far beyond any fancies and devisings of ours, and by institutions such as the Universities,* formed to defend and advance that very culture and many-sided development which it is the danger of Hebraising to make us neglect,—how much more must we tend to Hebraise when we lack these preventives. One may say that to be reared a member of an Establishment is in itself a lesson of religious moderation, and a help towards culture and harmonious perfection. Instead of battling for his own private forms for express-ing the inexpressible and defining the undefinable, a man takes those which have commended themselves most to the religious life of his nation; and while he may be sure that within those forms the religious side of his own nature may find its satisfaction, he has leisure and composure to satisfy other sides of his nature as well.

But with the member of a Nonconforming or self-made religious community how different! The sectary's *eigene grosse Erfindungen*, as Goethe calls them,*—the precious discoveries of himself and his friends for expressing the inexpressible and defining the undefinable in peculiar forms of their own, cannot but, as he has voluntarily chosen them, and is personally responsible for them, fill his whole mind. He is zealous to do battle for them and affirm them, for in affirming them he affirms himself, and that is what we all like.* Other sides of his being are thus neglected, because the religious side, always tending in every serious man to predominance over our other spiritual sides, is in him made quite absorbing and tyrannous by the condition of self-assertion and challenge which he has chosen for himself. And just what is not essential in religion he comes to mis-take for essential, and a thousand times the more readily because he has chosen it of himself; and religious activity he fancies to consist in battling for it. All this leaves him little leisure or inclination for culture; to which, besides, he has no great institutions not of his own making, like the Universities connected with the national Establish-ment, to invite him; but only such institutions as, like the order and discipline of his religion, he may have invented for himself, and invented under the sway of the narrow and tyrannous notions of religion fostered in him as we have seen. Thus, while a national Establishment of religion favours totality, *hole-and-corner* forms of religion (to use an expressive popular word) inevitably favour provincialism.

But the Nonconformists, and many of our Liberal friends along with them, have a plausible plan for getting rid of this provincialism, if, as they can hardly quite deny, it exists. 'Let us all be in the same boat,' they cry; 'open the Universities to everybody, and let there be no establishment of religion at all!' Open the Universities by all means; but, as to the second point about establishment, let us sift the proposal a little. It does seem at first a little like that proposal of the fox, who had lost his own tail, to put all the other foxes in the same boat by a general cutting off of tails; and we know that moralists have decided that the right course here was, not to adopt this plausible suggestion, and cut off tails all round, but rather that the other foxes should keep their tails, and that the fox without a tail should get one. And so we might be inclined to urge that, to cure the evil of the Nonconformists' provincialism, the right way can hardly be to provincialise us all round.

However, perhaps we shall not be provincialised. For the Rev. Edward White says that probably, 'when all good men alike are placed in a condition of religious equality, and the whole complicated iniquity of Government Church patronage is swept away, more of moral and ennobling influence than ever will be brought to bear upon the action of statesmen.' We already have an example of religious equality in our colonies.* 'In the colonies,' says *The Times*, 'we see religious communities unfettered by State-control, and the State relieved from one of the most troublesome and irritating of responsibilities.' But America is the great example alleged by those who are against establishments for religion. Our topic at this moment is the influence of religious establishments on culture; and it is remarkable that Mr Bright,* who has taken lately to representing himself as, above all, a promoter of reason and of the simple natural truth of things, and his policy as a fostering of the growth of intelligence,—just the aims, as is well known, of culture also,—Mr Bright, in a speech at Birmingham about education, seized on the very point which seems to concern our topic, when he said: 'I believe the people of the United States have offered to the world more valuable information during the last forty years than all Europe put together.' So America, without religious establishments, seems to get ahead of us all in culture *and* totality; and these are the cure for provincialism.

On the other hand, another friend of reason and the simple natural truth of things, Monsieur Renan,* says of America, in a book he has recently published, what seems to conflict violently with what Mr Bright says. Mr Bright affirms that, not only have the United States thus informed Europe, but they have done it without a great apparatus of higher and scientific instruction, and by dint of all classes in America being 'sufficiently educated to be able to read, and to comprehend, and to think; and that, I maintain, is the foundation of all subsequent progress.' And then comes Monsieur Renan, and says: 'The sound instruction of the people is an effect of the high culture of certain classes. The countries which, like the United States, have created a considerable popular instruction without any serious higher instruction, will long have to expiate this fault by their intellectual mediocrity, their vulgarity of manners, their superficial spirit, their lack of general intelligence.'[1]

Now, which of these two friends of culture are we to believe? Monsieur Renan seems more to have in his eye what we ourselves mean by culture; because Mr Bright always has in his eye what he calls 'a commendable interest' in politics and political agitations.* As he said only the other day at Birmingham: 'At this moment,—in fact, I may say at every moment in the history of a free country,—there is nothing that is so much worth discussing as politics.' And he keeps repeating, with all the powers of his noble oratory, the old story, how to the thoughtfulness and intelligence of the people of great towns we owe all our improvements in the last thirty years, and how these improvements have hitherto consisted in Parliamentary reform, and free trade, and abolition of Church rates, and so on; and how they are now about to consist in getting rid of minority-members, and in introducing a free breakfast-table, and in abolishing the Irish Church by the power of the Nonconformists' antipathy to establishments, and much more of the same kind. And though our pauperism and ignorance, and all the questions which are called social, seem now to be forcing themselves upon his mind, yet he still goes on with his glorifying of the great towns, and the Liberals,* and their operations for the last thirty years. It never seems to occur to him that the present troubled state of our social life has anything to do with the thirty years' blind worship of their nostrums by himself

---

[1] 'Les pays qui comme les États-Unis ont créé un enseignement populaire considérable sans instruction supérieure sérieuse, expieront longtemps encore leur faute par leur médiocrité intellectuelle, leur grossièreté de mœurs, leur esprit superficiel, leur manque d'intelligence générale.'

and our Liberal friends, or that it throws any doubts upon the sufficiency of this worship. But he thinks what is still amiss is due to the
stupidity of the Tories,* and will be cured by the thoughtfulness and
intelligence of the great towns, and by the Liberals going on glori-
ously with their political operations as before; or that it will cure
itself. So we see what Mr Bright means by thoughtfulness and intelligence, and in what manner, according to him, we are to grow in
them. And, no doubt, in America all classes read their newspaper
and take a commendable interest in politics more than here or
anywhere else in Europe.

But, in the following essay, we have been led to doubt the sufficiency of all this political operating of ours, pursued mechanically
as we pursue it; and we found that *general intelligence*, as Monsieur
Renan calls it, or, in our own words, a reference of all our operating
to a firm intelligible law of things, was just what we were without,
and that we were without it because we worshipped our machinery
so devoutly. Therefore, we conclude that Monsieur Renan, more
than Mr Bright, means by reason and intelligence the same thing
as we do; and when he says that America, that chosen home of
newspapers and politics, is without general intelligence; we think it
likely, from the circumstances of the case, that this is so; and that, in
culture and totality, America, instead of surpassing us all, falls short.

And,—to keep to our point of the influence of religious establishments upon culture and a high development of our humanity,—we
can surely see reasons why, with all her energy and fine gifts,
America does not show more of this development, or more promise
of this. In the following essay it will be seen how our society distrib-
utes itself into Barbarians, Philistines, and Populace,* and America is
just ourselves, with the Barbarians quite left out, and the Populace
nearly. This leaves the Philistines for the great bulk of the nation;—a
livelier sort of Philistine than ours, and with the pressure and false
ideal of our Barbarians taken away, but left all the more to himself
and to have his full swing. And as we have found that the strongest
and most vital part of English Philistinism was the Puritan and
Hebraising middle-class, and that its Hebraising keeps it from culture and totality, so it is notorious that the people of the United
States issues from this class, and reproduces its tendencies,—its narrow conception of man's spiritual range and of his one thing needful.
From Maine to Florida, and back again, all America Hebraises.*

Difficult as it is to speak of a people merely from what one reads, yet that, I think, one may, without much fear of contradiction say. I mean, when, in the United States, any spiritual side in a man is wakened to activity, it is generally the religious side, and the religious side in a narrow way. Social reformers go to Moses or St Paul for their doctrines, and have no notion there is anywhere else to go to; earnest young men at schools and universities, instead of conceiving salvation as a harmonious perfection only to be won by unreservedly cultivating many sides in us, conceive of it in the old Puritan fashion, and fling themselves ardently upon it in the old, false ways of this fashion, which we know so well, and such as Mr Hammond, the American revivalist,* has lately, at Mr Spurgeon's Tabernacle,* been refreshing our memory with. Now, if America thus Hebraises more than either England or Germany, will any one deny that the absence of religious establishments has much to do with it? We have seen how establishments tend to give us a sense of a historical life of the human spirit, outside and beyond our own fancies and feelings; how they thus tend to suggest new sides and sympathies in us to cultivate; how, further, by saving us from having to invent and fight for our own forms of religion, they give us leisure and calm to steady our view of religion itself,—the most overpowering of objects, as it is the grandest,—and to enlarge our first crude notions of the one thing needful.* But, in a serious people, where every one has to choose and strive for his own order and discipline of religion, the contention about these non-essentials occupies his mind, his first crude notions about the one thing needful do not get purged, and they invade the whole spiritual man in him, and then, making a solitude, they call it heavenly peace.*

I remember a Nonconformist manufacturer, in a town of the Midland counties, telling me that when he first came there, some years ago, the place had no Dissenters; but he had opened an Independent chapel in it, and now Church and Dissent were pretty equally divided, with sharp contests between them. I said, that seemed a pity. 'A pity?' cried he; 'not at all! Only think of all the zeal and activity which the collision calls forth!' 'Ah, but, my dear friend,' I answered, 'only think of all the nonsense which you now hold quite firmly, which you would never have held if you had not been contradicting your adversary in it all these years!' The more serious the people, and the more prominent the religious side in it, the greater is the danger of this side, if set to choose out forms for itself and fight for existence, swelling and spreading till it swallows all other spiritual sides up, intercepts and absorbs all nutriment which should have gone to them, and leaves Hebraism rampant in us and Hellenism stamped out.

Culture, and the harmonious perfection of our whole being, and what we call totality, then become secondary matters; and the institutions, which should develope these, take the same narrow and partial view of humanity and its wants as the free religious communities take. Just as the free churches of Mr Beecher* or Brother Noyes,* with their provincialism and want of centrality, make mere Hebraisers in religion, and not perfect men, so the university of Mr Ezra Cornell,* a really noble monument of his munificence, yet seems to rest on a provincial misconception of what culture truly is, and to be calculated to produce miners, or engineers, or architects, not sweetness and light.

And, therefore, when the Rev. Edward White asks the same kind of question about America that he has asked about England, and wants to know whether, without religious establishments, as much is not done in America for the higher national life as is done for that life here, we answer in the same way as we did before, that as much is not done. Because to enable and stir up people to read their Bible and the newspapers, and to get a practical knowledge of their business, does not serve to the higher spiritual life of a nation so much as culture, truly conceived, serves; and a true conception of culture is, as Monsieur Renan's words show, just what America fails in.

To the many who think that culture, and sweetness, and light, are all moonshine, this will not appear to matter much; but with us, who value them, and who think that we have traced much of our present discomfort to the want of them, it weighs a great deal. So not only do we say that the Nonconformists have got provincialism and lost totality by the want of a religious establishment, but we say that the very example which they bring forward to help their case makes against them; and that when they triumphantly show us America without religious establishments, they only show us a whole nation touched, amidst all its greatness and promise, with that provincialism which it is our aim to extirpate in the English Nonconformists.

But now to evince the disinterestedness* which culture, as I have said, teaches us. We have seen the narrowness generated in Puritanism by its hole-and-corner organisation, and we propose to cure it by bringing Puritanism more into contact with the main current of national life. Here we are fully at one with the Dean of Westminster; and, indeed, he and we were trained in the same school to mark the narrowness of Puritanism,* and to wish to cure it. But he and others would give to the present Anglican Establishment a character the most latitudinarian, as it is called, possible; availing themselves for this purpose of the diversity of tendencies and doctrines which does undoubtedly exist already in the Anglican formularies; and they would say to the Puritans: 'Come all of you into this liberally conceived Anglican Establishment.' But to say this is hardly, perhaps, to take sufficient account of the course of history, or of the strength of men's feelings in what concerns religion, or of the gravity which may have come to attach itself to points of religious order and discipline merely. When the Rev. Edward White talks of 'sweeping away the whole complicated iniquity of Government Church patronage,' he uses language which has been forced upon him by his position, but which is, as we have seen, devoid of any real solidity. But when he talks of the religious communities 'which have for three hundred years contended for the power of the congregation in the management of their own affairs,' then he talks history; and his language has behind it, in my opinion, facts which make the latitudinarianism of our Broad Churchmen* quite illusory. Certainly, culture will never make us think it an essential of religion whether we have in our Church discipline 'a popular authority of elders,' as Hooker calls it, or whether we have Episcopal jurisdiction. Certainly, Hooker himself did not think it an essential; for in the dedication of his *Ecclesiastical Polity*, speaking of these questions of Church discipline which gave occasion to his great work, he says they are 'in truth, for the greatest part, such silly things, that very easiness doth make them hard to be disputed of in serious manner.'* Hooker's great work against the impugners of the order and discipline of the Church of England was written (and this is too indistinctly seized by many who read it), not because Episcopalianism is essential, but because its impugners maintained that Presbyterianism is essential, and that Episcopalianism is sinful. Neither the one nor the other is either essential or sinful, and much may be said on behalf of both. But what is important to be remarked is that *both were in the Church of England at the Reformation*, and that Presbyterianism was only extruded gradually. We have mentioned Hooker, and nothing better illustrates what has just been asserted than the following incident in Hooker's own career, which every one has read, for it is related in Isaac Walton's* *Life of Hooker*, but of which, probably, the significance has been fully grasped by not one-half of those who have read it.

Hooker was through the influence of Archbishop Whitgift* appointed, in 1585, Master of the Temple; but a great effort had just been made to obtain the place for a Mr Walter Travers,* well known in that day, though now it is Hooker's name which alone preserves his. This Travers was then afternoon-lecturer at the Temple. The Master whose death made the vacancy, Alvey, recommended on his deathbed Travers for his successor, the society was favourable to him, and he had the support of the Lord Treasurer Burghley. After Hooker's appointment to the Mastership, Travers remained afternoon-lecturer, and combated in the afternoons the doctrine which Hooker preached in the mornings. Now, this Travers, originally a Fellow of Trinity College, Cambridge, afterwards afternoon-lecturer at the Temple, recommended for the Mastership by the foregoing Master, whose opinions, it is said, agreed with his, favoured by the society of the Temple, and supported by the Prime Minister,—this Travers was not an Episcopally ordained clergyman at all; he was a Presbyterian, a partisan of the Geneva church-discipline,* as it was then called, and 'had taken orders,' says Walton, 'by the Presbyters in Antwerp.' In another place Walton speaks of his orders yet more fully:—'He had disowned,' he says, 'the English Established Church and Episcopacy, and went to Geneva, and afterwards to Antwerp, to be ordained minister, as he was by Villers and Cartwright* and others the heads of a congregation there; and so came back again more confirmed for the discipline.'* Villers and Cartwright are in like manner examples of Presbyterianism within the Church of England, which was common enough at that time; but perhaps nothing can better give us a lively sense of its presence there than this history of Travers, which is as if Mr Binney* were now afternoon-reader at Lincoln's Inn or the Temple, were to be a candidate, favoured by the benchers and by the Prime Minister, for the Mastership, and were only kept out of the post by the accident of the Archbishop of Canterbury's influence with the Queen carrying a rival candidate.

Presbyterianism, with its popular principle of the power of the congregation in the management of their own affairs, was extruded from the Church of England, and men like Travers can no longer appear in her pulpits. Perhaps if a government like that of Elizabeth, with secular statesmen like the Cecils,* and ecclesiastical statesmen like Whitgift, could have been prolonged, Presbyterianism might, by a wise mixture of concession and firmness, have been absorbed in the Establishment. Lord Bolingbroke,* on a matter of this kind a very clear-judging and impartial witness, says, in a work far too little read, his *Remarks on English History:*—'The measures pursued and the temper observed in Queen Elizabeth's time tended to diminish the religious opposition by a slow, a gentle, and for that very reason an effectual progression. There was even room to hope that when the first fire of the Dissenters' zeal was passed, reasonable terms of union with the Established Church might be accepted by such of them as were not intoxicated with fanaticism. These were friends to order, though they disputed about it. If these friends of Calvin's discipline had been once incorporated with the Established Church, the remaining sectaries would have been of little moment, either for numbers or reputation; and the very means which were proper to gain these friends, were likewise the most effectual to hinder the increase of them, and of the other sectaries in the meantime.' The temper and ill judgment of the Stuarts made shipwreck of all policy of this kind. Yet speaking even of the time of the Stuarts, but their early time, Clarendon* says that if Bishop Andrewes* had succeeded Bancroft* at Canterbury, the disaffection of separatists might have been stayed and healed. This, however, was not to be; and Presbyterianism, after exercising for some years the law of the strongest, itself in Charles the Second's reign suffered under this law, and was finally cast out from the Church of England.*

Now the points of church discipline at issue between Presbyterianism and Episcopalianism are, as has been said, not essential. They might probably once have been settled in a sense altogether favourable to Episcopalianism. Hooker may have been right in thinking that there were in his time circumstances which made it essential that they should be settled in this sense, though the points in themselves were not essential. But by the very fact of the settlement not having then been effected, of the breach having gone on and widened, of the Nonconformists not having been amicably incorporated with the Establishment but violently cast out from it, the circumstances are now altogether altered. Isaac Walton, a fervent Churchman, complains that 'the principles of the Nonconformists grew at last to such a height and were vented so daringly, that, beside the loss of life and limbs, the Church and State were both forced to use such other severities as will not admit of an excuse, if it had not been to prevent confusion and the perilous consequences of it.'* But those very severities have of themselves made union on an Episcopalian footing impossible. Besides, Presbyterianism, the popular authority of elders, the power of the congregation in the management of their own affairs, has that warrant given to it by Scripture and by the proceedings of the early Christian Churches, it is so consonant with the spirit of Protestantism which made the Reformation and which has such strength in this country, it is so predominant in the practice of other reformed churches, it was so strong in the original reformed Church of England, that one cannot help doubting whether any settlement which suppressed it could have been really permanent, and whether it would not have kept appearing again and again, and causing dissension.

Well, then, if culture is the disinterested endeavour after man's perfection, will it not make us wish to cure the provincialism of the Nonconformists, not by making Churchmen provincial along with them, but by letting their popular church discipline, formerly found in the National Church, and still found in the affections and practice of a good part of the nation, appear in the National Church once more; and thus to bring Nonconformists into contact again, as their greater fathers were, with the main stream of national life? Why should not a Presbyterian or Congregational Church, based on this considerable and important, though not essential principle, of the congregation's power in the church management, be established,— with equal rank for its chiefs with the chiefs of Episcopacy, and with admissibility of its ministers, under a revised system of patronage and preferment, to benefices,—side by side with the Episcopal Church, as the Calvinist and Lutheran Churches are established side by side in France and Germany? Such a Congregational Church would unite the main bodies of Protestants who are now separatists; and separation would cease to be the law of their religious order. Then,—through this concession on a really considerable point of difference,—that endless splitting into hole-and-corner churches on quite inconsiderable points of difference, which must prevail so long as separatism is the first law of a Nonconformist's religious existence, would be checked. Culture would then find a place among English followers of the popular authority of elders, as it has long found it among the followers of Episcopal jurisdiction; and this we should gain by merely recognising, regularising, and restoring an element which appeared once in the reformed National Church, and which is considerable and national enough to have a sound claim to appear there still.

So far, then, is culture from making us unjust to the Nonconformists because it forbids us to worship their fetishes, that it even leads us to propose to do more for them than they themselves venture to claim. It leads us, also, to respect what is solid and respectable in their convictions, while their latitudinarian friends make light of it. Not that the forms in which the human spirit tries to express the inexpressible, or the forms by which man tries to worship, have or can have, as has been said, for the follower of perfection, anything necessary or eternal. If the New Testament and the practice of the primitive Christians sanctioned the popular form of church government a thousand times more expressly than they do, if the Church since Constantine* were a thousand times more of a departure from the scheme of primitive Christianity than it can be shown to be, that does not at all make, as is supposed by men in bondage to the letter, the popular form of church government alone and always sacred and binding, or the work of Constantine a thing to be regretted. What is alone and always sacred and binding for man is the climbing towards his total perfection, and the machinery by which he does this varies in value according as it helps him to do it. The planters of Christianity had their roots in deep and rich grounds of human life and achievement, both Jewish and also Greek; and had thus a comparatively firm and wide basis amidst all the vehement inspiration of their mighty movement and change. By their strong inspiration they carried men off the old basis of life and culture, whether Jewish or Greek, and generations arose who had their roots in neither world, and were in contact therefore with no full and great stream of human life. Christianity might have lost herself, if it had not been for some such change as that of the fourth century, in a multitude of hole-and-corner churches like the churches of English Nonconformity after its founders departed; churches without great men, and without furtherance for the higher life of humanity. At a critical moment came Constantine, and placed Christianity,—or let us rather say, placed the human spirit, whose totality was endangered,—in contact with the main current of human life. And his work was justified by its fruits, in men like Augustine* and Dante,* and indeed in all the great men of Christianity, Catholics or Protestants, ever since. And one may go beyond this. Monsieur Albert Réville,* whose religious writings are always interesting, says that the conception which cultivated and philosophical Jews now entertain of Christianity and its founder, is probably destined to become the conception which Christians themselves will entertain. Socinians* are fond of saying the same thing about the Socinian conception of Christianity. Even if this were true, it would still have been better for a man, through the last eighteen hundred years, to have been a Christian, and a member of one of the great Christian communions, than to have been a Jew or a Socinian; because the being in contact with the main stream of human life is of more moment for a man's total spiritual growth, and for his bringing to perfection the gifts committed to him, which is his business on earth, than any speculative opinion which he may hold or think he holds. Luther,—whom we have called a Philistine of genius, and who, because he was a Philistine, had a coarseness and lack of spiritual delicacy which have harmed his disciples, but who, because he was a genius, had splendid flashes of spiritual insight,—Luther says admirably in his Commentary on the Book of Daniel:* 'A God is simply *that* whereon the human heart rests with trust, faith, hope and love. If the resting is right, then the God too is right; if the resting is wrong, then the God too is illusory.' In other words, the worth of what a man thinks about God and the objects of religion depends on what the man *is*; and what the man *is*, depends upon his having more or less reached the measure of a perfect and total man.

All this is true; and yet culture, as we have seen, has more tenderness for scruples of the Nonconformists than have their Broad Church friends. That is because culture, disinterestedly trying, in its aim at perfection, to see things as they really are, sees how worthy and divine a thing is the religious side in man, though it is not the whole of man. And when Mr Greg,* who differs from us about edification, (and certainly we do not seem likely to agree with him as to what edifies), finding himself moved by some extraneous considerations or other to take a Church's part against its enemies, calls

taking a Church's part *returning to base uses*, culture teaches us how
out of place is this language, and that to use it shows an inadequate
conception of human nature, and that no Church will thank a man
for taking its part in this fashion, but will leave him with indifference
to the tender mercies of his Benthamite friends. But avoiding
Benthamism,* or an inadequate conception of the religious side in
man, culture makes us also avoid Mialism,* or an inadequate conception of man's totality. Therefore to the worth and grandeur of the
religious side in man, culture is rejoiced and willing to pay any
tribute, except the tribute of man's totality. True, the order and
liturgy of the Church of England one may be well contented to live
and to die with, and they are such as to inspire an affectionate
and revering attachment. True, the reproaches of Nonconformists
against this order for 'retaining badges of Antichristian recogni-
sance;' and for 'corrupting the right form of Church polity with
manifold Popish rites and ceremonies;' true, their assertion of the
essentialness of their own supposed Scriptural order, and their belief
in its eternal fitness, are founded on illusion. True, the whole attitude of horror and holy superiority assumed by Puritanism towards
the Church of Rome, is wrong and false, and well merits Sir Henry
Wotton's* rebuke: — 'Take heed of thinking that the farther you go
from the Church of Rome, the nearer you are to God.' True, one of
the best wishes one could form for Mr Spurgeon or Father Jackson*
is, that they might be permitted to learn on this side the grave (for if
they do not, a considerable surprise is certainly reserved for them
on the other) that Whitfield* and Wesley were not at all better than
St Francis,* and that they themselves are not at all better than
Lacordaire.* Yet, in spite of all this, so noble and divine a thing is
religion, so respectable is that earnestness which desires a prayer-
book with one strain of doctrine, so attaching is the order and discipline by which we are used to have our religion conveyed, so many
claims on our regard has that popular form of church government
for which Nonconformists contend, so perfectly compatible is it
with all progress towards perfection, that culture would make us shy
even to propose to Nonconformists the acceptance of the Anglican
prayer-book and the episcopal order; and would be forward to
wish them a prayer-book of their own approving, and the church
discipline to which they are attached and accustomed.

Only not at the price of Mialism; that is, of a doctrine which leaves the Nonconformists in holes and corners, out of contact with the main current of national life. One can lay one's finger, indeed, on the line by which this doctrine has grown up, and see how the essential part of Nonconformity is a popular church-discipline analogous to that of the other reformed churches, and how its voluntaryism is an accident. It contended for the establishment of its own church-discipline as the only true one; and beaten in this contention, and seeing its rival established, it came down to the more plausible pro- posal 'to place all good men alike in a condition of religious equality;' and this plan of proceeding, originally taken as a mere second-best, became, by long sticking to it and preaching it up, first fair, then righteous, then the only righteous, then at last necessary to salvation. This is the plan for remedying the Nonconformists' divorce from contact with the national life by divorcing churchmen too from con- tact with it; that is, as we have familiarly before put it, the tailless foxes are for cutting off tails all round. But this the other foxes could not wisely grant, unless it were proved that tails are of no value. And so, too, unless it is proved that contact with the main current of national life is of no value (and we have shown that it is of the greatest value), we cannot safely, even to please the Nonconformists in a matter where we would please them as much as possible, admit Mialism.

But now, as we have shown the disinterestedness which culture enjoins, and its obedience not to likings or dislikings, but to the aim of perfection, let us show its flexibility,—its independence of machinery.* That other and greater prophet of intelligence, and rea- son, and the simple natural truth of things,—Mr Bright,—means by these, as we have seen, a certain set of measures which suit the special ends of Liberal and Nonconformist partisans. For instance, reason and justice towards Ireland mean the abolishment of the ini- quitous Protestant ascendency in such a particular way as to suit the Nonconformists' antipathy to establishments. Reason and justice pursued in a different way, by distributing among the three main Churches of Ireland,—the Roman Catholic, the Anglican, and the Presbyterian,—the church property of Ireland, would immediately cease, for Mr Bright and the Nonconformists, to be reason and justice at all, and would become, as Mr Spurgeon says, 'a setting up of the Roman image.'* Thus we see that the sort of intelligence reached by culture is more disinterested than the sort of intelligence reached by belonging to the Liberal party in the great towns, and taking a commendable interest in politics. But still more striking is the difference between the two views of intelligence, when we see that culture not only makes a quite disinterested choice of the machinery proper to carry us towards sweetness and light, and to make reason and the will of God prevail,* but by even this machinery does not hold stiffly and blindly, and easily passes on beyond it to that for the sake of which it chose it.

For instance: culture leads us to think that the ends of human perfection might be best served by establishing,—that is, by bringing into contact with the main current of the national life,—in Ireland the Roman Catholic and the Presbyterian Churches along with the Anglican Church; and, in England, a Presbyterian or Congregational Church of like rank and *status* with our Episcopalian one. It leads us to think that we should really, in this way, be working to make reason and the will of God prevail; because we should be making Roman Catholics better citizens, and Nonconformists,—nay, and Churchmen along with them,—larger-minded and more complete men. But undoubtedly there are great difficulties in such a plan as this; and the plan is not one which looks very likely to be adopted. It is a plan more for a time of creative statesmen, like the time of Elizabeth, than for a time of instrumental statesmen like the present. The Churchman must rise above his ordinary self in order to favour it; and the Nonconformist has worshipped his fetish of separatism so long that he is likely to wish still to remain, like Ephraim, 'a wild ass alone by himself.'* The centre of power being where it is, our instrumental statesmen have every temptation, as is shown more at large in the following essay, in the first place, to 'relieve themselves,' as *The Times* says, 'of troublesome and irritating responsibilities;' in the second place, when they must act, to go along, as they do, with the ordinary self of those on whose favour they depend, to adopt as their own its desires, and to serve them with fidelity, and even, if possible, with impulsiveness. This is the more easy for them, because there are not wanting,—and there never will be wanting,—thinkers like Mr Baxter, Mr Charles Buxton, and the Dean of Canterbury, to swim with the stream, but to swim with it philosophically; to call the desires of the ordinary self of any great section of the community edicts of the national mind and laws of human progress, and to give them a general, a philosophic, and an imposing expression. A generous statesman may honestly, therefore, soon unlearn any dis-position to put his tongue in his cheek in advocating these desires, and may advocate them with fervour and impulsiveness. Therefore a plan such as that which we have indicated does not seem a plan so likely to find favour as a plan for abolishing the Irish Church by the power of the Nonconformists' antipathy to establishments.

But to tell us that our fond dreams are on that account shattered is inexact, and is the sort of language which ought to be addressed to the promoters of intelligence through public meetings and a com-mendable interest in politics, when they fail in their designs, and not to us. For we are fond stickers to no machinery, not even our own; and we have no doubt that perfection can be reached without it,— with free churches as with established churches, and with instru-mental statesmen as with creative statesmen. But it can never be reached without seeing things as they really are; and it is to this, therefore, and to no machinery in the world, that culture sticks fondly. It insists that men should not mistake, as they are prone to mistake, their natural taste for the bathos for a relish for the sublime;* and if statesmen, either with their tongue in their cheek or through a generous impulsiveness, tell them their natural taste for the bathos is a relish for the sublime, there is the more need for culture to tell them the contrary. It is delusion on this point which is fatal, and against delusion on this point culture works. It is not fatal to our Liberal friends to labour for free trade, extension of the suffrage, and abolition of church-rates, instead of graver social ends; but it is fatal to them to be told by their flatterers, and to believe, with our pauperism increasing more rapidly than our population, that they have performed a great, an heroic work, by occupying themselves exclusively, for the last thirty years, with these Liberal nostrums, and that the right and good course for them now is to go on occupying themselves with the like for the future. It is not fatal to Americans to have no religious establishments and no effective centres of high culture; but it is fatal to them to be told by their flatterers, and to believe, that they are the most intelligent people in the whole world, when of intelligence, in the true and fruitful sense of the word, they even singularly, as we have seen, come short. It is not fatal to the Nonconformists to remain with their separated churches; but it is fatal to them to be told by their flatterers, and to believe, that theirs is the one pure and Christ-ordained way of worshipping God, that provincialism and loss of totality have not come to them from following it, or that provincialism and loss of totality are not evils. It is not fatal to the English nation to abolish the Irish Church by the power of the Nonconformists' antipathy to establishments; but it is fatal to it to be told by its flatterers, and to believe, that it is abolishing it through reason and justice, when it is really abolishing it through this power; or to expect the fruits of reason and justice from anything but the spirit of reason and justice themselves.

Now culture, because of its keen sense of what is really fatal, is all the more disposed to be pliant and easy about what is not fatal. And because machinery is the bane of politics, and an inward working, and not machinery, is what we most want, we keep advising our ardent young Liberal friends to think less of machinery, to stand more aloof from the arena of politics at present, and rather to try and promote, with us, an inward working. They do not listen to us, and they rush into the arena of politics, where their merits, indeed, seem to be little appreciated as yet; and then they complain of the reformed constituencies, and call the new Parliament a Philistine Parliament.* As if a nation, nourished and reared in Hebraising, could give us, just yet, anything better than a Philistine Parliament!—for would a Barbarian Parliament be even so good, or a Populace Parliament? For our part, we rejoice to see our dear old friends, the Hebraising Philistines, gathered in force in the Valley of Jehoshaphat* before their final conversion, which will certainly come; but for this conversion we must not try to oust them from their places, and to contend for machinery with them, but we must work on them inwardly and cure them of Hebraising.

Yet *the days of Israel are innumerable*;* and in its blame of Hebraising too, and in its praise of Hellenising, culture must not fail to keep its flexibility, and to give to its judgments that passing and provisional character which we have seen it impose on its preferences and rejections of machinery. Now, and for us, it is a time to Hellenise, and to praise knowing; for we have Hebraised too much, and have overvalued doing. But the habits and discipline received from Hebraism remain for our race an eternal possession; and, as humanity is constituted, one must never assign them the second rank to-day, without being ready to restore them to the first rank to-morrow. To walk staunchly by the best light one has,* to be strict and sincere with oneself, not to be of the number of those who say and do not, to be in earnest,—this is the discipline by which alone man is enabled to rescue his life from thraldom to the passing moment and to his bodily senses, to ennoble it, and to make it eternal. And this discipline has been nowhere so effectively taught as in the school of Hebraism. Sophocles and Plato knew as well as the author of the Epistle to the Hebrews that 'without holiness no man shall see God,'* and their notion of what goes to make up holiness was larger than his. But the intense and convinced energy with which the Hebrew, both of the Old and of the New Testament, threw himself upon his ideal, and which inspired the incomparable definition of the great Christian virtue, Faith,—*the substance of things hoped for, the evidence of things not seen,*—this energy of faith in its ideal has belonged to Hebraism alone. As our idea of holiness enlarges, and our scope of perfection widens beyond the narrow limits to which the over-rigour of Hebraising has tended to confine it, we shall come again to Hebraism for that devout energy in embracing our ideal, which alone can give to man the happiness of doing what he knows. 'If ye know these things, happy are ye if ye do them!'*—the last word for infirm humanity will always be that. For this word, reiterated with a power now sublime, now affecting, but always admirable, our race will, as long as the world lasts, return to Hebraism; and the Bible, which preaches this word, will forever remain, as Goethe called it, not only a national book, but the Book of the Nations.'* Again and again, after what seemed breaches and separations, the prophetic promise to Jerusalem will still be true:—*Lo, thy sons come, whom thou sentest away; they come gathered from the west unto the east by the word of the Holy One, rejoicing in the remembrance of God.**

INTRODUCTION

IN one of his speeches a year or two ago,* that fine speaker and famous Liberal, Mr Bright, took occasion to have a fling at the friends and preachers of culture. 'People who talk about what they call *culture!*' said he contemptuously; 'by which they mean a smattering of the two dead languages of Greek and Latin.' And he went on to remark, in a strain with which modern speakers and writers have made us very familiar, how poor a thing this culture is, how little good it can do to the world, and how absurd it is for its possessors to set much store by it. And the other day a younger Liberal than Mr Bright, one of a school whose mission it is to bring into order and system that body of truth of which the earlier Liberals merely touched the outside, a member of the University of Oxford, and a very clever writer, Mr Frederic Harrison,* developed, in the systematic and stringent manner of his school, the thesis which Mr Bright had propounded in only general terms. 'Perhaps the very silliest cant of the day,' said Mr Frederic Harrison, 'is the cant about culture. Culture is a desirable quality in a critic of new books, and sits well on a possessor of *belles lettres*; but as applied to politics, it means simply a turn for small faultfinding, love of selfish ease, and indecision in action. The man of culture is in politics one of the poorest mortals alive. For simple pedantry and want of good sense no man is his equal. No assumption is too unreal, no end is too unpractical for him. But the active exercise of politics requires common sense, sympathy, trust, resolution and enthusiasm, qualities which your man of culture has carefully rooted up, lest they damage the delicacy of his critical olfactories. Perhaps they are the only class of responsible beings in the community who cannot with safety be entrusted with power.'

Now for my part I do not wish to see men of culture asking to be entrusted with power; and, indeed, I have freely said, that in my opinion the speech most proper, at present, for a man of culture to make to a body of his fellow-countrymen who get him into a committee-room, is Socrates's: *Know thyself!** and this is not a speech to be made by men wanting to be entrusted with power. For this very indifference to direct political action I have been taken to task by the *Daily Telegraph*, coupled, by a strange perversity of fate,

with just that very one of the Hebrew prophets whose style I admire
the least, and called 'an elegant Jeremiah.'* It is because I say (to use
the words which the *Daily Telegraph* puts in my mouth):—'You
mustn't make a fuss because you have no vote,—that is vulgarity;
you mustn't hold big meetings to agitate for reform bills and to
repeal corn laws,—that is the very height of vulgarity,'—it is for this
reason that I am called, sometimes an elegant Jeremiah, sometimes a
spurious Jeremiah, a Jeremiah about the reality of whose mission the
writer in the *Daily Telegraph* has his doubts. It is evident, therefore,
that I have so taken my line as not to be exposed to the whole brunt
of Mr Frederic Harrison's censure. Still, I have often spoken in
praise of culture; I have striven to make all my works and ways serve
the interests of culture; I take culture to be something a great deal
more than what Mr Frederic Harrison and others call it: 'a desirable
quality in a critic of new books.' Nay, even though to a certain extent
I am disposed to agree with Mr Frederic Harrison, that men of
culture are just the class of responsible beings in this community of
ours who cannot properly, at present, be entrusted with power, I am
not sure that I do not think this the fault of our community rather
than of the men of culture. In short, although, like Mr Bright and
Mr Frederic Harrison, and the editor of the *Daily Telegraph*, and a
large body of valued friends of mine, I am a liberal, yet I am a liberal
tempered by experience, reflection, and renouncement, and I am,
above all, a believer in culture. Therefore I propose now to try and
enquire, in the simple unsystematic way* which best suits both my
taste and my powers, what culture really is, what good it can do, what
is our own special need of it; and I shall seek to find some plain
grounds on which a faith in culture—both my own faith in it and
the faith of others,—may rest securely.

CHAPTER I

THE disparagers of culture make its motive curiosity;* sometimes,
indeed, they make its motive mere exclusiveness and vanity. The
culture which is supposed to plume itself on a smattering of Greek
and Latin is a culture which is begotten by nothing so intellectual as
curiosity; it is valued either out of sheer vanity and ignorance, or else
as an engine of social and class distinction, separating its holder, like

a badge or title, from other people who have not got it. No serious man would call this *culture*, or attach any value to it, as culture, at all. To find the real ground for the very differing estimate which serious people will set upon culture, we must find some motive for culture in the terms of which may lie a real ambiguity; and such a motive the word *curiosity* gives us. I have before now pointed out* that in English we do not, like the foreigners, use this word in a good sense as well as in a bad sense; with us the word is always used in a somewhat disapproving sense; a liberal and intelligent eagerness about the things of the mind may be meant by a foreigner when he speaks of curiosity, but with us the word always conveys a certain notion of frivolous and unedifying activity. In the *Quarterly Review*, some little time ago, was an estimate of the celebrated French critic, Monsieur Sainte-Beuve,* and a very inadequate estimate it, in my judgment, was. And its inadequacy consisted chiefly in this: that in our English way it left out of sight the double sense really involved in the word *curiosity*, thinking enough was said to stamp Monsieur Sainte-Beuve with blame if it was said that he was impelled in his operations as a critic by curiosity, and omitting either to perceive that Monsieur Sainte-Beuve himself, and many other people with him, would consider that this was praiseworthy and not blameworthy, or to point out why it ought really to be accounted worthy of blame and not of praise. For as there is a curiosity about intellectual matters which is futile, and merely a disease, so there is certainly a curiosity,—a desire after the things of the mind simply for their own sakes and for the pleasure of seeing them as they are,*—which is, in an intelligent being, natural and laudable. Nay, and the very desire to see things as they are implies a balance and regulation of mind which is not often attained without fruitful effort, and which is the very opposite of the blind and diseased impulse of mind which is what we mean to blame when we blame curiosity. Montesquieu* says:—'The first motive which ought to impel us to study is the desire to augment the excellence of our nature, and to render an intelligent being yet more intelligent.' This is the true ground to assign for the genuine scientific passion, however manifested, and for culture, viewed simply as a fruit of this passion; and it is a worthy ground, even though we let the term *curiosity* stand to describe it.

But there is of culture another view, in which not solely the scientific passion, the sheer desire to see things as they are, natural and proper in an intelligent being, appears as the ground of it. There is a view in which all the love of our neighbour, the impulses towards action, help, and beneficence, the desire for stopping human error, clearing human confusion, and diminishing the sum of human misery, the noble aspiration to leave the world better and happier than we found it,—motives eminently such as are called social,—come in as part of the grounds of culture, and the main and pre-eminent part. Culture is then properly described not as having its origin in curiosity, but as having its origin in the love of perfection; it is *a study of perfection*. It moves by the force, not merely or primarily of the scientific passion for pure knowledge, but also of the moral and social passion for doing good. As, in the first view of it, we took for its worthy motto Montesquieu's words: 'To render an intelligent being yet more intelligent!' so, in the second view of it, there is no better motto which it can have than these words of Bishop Wilson: 'To make reason and the will of God prevail!'* Only, whereas the passion for doing good is apt to be overhasty in determining what reason and the will of God say, because its turn is for acting rather than thinking, and it wants to be beginning to act; and whereas it is apt to take its own conceptions, which proceed from its own state of development and share in all the imperfections and immaturities of this, for a basis of action; what distinguishes culture is, that it is possessed by the scientific passion, as well as by the passion of doing good; that it has worthy notions of reason and the will of God, and does not readily suffer its own crude conceptions to substitute themselves for them; and that, knowing that no action or institution can be salutary and stable which are not based on reason and the will of God, it is not so bent on acting and instituting, even with the great aim of diminishing human error and misery ever before its thoughts, but that it can remember that acting and instituting are of little use, unless we know how and what we ought to act and to institute.

This culture is more interesting and more far-reaching than that other, which is founded solely on the scientific passion for knowing. But it needs times of faith and ardour,* times when the intellectual horizon is opening and widening all round us, to flourish in. And is not the close and bounded intellectual horizon within which we have long lived and moved now lifting up, and are not new lights finding free passage to shine in upon us? For a long time there was no passage for them to make their way in upon us, and then it was of no use to think of adapting the world's action to them. Where was the hope of making reason and the will of God prevail among people who had a routine which they had christened reason and the will of God,* in which they were inextricably bound, and beyond which they had no power of looking? But now the iron force of adhesion to the old routine,—social, political, religious,—has wonderfully yielded; the iron force of exclusion of all which is new has wonderfully yielded; the danger now is, not that people should obstinately refuse to allow anything but their old routine to pass for reason and the will of God, but either that they should allow some novelty or other to pass for these too easily, or else that they should underrate the importance of them altogether, and think it enough to follow action for its own sake, without troubling themselves to make reason and the will of God prevail therein. Now, then, is the moment for culture to be of service, culture which believes in making reason and the will of God prevail, believes in perfection, is the study and pursuit of perfection, and is no longer debarred, by a rigid invincible exclusion of whatever is new, from getting acceptance for its ideas, simply because they are new.

The moment this view of culture is seized, the moment it is regarded not solely as the endeavour to see things as they are, to draw towards a knowledge of the universal order which seems to be intended and aimed at in the world, and which it is a man's happiness to go along with or his misery to go counter to,—to learn, in short, the will of God,—the moment, I say, culture is considered not merely as the endeavour to *see* and *learn* this, but as the endeavour, also, to make it *prevail*, the moral, social, and beneficent character of culture becomes manifest. The mere endeavour to see and learn it for our own personal satisfaction is indeed a commencement for making it prevail, a preparing the way for this, which always serves this, and is wrongly, therefore, stamped with blame absolutely in itself, and not only in its caricature and degeneration. But perhaps it has got stamped with blame, and disparaged with the dubious title of curiosity, because in comparison with this wider endeavour of such great and plain utility it looks selfish, petty, and unprofitable.

And religion, the greatest and most important of the efforts by which the human race has manifested its impulse to perfect itself,— religion, that voice of the deepest human experience,—does not only enjoin and sanction the aim which is the great aim of culture, the aim of setting ourselves to ascertain what perfection is and to make it prevail; but also, in determining generally in what human perfection consists, religion comes to a conclusion identical with that which culture,—seeking the determination of this question through all the voices of human experience which have been heard upon it, art, science, poetry, philosophy, history, as well as religion, in order to give a greater fulness and certainty to its solution,—likewise reaches. Religion says: *The kingdom of God is within you,** and culture, in like manner, places human perfection in an *internal* condition, in the growth and predominance of our humanity proper, as distinguished from our animality, in the ever-increasing efficaciousness and in the general harmonious expansion of those gifts of thought and feeling which make the peculiar dignity, wealth, and happiness of human nature. As I have said on a former occasion:* 'It is in making endless additions to itself, in the endless expansion of its powers, in endless growth in wisdom and beauty, that the spirit of the human race finds its ideal. To reach this ideal, culture is an indispensable aid, and that is the true value of culture.' Not a having and a resting, but a growing and a becoming, is the character of perfection as culture conceives it; and here, too, it coincides with religion. And because men are all members of one great whole, and the sympathy which is in human nature will not allow one member to be indifferent to the rest, or to have a perfect welfare independent of the rest, the expansion of our humanity, to suit the idea of perfection which culture forms, must be a *general* expansion. Perfection, as culture conceives it, is not possible while the individual remains isolated: the individual is obliged, under pain of being stunted and enfeebled in his own development if he disobeys, to carry others along with him in his march towards perfection,* to be continually doing all he can to enlarge and increase the volume of the human stream sweeping thitherward; and here, once more, it lays on us the same obligation as religion, which says, as Bishop Wilson has admirably put it, that 'to promote the kingdom of God is to increase and hasten one's own happiness.'* Finally, perfection,—as culture, from a thorough disinterested study of human nature and human experience, learns to conceive it,—is an harmonious expansion* of *all* the powers which make the beauty and worth of human nature, and is not consistent with the over-development of any one power at the expense of the rest Here it goes beyond religion, as religion is generally conceived by us.*

If culture, then, is a study of perfection, and of harmonious perfection, general perfection, and perfection which consists in becoming something rather than in having something, in an inward condition of the mind and spirit, not in an outward set of circumstances,—it is clear that culture, instead of being the frivolous and useless thing which Mr Bright, and Mr Frederic Harrison, and many other liberals are apt to call it, has a very important function to fulfil for mankind. And this function is particularly important in our modern world, of which the whole civilisation is, to a much greater degree than the civilisation of Greece and Rome, mechanical and external, and tends constantly to become more so. But above all in our own country has culture a weighty part to perform, because here that mechanical character, which civilisation tends to take everywhere, is shown in the most eminent degree. Indeed nearly all the characters of perfection, as culture teaches us to fix them, meet in this country with some powerful tendency which thwarts them and sets them at defiance. The idea of perfection as an *inward* condition of the mind and spirit is at variance with the mechanical and material civilisation in esteem with us, and nowhere, as I have said, so much in esteem as with us. The idea of perfection as a *general* expansion of the human family is at variance with our strong individualism, our hatred of all limits to the unrestrained swing of the individual's personality, our maxim of 'every man for himself.'* The idea of perfection as an *harmonious* expansion of human nature is at variance with our want of flexibility, with our inaptitude for seeing more than one side of a thing, with our intense energetic absorption in the particular pursuit we happen to be following. So culture has a rough task to achieve in this country, and its preachers have, and are likely long to have, a hard time of it, and they will much oftener be regarded, for a great while to come, as elegant or spurious Jeremiahs, than as friends and benefactors. That, however, will not prevent their doing in the end good service if they persevere; and meanwhile, the mode of action they have to pursue, and the sort of habits they must fight against, should be made quite clear to every one who may be willing to look at the matter attentively and dispassionately.

Faith in machinery is, I said, our besetting danger;* often in machinery most absurdly disproportioned to the end which this machinery, if it is to do any good at all, is to serve; but always in machinery, as if it had a value in and for itself. What is freedom but machinery? what is population but machinery? what is coal but machinery? what are railroads but machinery? what is wealth but machinery? what are religious organisations but machinery? Now almost every voice in England is accustomed to speak of these things as if they were precious ends in themselves, and therefore had some of the characters of perfection indisputably joined to them. I have once before noticed Mr Roebuck's stock argument* for proving the greatness and happiness of England as she is, and for quite stopping the mouths of all gainsayers. Mr Roebuck is never weary of reiterating this argument of his, so I do not know why I should be weary of noticing it. 'May not every man in England say what he likes?'— Mr Roebuck perpetually asks; and that, he thinks, is quite sufficient, and when every man may say what he likes, our aspirations ought to be satisfied. But the aspirations of culture, which is the study of perfection, are not satisfied, unless what men say, when they may say what they like, is worth saying,—has good in it, and more good than bad. In the same way *The Times*,* replying to some foreign strictures on the dress, looks, and behaviour of the English abroad, urges that the English ideal is that every one should be free to do and to look just as he likes. But culture indefatigably tries, not to make what each raw person may like, the rule by which he fashions himself; but to draw ever nearer to a sense of what is indeed beautiful, graceful, and becoming, and to get the raw person to like that. And in the same way with respect to railroads and coal. Every one must have observed the strange language current during the late discussions as to the possible failure of our supplies of coal.* Our coal, thousands of people were saying, is the real basis of our national greatness; if our coal runs short, there is an end of the greatness of England. But what *is* greatness?—culture makes us ask. Greatness is a spiritual condition worthy to excite love, interest, and admiration; and the outward proof of possessing greatness is that we excite love, interest, and admiration. If England were swallowed up by the sea to-morrow, which of the two, a hundred years hence, would most excite the love, interest, and admiration of mankind,—would most, therefore, show the evidences of having possessed greatness,—the England of the last twenty years, or the England of Elizabeth,* of a time of splendid spiritual effort, but when our coal, and our industrial operations depending on coal, were very little developed? Well then, what an unsound habit of mind it must be which makes us talk of things like coal or iron as constituting the greatness of England, and how salutary a friend is culture, bent on seeing things as they are, and thus dissipating delusions of this kind and fixing standards of perfection that are real!

Wealth, again, that end to which our prodigious works for material advantage are directed,—the commonest of commonplaces tells us how men are always apt to regard wealth as a precious end in itself; and certainly they have never been so apt thus to regard it as they are in England at the present time. Never did people believe anything more firmly, than nine Englishmen out of ten at the present day believe that our greatness and welfare are proved by our being so very rich. Now, the use of culture is that it helps us, by means of its spiritual standard of perfection, to regard wealth as but machinery, and not only to say as a matter of words that we regard wealth as but machinery, but really to perceive and feel that it is so. If it were not for this purging effect wrought upon our minds by culture, the whole world, the future as well as the present, would inevitably belong to the Philistines. The people who believe most that our greatness and welfare are proved by our being very rich, and who most give their lives and thoughts to becoming rich, are just the very people whom we call the Philistines. Culture says: 'Consider these people, then, their way of life, their habits, their manners, the very tones of their voice; look at them attentively; observe the literature they read, the things which give them pleasure, the words which come forth out of their mouths, the thoughts which make the furniture of their minds; would any amount of wealth be worth having with the condition that one was to become just like these people by having it?' And thus culture begets a dissatisfaction which is of the highest possible value in stemming the common tide of men's thoughts in a wealthy and industrial community, and which saves the future, as one may hope, from being vulgarised, even if it cannot save the present.

Population, again, and bodily health and vigour, are things which are nowhere treated in such an unintelligent, misleading, exaggerated way as in England. Both are really machinery; yet how many people all around us do we see rest in them and fail to look beyond them! Why, I have heard people, fresh from reading certain articles of *The Times* on the Registrar-General's returns of marriages and births* in this country, who would talk of large families in quite a solemn strain, as if they had something in itself beautiful, elevating, and meritorious in them; as if the British Philistine would have only to present himself before the Great Judge with his twelve children, in order to be received among the sheep as a matter of right! But bodily health and vigour, it may be said, are not to be classed with wealth and population as mere machinery; they have a more real and essential value. True; but only as they are more intimately connected with a perfect spiritual condition than wealth or population are. The moment we disjoin them from the idea of a perfect spiritual condition, and pursue them, as we do pursue them, for their own sake and as ends in themselves, our worship of them becomes as mere worship of machinery, as our worship of wealth or population, and as unintelligent and vulgarising a worship as that is. Every one with anything like an adequate idea of human perfection has distinctly marked this subordination to higher and spiritual ends of the cultivation of bodily vigour and activity. 'Bodily exercise profiteth little; but godliness is profitable unto all things,'* says the author of the Epistle to Timothy. And the utilitarian Franklin* says just as explicitly:— 'Eat and drink such an exact quantity as suits the constitution of thy body, *in reference to the services of the mind.*' But the point of view of culture, keeping the mark of human perfection simply and broadly in view, and not assigning to this perfection, as religion or utilitarianism assign to it, a special and limited character,—this point of view, I say, of culture is best given by these words of Epictetus:*—'It is a sign of ἀφυΐα,' says he,—that is, of a nature not finely tempered,— 'to give yourselves up to things which relate to the body; to make, for instance, a great fuss about exercise, a great fuss about eating, a great fuss about drinking, a great fuss about walking, a great fuss about riding. All these things ought to be done merely *by the way*: the formation of the spirit and character must be our real concern.' This is admirable; and, indeed, the Greek words ἀφυΐα, εὐφυΐα, a finely tempered nature, a coarsely tempered nature, give exactly the notion of perfection as culture brings us to conceive of it: a perfection in which the characters of beauty and intelligence are both present, which unites 'the two noblest of things,'—as Swift, who of one of the two, at any rate, had himself all too little, most happily calls them in his *Battle of the Books*,*—'the two noblest of things, *sweetness and light*.' The εὐφυής is the man who tends towards sweetness and light; the ἀφυής is precisely our Philistine. The immense spiritual significance of the Greeks is due to their having been inspired with this central and happy idea of the essential character of human perfection; and Mr Bright's misconception of culture, as a smattering of Greek and Latin, comes itself, after all, from this wonderful significance of the Greeks having affected the very machinery of our education, and is in itself a kind of homage to it.

It is by thus making sweetness and light to be characters of perfection, that culture is of like spirit with poetry, follows one law with poetry. I have called religion a more important manifestation of human nature than poetry, because it has worked on a broader scale for perfection, and with greater masses of men. But the idea of beauty and of a human nature perfect on all its sides, which is the dominant idea of poetry, is a true and invaluable idea, though it has not yet had the success that the idea of conquering the obvious faults of our animality, and of a human nature perfect on the moral side, which is the dominant idea of religion, has been enabled to have; and it is destined, adding to itself the religious idea of a devout energy, to transform and govern the other. The best art and poetry of the Greeks, in which religion and poetry are one, in which the idea of beauty and of a human nature perfect on all sides adds to itself a religious and devout energy, and works in the strength of that, is on this account of such surpassing interest and instructiveness for us, though it was,—as, having regard to the human race in general, and, indeed, having regard to the Greeks themselves, we must own,—a premature attempt, an attempt which for success needed the moral and religious fibre in humanity to be more braced and developed than it had yet been. But Greece did not err in having the idea of beauty, harmony, and complete human perfection, so present and paramount; it is impossible to have this idea too present and paramount; only the moral fibre must be braced too. And we, because we have braced the moral fibre, are not on that account in the right way, if at the same time the idea of beauty, harmony, and complete human perfection, is wanting or misapprehended amongst us; and evidently it *is* wanting or misapprehended at present. And when we rely as we do on our religious organisations, which in themselves do not and cannot give us this idea, and think we have done enough if we make them spread and prevail, then, I say, we fall into our common fault of overvaluing machinery.

Nothing is more common than for people to confound the inward peace and satisfaction which follows the subduing of the obvious faults of our animality with what I may call absolute inward peace and satisfaction,—the peace and satisfaction which are reached as we draw near to complete spiritual perfection, and not merely to moral perfection, or rather to relative moral perfection. No people in the world have done more and struggled more to attain this relative moral perfection than our English race has; for no people in the world has the command to *resist the Devil*, to *overcome the Wicked One*,* in the nearest and most obvious sense of those words, had such a pressing force and reality. And we have had our reward, not only in the great worldly prosperity which our obedience to this command has brought us, but also, and far more, in great inward peace and satisfaction. But to me few things are more pathetic than to see people, on the strength of the inward peace and satisfaction which their rudimentary efforts towards perfection have brought them, use, concerning their incomplete perfection and the religious organisations within which they have found it, language which properly applies only to complete perfection, and is a far-off echo of the human soul's prophecy of it. Religion itself, I need hardly say, supplies in abundance this grand language, which is really the severest criticism of such an incomplete perfection as alone we have yet reached through our religious organisations.

The impulse of the English race towards moral development and self-conquest has nowhere so powerfully manifested itself as in Puritanism; nowhere has Puritanism found so adequate an expression as in the religious organisation of the Independents.* The modern Independents have a newspaper, the *Nonconformist*,* written with great sincerity and ability. The motto, the standard, the profession of faith which this organ of theirs carries aloft, is: 'The Dissidence of Dissent and the Protestantism of the Protestant religion.' There is sweetness and light, and an ideal of complete harmonious human perfection! One need not go to culture and poetry to find language to judge it. Religion, with its instinct for perfection, supplies language to judge it: 'Finally, be of one mind, united in feeling,'* says St Peter. There is an ideal which judges the Puritan ideal—'The Dissidence of Dissent and the Protestantism of the Protestant religion!' And religious organisations like this are what people believe in, rest in, would give their lives for! Such, I say, is the wonderful virtue of even the beginnings of perfection, of having conquered even the plain faults of our animality, that the religious organisation which has helped us to do it can seem to us something precious, salutary, and to be propagated, even when it wears such a brand of imperfection on its forehead as this. And men have got such a habit of giving to the language of religion a special application, of making it a mere jargon, that for the condemnation which religion itself passes on the short-comings of their religious organisations they have no ear; they are sure to cheat themselves and to explain this condemnation away. They can only be reached by the criticism which culture, like poetry, speaking a language not to be sophisticated, and resolutely testing these organisations by the ideal of a human perfection complete on all sides, applies to them.

But men of culture and poetry, it will be said, are again and again failing, and failing conspicuously, in the necessary first stage to per-fection, in the subduing of the great obvious faults of our animality, which it is the glory of these religious organisations to have helped us to subdue. True, they do often so fail: they have often been with-out the virtues as well as the faults of the Puritan; it has been one of their dangers that they so felt the Puritan's faults that they too much neglected the practice of his virtues. I will not, however, exculpate them at the Puritan's expense; they have often failed in morality, and morality is indispensable; they have been punished for their failure, as the Puritan has been rewarded for his performance. They have been punished wherein they erred; but their ideal of beauty and sweetness and light, and a human nature complete on all its sides, remains the true ideal of perfection still; just as the Puritan's ideal of perfection remains narrow and inadequate, although for what he did well he has been richly rewarded. Notwithstanding the mighty results of the Pilgrim Fathers'* voyage, they and their standard of perfection are rightly judged when we figure to ourselves Shake-speare or Virgil,*—souls in whom sweetness and light, and all that in human nature is most humane, were eminent,—accompanying them on their voyage, and think what intolerable company Shake-speare and Virgil would have found them! In the same way let us judge the religious organisations which we see all around us. Do not let us deny the good and the happiness which they have accom-plished; but do not let us fail to see clearly that their idea of human perfection is narrow and inadequate, and that the Dissidence of

Dissent and the Protestantism of the Protestant religion will never
bring humanity to its true goal. As I said with regard to wealth,—let
us look at the life of those who live in and for it;—so I say with regard
to the religious organisations. Look at the life imagined in such a
newspaper as the *Nonconformist*;—a life of jealousy of the Establishment, disputes, tea-meetings, openings of chapels, sermons; and then
think of it as an ideal of a human life completing itself on all sides,
and aspiring with all its organs after sweetness, light, and perfection!

Another newspaper, representing, like the *Nonconformist*, one of
the religious organisations of this country, was a short time ago
giving an account of the crowd at Epsom on the Derby day,* and of all
the vice and hideousness which was to be seen in that crowd; and
then the writer turned suddenly round upon Professor Huxley, and
asked him how he proposed to cure all this vice and hideousness
without religion. I confess I felt disposed to ask the asker this question: And how do you propose to cure it with such a religion as
yours? How is the ideal of a life so unlovely, so unattractive, so
narrow, so far removed from a true and satisfying ideal of human
perfection, as is the life of your religious organisation as you yourself
image it, to conquer and transform all this vice and hideousness?
Indeed, the strongest plea for the study of perfection as pursued by
culture, the clearest proof of the actual inadequacy of the idea of
perfection held by the religious organisations,—expressing, as I have
said, the most wide-spread effort which the human race has yet
made after perfection,—is to be found in the state of our life and
society with these in possession of it, and having been in possession
of it I know not how many hundred years. We are all of us included
in some religious organisation or other; we all call ourselves, in
the sublime and aspiring language of religion which I have before
noticed, *children of God*.* Children of God;—it is an immense preten-
sion!—and how are we to justify it? By the works which we do, and
the words which we speak. And the work which we collective children of God do, our grand centre of life, our *city* which we have
builded for us to dwell in,* is London! London, with its unutterable
external hideousness, and with its internal canker of *publicé egestas,
privatim opulentia*,*—to use the words which Sallust puts into Cato's
mouth about Rome,—unequalled in the world! The word, again,
which we children of God speak, the voice which most hits our
collective thought, the newspaper with the largest circulation in

England, nay, with the largest circulation in the whole world, is the *Daily Telegraph*! I say that when our religious organisations,—which I admit to express the most considerable effort after perfection that our race has yet made,—land us in no better result than this, it is high time to examine carefully their idea of perfection, to see whether it does not leave out of account sides and forces of human nature which we might turn to great use; whether it would not be more operative if it were more complete. And I say that the English reliance on our religious organisations and on their ideas of human perfection just as they stand, is like our reliance on freedom, on muscular Christianity,* on population, on coal, on wealth,—mere belief in machinery, and unfruitful; and that it is wholesomely counteracted by culture, bent on seeing things as they are, and on drawing the human race onwards to a more complete perfection.

Culture, however, shows its single-minded love of perfection, its desire simply to make reason and the will of God prevail, its freedom from fanaticism, by its attitude towards all this machinery, even while it insists that it *is* machinery. Fanatics, seeing the mischief men do themselves by their blind belief in some machinery or other,— whether it is wealth and industrialism, or whether it is the cultivation of bodily strength and activity, or whether it is a political organisation, or whether it is a religious organisation,—oppose with might and main the tendency to this or that political and religious organisation, or to games and athletic exercises, or to wealth and industrialism, and try violently to stop it. But the flexibility which sweetness and light give, and which is one of the rewards of culture pursued in good faith, enables a man to see that a tendency may be necessary, and even, as a preparation for something in the future, salutary, and yet that the generations or individuals who obey this tendency are sacrificed to it, that they fall short of the hope of perfection by following it; and that its mischiefs are to be criticised, lest it should take too firm a hold and last after it has served its purpose. Mr Gladstone well pointed out, in a speech at Paris,*—and others have pointed out the same thing,—how necessary is the present great movement towards wealth and industrialism, in order to lay broad foundations of material well-being for the society of the future. The worst of these justifications is, that they are generally addressed to the very people engaged, body and soul, in the movement in question; at all events, they are always seized with the greatest avidity by these people, and taken by them as quite justifying their life; and that thus they tend to harden them in their sins. Now, culture admits the necessity of the movement towards fortune-making and exaggerated industrialism, readily allows that the future may derive benefit from it; but insists, at the same time, that the passing generations of industrialists,—forming, for the most part, the stout main body of Philistinism,—are sacrificed to it. In the same way, the result of all the games and sports which occupy the passing generation of boys and young men may be the establishment of a better and sounder physical type for the future to work with. Culture does not set itself against the games and sports; it congratulates the future, and hopes it will make a good use of its improved physical basis; but it points out that our passing generation of boys and young men is, meantime, sacrificed. Puritanism was necessary to develop the moral fibre of the English race, Nonconformity to break the yoke of ecclesiastical domination over men's minds and to prepare the way for freedom of thought in the distant future; still, culture points out that the harmonious perfection of generations of Puritans and Nonconformists have been, in consequence, sacrificed. Freedom of speech is necessary for the society of the future, but the young lions of the *Daily Telegraph** in the meanwhile are sacrificed. A voice for every man in his country's government is necessary for the society of the future, but meanwhile Mr Beales* and Mr Bradlaugh* are sacrificed.

Oxford, the Oxford of the past,* has many faults; and she has heavily paid for them in defeat, in isolation, in want of hold upon the modern world. Yet we in Oxford, brought up amidst the beauty and sweetness of that beautiful place, have not failed to seize one truth:— the truth that beauty and sweetness are essential characters of a complete human perfection. When I insist on this, I am all in the faith and tradition of Oxford. I say boldly that this our sentiment for beauty and sweetness, our sentiment against hideousness and rawness, has been at the bottom of our attachment to so many beaten causes, of our opposition to so many triumphant movements. And the sentiment is true, and has never been wholly defeated, and has shown its power even in its defeat. We have not won our political battles, we have not carried our main points, we have not stopped our adversaries' advance, we have not marched victoriously with the modern world; but we have told silently upon the mind of the country, we have prepared currents of feeling which sap our adversaries' position when it seems gained, we have kept up our own communications with the future. Look at the course of the great movement which shook Oxford to its centre* some thirty years ago! It was directed, as any one who reads Dr Newman's *Apology* may see, against what in one word may be called 'liberalism.' Liberalism prevailed;* it was the appointed force to do the work of the hour; it was necessary, it was inevitable that it should prevail. The Oxford movement was broken, it failed; our wrecks are scattered on every shore:

> Quæ regio in terris nostri non plena laboris?*

But what was it, this liberalism, as Dr Newman saw it, and as it really broke the Oxford movement? It was the great middle-class liberalism, which had for the cardinal points of its belief the Reform Bill of 1832, and local self-government, in politics; in the social sphere, free-trade, unrestricted competition, and the making of large industrial fortunes; in the religious sphere, the Dissidence of Dissent and the Protestantism of the Protestant religion. I do not say that other and more intelligent forces than this were not opposed to the Oxford movement: but this was the force which really beat it; this was the force which Dr Newman felt himself fighting with; this was the force which till only the other day seemed to be the paramount force in this country, and to be in possession of the future; this was the force whose achievements fill Mr Lowe* with such inexpressible admiration, and whose rule he was so horror-struck to see threatened. And where is this great force of Philistinism now? It is thrust into the second rank, it is become a power of yesterday, it has lost the future. A new power* has suddenly appeared, a power which it is impossible yet to judge fully, but which is certainly a wholly different force from middle-class liberalism; different in its cardinal points of belief, different in its tendencies in every sphere. It loves and admires neither the legislation of middle-class Parliaments, nor the local self-government of middle-class vestries, nor the unrestricted competition of middle-class industrialists, nor the dissidence of middle-class Dissent and the Protestantism of middle-class Protestant religion. I am not now praising this new force, or saying that its own ideals are better; all I say is, that they are wholly different. And who will estimate how much the currents of feeling created by Dr Newman's movement, the keen desire for beauty and sweetness which it nourished, the deep aversion it manifested to the hardness and vulgarity of middle-class liberalism, the strong light it turned on the hideous and grotesque illusions of middle-class Protestantism,— who will estimate how much all these contributed to swell the tide of secret dissatisfaction which has mined the ground under the self-confident liberalism of the last thirty years, and has prepared the way for its sudden collapse and supersession? It is in this manner that the sentiment of Oxford for beauty and sweetness conquers, and in this manner long may it continue to conquer!

In this manner it works to the same end as culture, and there is plenty of work for it yet to do. I have said that the new and more democratic force which is now superseding our old middle-class liberalism cannot yet be rightly judged. It has its main tendencies still to form. We hear promises of its giving us administrative reform, law reform, reform of education, and I know not what; but those promises come rather from its advocates, wishing to make a good plea for it and to justify it for superseding middle-class liberalism, than from clear tendencies which it has itself yet developed. But meanwhile it has plenty of well-intentioned friends against whom culture may with advantage continue to uphold steadily its ideal of human perfection; that this is *an inward spiritual activity, having for its characters increased sweetness, increased light, increased life, increased sympathy*. Mr Bright, who has a foot in both worlds, the world of middle-class liberalism and the world of democracy, but who brings most of his ideas from the world of middle-class liberalism in which he was bred, always inclines to inculcate that faith in machinery to which, as we have seen, Englishmen are so prone, and which has been the bane of middle-class liberalism. He complains with a sorrowful indignation of people who 'appear to have no proper estimate of the value of the franchise;' he leads his disciples to believe,—what the Englishman is always too ready to believe,—that the having a vote, like the having a large family, or a large business, or large muscles, has in itself some edifying and perfecting effect upon human nature. Or else he cries out to the democracy,—'the men,' as he calls them, 'upon whose shoulders the greatness of England rests,'—he cries out to them: 'See what you have done! I look over this country and see the cities you have built, the railroads you have made, the manufactures you have produced, the cargoes which freight the ships of the greatest mercantile navy the world has ever seen! I see that you have converted by your labours what was once a wilderness, these islands, into a fruitful garden; I know that you have created this wealth, and are a nation whose name is a word of power throughout all the world.'* Why, this is just the very style of laudation with which Mr Roebuck or Mr Lowe debauch the minds of the middle classes, and make such Philistines of them. It is the same fashion of teaching a man to value himself not on what he *is*, not on his progress in sweetness and light, but on the number of the railroads he has constructed, or the bigness of the Tabernacle* he has built. Only the middle classes are told they have done it all with their energy,* self-reliance, and capital, and the democracy are told they have done it all with their hands and sinews. But teaching the democracy to put its trust in achievements of this kind is merely training them to be Philistines to take the place of the Philistines whom they are superseding; and they too, like the middle class, will be encouraged to sit down at the banquet of the future without having on a wedding garment,* and nothing excellent can then come from them. Those who know their besetting faults, those who have watched them and listened to them, or those who will read the instructive account recently given of them by one of themselves, the *Journeyman Engineer*,* will agree that the idea which culture sets before us of perfection,—an increased spiritual activity, having for its characters increased sweetness, increased light, increased life, increased sympathy,—is an idea which the new democracy needs far more than the idea of the blessedness of the franchise, or the wonderfulness of their own industrial performances.

Other well-meaning friends of this new power are for leading it, not in the old ruts of middle-class Philistinism, but in ways which are naturally alluring to the feet of democracy, though in this country they are novel and untried ways. I may call them the ways of Jacobinism.* Violent indignation with the past, abstract systems of renovation applied wholesale, a new doctrine drawn up in black and white for elaborating down to the very smallest details a rational society for the future,—these are the ways of Jacobinism. Mr Frederic Harrison and other disciples of Comte,*—one of them, Mr Congreve,* is an old acquaintance of mine, and I am glad to have an opportunity of pub-licly expressing my respect for his talents and character,—are among the friends of democracy who are for leading it in paths of this kind. Mr Frederic Harrison is very hostile to culture, and from a natural enough motive; for culture is the eternal opponent of the two things which are the signal marks of Jacobinism,—its fierceness, and its addiction to an abstract system. Culture is always assigning to system-makers and systems a smaller share in the bent of human destiny than their friends like. A current in people's minds sets towards new ideas; people are dissatisfied with their old narrow stock of Philistine ideas, Anglo-Saxon ideas, or any other; and some man, some Bentham* or Comte, who has the real merit of having early and strongly felt and helped the new current, but who brings plenty of narrownesses and mistakes of his own into his feeling and help of it, is credited with being the author of the whole current, the fit person to be entrusted with its regulation and to guide the human race. The excellent German historian of the mythology of Rome, Preller,* relating the introduction at Rome under the Tarquins of the worship of Apollo, the god of light, healing, and reconciliation, observes that it was not so much the Tarquins who brought to Rome the new worship of Apollo, as a current in the mind of the Roman people which set powerfully at that time towards a new worship of this kind, and away from the old run of Latin and Sabine religious ideas. In a similar way, culture directs our attention to the current in human affairs, and to its continual working, and will not let us rivet our faith upon any one man and his doings. It makes us see, not only his good side, but also how much in him was of necessity limited and transient; nay, it even feels a pleasure, a sense of an increased freedom and of an ampler future, in so doing. I remember, when I was under the influence of a mind to which I feel the greatest obligations, the mind of a man who was the very incarnation of sanity and clear sense, a man the most considerable, it seems to me, whom America has yet produced,—Benjamin Franklin,*—I remember the relief with which, after long feeling the sway of Franklin's imperturbable common-sense, I came upon a project of his for a new version of the Book of Job, to replace the old version, the style of which, says Franklin, has become obsolete, and thence less agreeable. 'I give,' he continues, 'a few verses, which may serve as a sample of the kind of version I would recommend.' We all recollect the famous verse in our translation: 'Then Satan answered the Lord and said: "Doth Job fear God for nought?"' Franklin makes this: 'Does Your Majesty imagine that Job's good conduct is the effect of mere personal attachment and affection?' I well remember how when first I read that, I drew a deep breath of relief, and said to myself: 'After all, there is a stretch of humanity beyond Franklin's victorious good sense!' So, after hearing Bentham cried loudly up as the renovator of modern society, and Bentham's mind and ideas proposed as the rulers of our future, I open the *Deontology*.* There I read: 'While Xenophon was writing his history and Euclid teaching geometry, Socrates and Plato were talking nonsense under pretence of talking wisdom and morality. This morality of theirs consisted in words; this wisdom of theirs was the denial of matters known to every man's experience.' From the moment of reading that, I am delivered from the bondage of Bentham! the fanaticism of his adherents can touch me no longer; I feel the inadequacy of his mind and ideas for being the rule of human society, for perfection. Culture tends always thus to deal with the men of a system, of disciples, of a school; with men like Comte, or the late Mr Buckle,* or Mr Mill.* However much it may find to admire in these personages, or in some of them, it nevertheless remembers the text: 'Be not ye called Rabbi!'* and it soon passes on from any Rabbi. But Jacobinism loves a Rabbi; it does not want to pass on from its Rabbi in pursuit of a future and still unreached perfection; it wants its Rabbi and his ideas to stand for perfection, that they may with the more authority recast the world; and for Jacobinism, therefore, culture,—eternally passing onwards and seeking,—is an impertinence and an offence. But culture, just because it resists this tendency of Jacobinism to impose on us a man with limitations and errors of his own along with the true ideas of which he is the organ, really does the world and Jacobinism itself a service.

So, too, Jacobinism, in its fierce hatred of the past and of those whom it makes liable for the sins of the past, cannot away with culture,—culture with its inexhaustible indulgence, its consideration of circumstances, its severe judgment of actions joined to its merciful judgment of persons. 'The man of culture is in politics,' cries Mr Frederic Harrison, 'one of the poorest mortals alive!' Mr Frederic Harrison wants to be doing business, and he complains that the man of culture stops him with a 'turn for small fault-finding, love of selfish ease, and indecision in action.' Of what use is culture, he asks, except for 'a critic of new books or a professor of *belles lettres*?' Why, it is of use because, in presence of the fierce exasperation which breathes, or rather, I may say, hisses, through the whole production in which Mr Frederic Harrison asks that question, it reminds us that the perfection of human nature is sweetness and light. It is of use because, like religion,—that other effort after perfection,—it testifies that, where bitter envying and strife are, there is confusion and every evil work.

The pursuit of perfection, then, is the pursuit of sweetness and light. He who works for sweetness works in the end for light also; he who works for light works in the end for sweetness also. But he who works for sweetness and light united, works to make reason and the will of God prevail. He who works for machinery, he who works for hatred, works only for confusion. Culture looks beyond machinery, culture hates hatred; culture has but one great passion, the passion for sweetness and light. Yes, it has one yet greater!—the passion for making them *prevail*. It is not satisfied till we *all* come to a perfect man; it knows that the sweetness and light of the few must be imperfect until the raw and unkindled masses of humanity are touched with sweetness and light. If I have not shrunk from saying that we must work for sweetness and light, so neither have I shrunk from saying that we must have a broad basis, must have sweetness and light for as many as possible. Again and again* I have insisted how those are the happy moments of humanity, how those are the marking epochs of a people's life, how those are the flowering times for literature and art and all the creative power of genius, when there is a *national* glow of life and thought, when the whole of society is in the fullest measure permeated by thought, sensible to beauty, intelligent and alive. Only it must be *real* thought and *real* beauty; *real* sweetness and *real* light. Plenty of people will try to give the masses, as they call them, an intellectual food prepared and adapted in the way they think proper for the actual condition of the masses. The ordinary popular literature is an example of this way of working on the masses. Plenty of people will try to indoctrinate the masses with the set of ideas and judgments constituting the creed of their own profession or party. Our religious and political organisations give an example of this way of working on the masses. I condemn neither way; but culture works differently. It does not try to teach down to the level of inferior classes; it does not try to win them for this or that sect of its own, with ready-made judgments and watchwords. It seeks to do away with classes;* to make all live in an atmosphere of sweetness and light, and use ideas, as it uses them itself, freely,—to be nourished and not bound by them.

This is the *social idea*; and the men of culture are the true apostles of equality. The great men of culture are those who have had a passion for diffusing, for making prevail, for carrying from one end of society to the other, the best knowledge, the best ideas of their time; who have laboured to divest knowledge of all that was harsh, uncouth, difficult, abstract, professional, exclusive; to humanise it, to make it efficient outside the clique of the cultivated and learned, yet still remaining the *best* knowledge and thought of the time, and a true source, therefore, of sweetness and light. Such a man was Abelard* in the Middle Ages, in spite of all his imperfections; and thence the boundless emotion and enthusiasm which Abelard excited. Such were Lessing* and Herder* in Germany, at the end of the last century; and their services to Germany were in this way inestimably precious. Generations will pass, and literary monuments will accumulate, and works far more perfect than the works of Lessing and Herder will be produced in Germany; and yet the names of these two men will fill a German with a reverence and enthusiasm such as the names of the most gifted masters will hardly awaken. Because they *humanised* knowledge; because they broadened the basis of life and intelligence; because they worked powerfully to diffuse sweetness and light, to make reason and the will of God prevail. With Saint Augustine* they said: 'Let us not leave Thee alone to make in the secret of thy knowledge, as thou didst before the creation of the firmament, the division of light from darkness; let the children of thy spirit, placed in their firmament, make their light shine upon the earth, mark the division of night and day, and announce the revolution of the times; for the old order is passed, and the new arises; the night is spent, the day is come forth; and thou shalt crown the year with thy blessing, when thou shalt send forth labourers into thy harvest sown by other hands than theirs; when thou shalt send forth new labourers to new seed-times, whereof the harvest shall be not yet.'

CHAPTER II

I HAVE been trying to show that culture is, or ought to be, the study and pursuit of perfection; and that of perfection as pursued by culture, beauty and intelligence, or, in other words, sweetness and light, are the main characters. But hitherto I have been insisting chiefly on beauty, or sweetness, as a character of perfection. To complete rightly my design, it evidently remains to speak also of intelligence, or light, as a character of perfection. First, however, I ought perhaps to notice that, both here and on the other side of the Atlantic, all sorts of objections are raised against the 'religion of culture,'* as the objectors mockingly call it, which I am supposed to be promulgating. It is said to be a religion proposing parmaceti, or some scented salve or other, as a cure for human miseries; a religion breathing a spirit of culti-vated inaction, making its believer refuse to lend a hand at uprooting the definite evils on all sides of us, and filling him with antipathy against the reforms and reformers which try to extirpate them. In general, it is summed up as being not practical, or,—as some critics more familiarly put it,—all moonshine. That Alcibiades,* the editor of the *Morning Star*,* taunts me, as its promulgator, with living out of the world and knowing nothing of life and men. That great austere toiler, the editor of the *Daily Telegraph*,* upbraids me,—but kindly, and more in sorrow than in anger,—for trifling with aesthetics and poetical fancies, while he himself, in that arsenal of his in Fleet Street, is bearing the burden and heat of the day. An intelligent American newspaper, the *Nation*,* says that it is very easy to sit in one's study and find fault with the course of modern society, but the thing is to propose practical improvements for it. While, finally, Mr Frederic Harrison, in a very good-tempered and witty satire, which makes me quite understand his having apparently achieved such a conquest of my young Prussian friend, Arminius,* at last gets moved to an almost stern moral impatience, to behold, as he says, 'Death, sin, cruelty stalk among us, filling their maws with innocence and youth,' and me, in the midst of the general tribulation, handing out my pouncet-box.

It is impossible that all these remonstrances and reproofs should not affect me, and I shall try my very best, in completing my design and in speaking of light as one of the characters of perfection, and of culture as giving us light, to profit by the objections I have heard and read, and to drive at practice as much as I can, by showing the communications and passages into practical life from the doctrine which I am inculcating.

It is said that a man with my theories of sweetness and light is full of antipathy against the rougher or coarser movements going on around him, that he will not lend a hand to the humble operation of uprooting evil by their means, and that therefore the believers in action grow impatient with them. But what if rough and coarse action, ill-calculated action, action with insufficient light, is, and has for a long time been, our bane? What if our urgent want now is, not to act at any price, but rather to lay in a stock of light for our difficulties? In that case, to refuse to lend a hand to the rougher and coarser movements going on round us, to make the primary need, both for oneself and others, to consist in enlightening ourselves and qualifying ourselves to act less at random, is surely the best, and in real truth the most practical line, our endeavours can take. So that if I can show what my opponents call rough or coarse action, but what I would rather call random and ill-regulated action,—action with insufficient light, action pursued because we like to be doing something and doing it as we please, and do not like the trouble of thinking, and the severe constraint of any kind of rule,—if I can show this to be, at the present moment, a practical mischief and danger to us, then I have found a practical use for light in correcting this state of things, and have only to exemplify how, in cases which fall under everybody's observation, it may deal with it.

When I began to speak of culture, I insisted on our bondage to machinery, on our proneness to value machinery as an end in itself, without looking beyond it to the end for which alone, in truth, it is valuable. Freedom, I said, was one of those things which we thus worshipped in itself, without enough regarding the ends for which freedom is to be desired. In our common notions and talk about freedom, we eminently show our idolatry of machinery. Our prevalent notion is,—and I quoted a number of instances to prove it,—that it is a most happy and important thing for a man merely to be able to do as he likes. On what he is to do when he is thus free to do as he likes, we do not lay so much stress. Our familiar praise of the British Constitution* under which we live, is that it is a system of checks,—a system which stops and paralyses any power in interfering with the free action of individuals. To this effect Mr Bright, who loves to walk in the old ways of the Constitution, said forcibly in one of his great speeches,* what many other people are every day saying less forcibly, that the central idea of English life and politics is *the assertion of personal liberty*. Evidently this is so; but evidently, also, as feudalism, which with its ideas and habits of subordination was for many centuries silently behind the British Constitution, dies out, and we are left with nothing but our system of checks, and our notion of its being the great right and happiness of an Englishman to do as far as possible what he likes, we are in danger of drifting towards anarchy. We have not the notion, so familiar on the Continent and to antiquity, of *the State*—the nation, in its collective and corporate character,* entrusted with stringent powers for the general advantage, and controlling individual wills in the name of an interest wider than that of individuals. We say, what is very true, that this notion is often made instrumental to tyranny; we say that a State is in reality made up of the individuals who compose it, and that every individual is the best judge of his own interests. Our leading class is an aristocracy, and no aristocracy likes the notion of a State-authority greater than itself, with a stringent administrative machinery superseding the decorative inutilities of lord-lieutenancy, deputy-lieutenancy, and the *posse comitatûs*,* which are all in its own hands. Our middle-class, the great representative of trade and Dissent, with its maxims of every man for himself in business, every man for himself in religion, dreads a powerful administration which might somehow interfere with it; and besides, it has its own decorative inutilities of vestrymanship and guardianship,* which are to this class what lord-lieutenancy and the county magistracy are to the aristocratic class, and a stringent administration might either take these functions out of its hands, or prevent its exercising them in its own comfortable, independent manner, as at present.

Then as to our working-class. This class, pressed constantly by the hard daily compulsion of material wants, is naturally the very centre and stronghold of our national idea, that it is man's ideal right and felicity to do as he likes. I think I have somewhere related how Monsieur Michelet said to me of the people of France,* that it was 'a nation of barbarians civilised by the conscription.' He meant that through their military service the idea of public duty and of discipline was brought to the mind of these masses, in other respects so raw and uncultivated. Our masses are quite as raw and uncultivated as the French; and, so far from their having the idea of public duty and of discipline, superior to the individual's self-will, brought to their mind by a universal obligation of military service, such as that of the conscription,—so far from their having this, the very idea of a conscription is so at variance with our English notion of the prime right and blessedness of doing as one likes, that I remember the manager of the Clay Cross works in Derbyshire told me during the Crimean war, when our want of soldiers was much felt and some people were talking of a conscription, that sooner than submit to a conscription the population of that district would flee to the mines, and lead a sort of Robin Hood life under ground.

For a long time, as I have said, the strong feudal habits of subordination and deference continued to tell upon the working-class. The modern spirit has now almost entirely dissolved those habits, and the anarchical tendency of our worship of freedom in and for itself, of our superstitious faith, as I say, in machinery, is becoming very manifest. More and more, because of this our blind faith in machinery, because of our want of light to enable us to look beyond machinery to the end for which machinery is valuable, this and that man, and this and that body of men, all over the country, are beginning to assert and put in practice an Englishman's right to do what he likes; his right to march where he likes,* meet where he likes, enter where he likes, hoot as he likes, threaten as he likes, smash as he likes. All this, I say, tends to anarchy; and though a number of excellent people, and particularly my friends of the liberal or progressive party, as they call themselves, are kind enough to reassure us by saying that these are trifles, that a few transient outbreaks of rowdyism signify nothing, that our system of liberty is one which itself cures all the evils which it works, that the educated and intelligent classes stand in overwhelming strength and majestic repose,* ready, like our military force in riots, to act at a moment's notice,—yet one finds that one's liberal friends generally say this because they have such faith in themselves and their nostrums, when they shall return, as the public welfare requires, to place and power. But this faith of theirs one cannot exactly share, when one has so long had them and their nostrums at work, and sees that they have not prevented our coming to our present embarrassed condition; and one finds, also, that the outbreaks of rowdyism tend to become less and less of trifles, to become more frequent rather than less frequent; and that meanwhile our educated and intelligent classes remain in their majestic repose, and somehow or other, whatever happens, their overwhelming strength, like our military force in riots, never does act.

How, indeed, *should* their overwhelming strength act, when the man who gives an inflammatory lecture,* or breaks down the Park railings,* or invades a Secretary of State's office,* is only following an

Englishman's impulse to do as he likes; and our own conscience tells us that we ourselves have always regarded this impulse as something primary and sacred? Mr Murphy lectures at Birmingham, and showers on the Catholic population of that town, 'words,' says Mr Hardy,* 'only fit to be addressed to thieves or murderers.' What then? Mr Murphy* has his own reasons of several kinds. He suspects the Roman Catholic Church of designs upon Mrs Murphy; and he says, if mayors and magistrates do not care for their wives and daughters, he does. But, above all, he is doing as he likes, or, in worthier language, asserting his personal liberty. 'I will carry out my lectures if they walk over my body as a dead corpse; and I say to the Mayor of Birmingham that he is my servant while I am in Birmingham, and as my servant he must do his duty and protect me.' Touching and beautiful words, which find a sympathetic chord in every British bosom! The moment it is plainly put before us that a man is asserting his personal liberty, we are half disarmed; because we are believers in freedom, and not in some dream of a right reason to which the assertion of our freedom is to be subordinated. Accordingly, the Secretary of State had to say that although the lecturer's language was 'only fit to be addressed to thieves or murderers,' yet, 'I do not think he is to be deprived, I do not think that anything I have said could justify the inference that he is to be deprived, of the right of protection in a place built by him for the purpose of these lectures; because the language was not language which afforded grounds for a criminal prosecution.' No, nor to be silenced by Mayor, or Home Secretary, or any administrative authority on earth, simply on their notion of what is discreet and reasonable! This is in perfect consonance with our public opinion, and with our national love for the assertion of personal liberty.

In quite another department of affairs, an experienced and distinguished Chancery Judge* relates an incident which is just to the same effect as this of Mr Murphy. A testator bequeathed 300*l.* a year, to be for ever applied as a pension to some person who had been unsuccessful in literature, and whose duty should be to support and diffuse, by his writings, the testator's own views, as enforced in the testator's publications. This bequest was appealed against in the Court of Chancery, on the ground of its absurdity; but, being only absurd, it was upheld, and the so-called charity was established. Having, I say, at the bottom of our English hearts a very strong belief in freedom, and a very weak belief in right reason, we are soon silenced when a man pleads the prime right to do as he likes, because this is the prime right for ourselves too; and even if we attempt now and then to mumble something about reason, yet we have ourselves thought so little about this and so much about liberty, that we are in conscience forced, when our brother Philistine with whom we are meddling turns boldly round upon us and asks: *Have you any light?*—to shake our heads ruefully, and to let him go his own way after all.

There are many things to be said on behalf of this exclusive attention of ours to liberty, and of the relaxed habits of government which it has engendered. It is very easy to mistake or to exaggerate the sort of anarchy from which we are in danger through them. We are not in danger from Fenianism,* fierce and turbulent as it may show itself; for against this our conscience is free enough to let us act resolutely and put forth our overwhelming strength the moment there is any real need for it. In the first place, it never was any part of our creed that the great right and blessedness of an Irishman, or, indeed, of anybody on earth except an Englishman, is to do as he likes,* and we can have no scruple at all about abridging, if necessary, a non-Englishman's assertion of personal liberty. The British Constitution, its checks, and its prime virtues, are for Englishmen. We may extend them to others out of love and kindness; but we find no real divine law written on our hearts constraining us so to extend them. And then the difference between an Irish Fenian and an English rough is so immense, and the case, in dealing with the Fenian, so much more clear! He is so evidently desperate and dangerous, a man of a conquered race, a Papist, with centuries of ill-usage to inflame him against us, with an alien religion established in his country by us at his expense, with no admiration of our institutions, no love of our virtues, no talents for our business, no turn for our comfort! Show him our symbolical Truss Manufactory on the finest site in Europe,* and tell him that British industrialism and individualism can bring a man to that, and he remains cold! Evidently, if we deal tenderly with a sentimentalist like this, it is out of pure philanthropy. But with the Hyde Park rioter how different! He is our own flesh and blood; he is a Protestant; he is framed by nature to do as we do, hate what we hate, love what we love; he is capable of feeling the symbolical force of the Truss Manufactory; the question of questions, for him, is a wages' question. That beautiful sentence Sir Daniel Gooch* quoted to the Swindon workmen, and which I treasure as Mrs Gooch's Golden Rule, or the Divine Injunction 'Be ye Perfect' done into British,—the sentence Sir Daniel Gooch's mother repeated to him every morning when he was a boy going to work: '*Ever remember, my dear Dan, that you should look forward to being some day manager of that concern!'*—this fruitful maxim is perfectly fitted to shine forth in the heart of the Hyde Park rough also, and to be his guiding-star through life. He has no visionary schemes of revolution and transformation, though of course he would like his class to rule, as the aristocratic class like their class to rule, and the middle-class theirs. Meanwhile, our social machine is a little out of order; there are a good many people in our paradisiacal centres of industrialism and individualism taking the bread out of one another's mouths; the rioter has not yet quite found his groove and settled down to his work, and so he is just asserting his personal liberty a little, going where he likes, assembling where he likes, bawling as he likes, hustling as he likes. Just as the rest of us,—as the country squires in the aristocratic class, as the political dissenters in the middle-class,— he has no idea of a *State*, of the nation in its collective and corporate character controlling, as government, the free swing of this or that one of its members in the name of the higher reason of all of them, his own as well as that of others. He sees the rich, the aristocratic class, in occupation of the executive government, and so if he is stopped from making Hyde Park a bear-garden or the streets impassable, he says he is being butchered by the aristocracy.*

His apparition is somewhat embarrassing, because too many cooks spoil the broth; because, while the aristocratic and middle classes have long been doing as they like with great vigour, he has been too undeveloped and submissive hitherto to join in the game; and now, when he does come, he comes in immense numbers, and is rather raw and rough. But he does not break many laws, or not many at one time; and, as our laws were made for very different circumstances from our present (but always with an eye to Englishmen doing as they like), and as the clear letter of the law must be against our Englishman who does as he likes and not only the spirit of the law and public policy, and as Government must neither have any dis- cretionary power nor act resolutely on its own interpretation of the law if any one disputes it, it is evident our laws give our playful giant, in doing as he likes, considerable advantage. Besides, even if he can be clearly proved to commit an illegality in doing as he likes, there is always the resource of not putting the law in force, or of abolishing it. So he has his way, and if he has his way he is soon satisfied for the time; however, he falls into the habit of taking it oftener and oftener, and at last begins to create by his operations a confusion of which mischievous people can take advantage, and which at any rate, by troubling the common course of business throughout the country tends to cause distress, and so to increase the sort of anarchy and social disintegration which had previously commenced. And thus that profound sense of settled order and security, without which a society like ours cannot live and grow at all, is beginning to threaten us with taking its departure.

Now, if culture, which simply means trying to perfect oneself, and one's mind as part of oneself, brings us light, and if light shows us that there is nothing so very blessed in merely doing as one likes, that the worship of the mere freedom to do as one likes is worship of machinery, that the really blessed thing is to like what right reason ordains, and to follow her authority, then we have got a practical benefit out of culture. We have got a much wanted principle, a principle of authority, to counteract the tendency to anarchy which seems to be threatening us.

But how to organise this authority, or to what hands to entrust the wielding of it? How to get your *State*, summing up the right reason of the community, and giving effect to it, as circumstances may require, with vigour? And here I think I see my enemies waiting for me with a hungry joy in their eyes. But I shall elude them.

The *State*, the power most representing the right reason of the nation, and most worthy, therefore, of ruling,—of exercising, when circumstances require it, authority over us all,—is for Mr Carlyle* the aristocracy. For Mr Lowe, it is the middle-class with its incomparable Parliament. For the Reform League, it is the working-class, with its 'brightest powers of sympathy and readiest powers of action.' Now, culture, with its disinterested pursuit of perfection, culture, simply trying to see things as they are, in order to seize on the best and to make it prevail, is surely well fitted to help us to judge rightly, by all the aids of observing, reading, and thinking, the qualifications and titles to our confidence of these three candidates for authority, and can thus render us a practical service of no mean value.

So when Mr Carlyle, a man of genius to whom we have all at one time or other been indebted for refreshment and stimulus, says we should give rule to the aristocracy, mainly because of its dignity and politeness, surely culture is useful in reminding us, that in our idea of perfection the characters of beauty and intelligence are both of them present, and sweetness and light, the two noblest of things, are united. Allowing, therefore, with Mr Carlyle, the aristocratic class to possess sweetness, culture insists on the necessity of light also, and shows us that aristocracies, being by the very nature of things inaccessible to ideas, unapt to see how the world is going, must be somewhat wanting in light, and must therefore be, at a moment when light is our great requisite, inadequate to our needs. Aristocracies, those children of the established fact, are for epochs of concentration. In epochs of expansion,* epochs such as that in which we now live, epochs when always the warning voice is again heard: *Now is the judgment of this world*—in such epochs aristocracies, with their natural clinging to the established fact, their want of sense for the flux of things, for the inevitable transitoriness of all human institutions, are bewildered and helpless. Their serenity, their high spirit, their power of haughty resistance,—the great qualities of an aristocracy, and the secret of its distinguished manners and dignity,— these very qualities, in an epoch of expansion, turn against their possessors. Again and again I have said how the refinement of an aristocracy may be precious and educative to a raw nation as a kind of shadow of true refinement; how its serenity and dignified freedom from petty cares may serve as a useful foil to set off the vulgarity and hideousness of that type of life which a hard middle-class tends to establish, and to help people to see this vulgarity and hideousness in their true colours. From such an ignoble spectacle as that of poor Mrs Lincoln,*—a spectacle to vulgarise a whole nation,—aristocracies undoubtedly preserve us. But the true grace and serenity is that of which Greece and Greek art suggest the admirable ideals of perfection,—a serenity which comes from having made order among ideas and harmonised them; whereas the serenity of aristocracies, at least the peculiar serenity of aristocracies of Teutonic origin, appears to come from their never having had any ideas to trouble them. And so, in a time of expansion like the present, a time for ideas, one gets, perhaps, in regarding an aristocracy, even more than the idea of serenity, the idea of futility and sterility. One has often wondered whether upon the whole earth there is anything so unintelligent, so unapt to perceive how the world is really going, as an ordinary young Englishman of our upper class. Ideas he has not, and neither has he that seriousness of our middle-class, which is, as I have often said, the great strength of this class, and may become its salvation. Why, a man may hear a young Dives* of the aristocratic class, when the whim takes him to sing the praises of wealth and material comfort, sing them with a cynicism from which the conscience of the veriest Philistine of our industrial middle-class would recoil in affright. And when, with the natural sympathy of aristocracies for firm dealing with the multitude, and his uneasiness at our feeble dealing with it at home, an unvarnished young Englishman of our aristocratic class applauds the absolute rulers on the Continent, he in general manages completely to miss the grounds of reason and intelligence which alone can give any colour of justification, any possibility of existence, to those rulers, and applauds them on grounds which it would make their own hair stand on end to listen to.

And all this time, we are in an epoch of expansion; and the essence of an epoch of expansion is a movement of ideas, and the one salvation of an epoch of expansion is a harmony of ideas. The very principle of the authority which we are seeking as a defence against anarchy is right reason, ideas, light. The more, therefore, an aristocracy calls to its aid its innate forces,—its impenetrability, its high spirit, its power of haughty resistance,—to deal with an epoch of expansion, the graver is the danger, the greater the certainty of explosion, the surer the aristocracy's defeat; for it is trying to do violence to nature instead of working along with it. The best powers shown by the best men of an aristocracy at such an epoch are, it will be observed, non-aristocratical powers, powers of industry, powers of intelligence; and these powers, thus exhibited, tend really not to strengthen the aristocracy, but to take their owners out of it, to expose them to the dissolving agencies of thought and change, to make them men of the modern spirit and of the future. If, as sometimes happens, they add to their non-aristocratical qualities of labour and thought, a strong dose of aristocratical qualities also,—of pride, defiance, turn for resistance—this truly aristocratical side of them, so far from adding any strength to them really neutralises their force and makes them impracticable and ineffective.

Knowing myself to be indeed sadly to seek, as one of my many

critics says,* in 'a philosophy with coherent, interdependent, subordinate and derivative principles,' I continually have recourse to a
plain man's expedient of trying to make what few simple notions I
have, clearer, and more intelligible to myself, by means of example
and illustration. And having been brought up at Oxford in the bad
old times, when we were stuffed with Greek and Aristotle, and
thought nothing of preparing ourselves,—as after Mr Lowe's great
speech at Edinburgh* we shall do,—to fight the battle of life with the
German waiters, my head is still full of a lumber of phrases we learnt
at Oxford from Aristotle, about virtue being in a mean, and about
excess and defect, and so on. Once when I had had the advantage
of listening to the Reform debates in the House of Commons,
having heard a number of interesting speakers, and among them
Lord Elcho and Sir Thomas Bateson, I remember it struck me,
applying Aristotle's machinery of the mean* to my ideas about our
aristocracy, that Lord Elcho was exactly the perfection, or happy
mean, or virtue, of aristocracy, and Sir Thomas Bateson the excess;
and I fancied that by observing these two we might see both the
inadequacy of aristocracy to supply the principle of authority needful for our present wants, and the danger of its trying to supply it
when it was not really competent for the business. On the one hand,
in Lord Elcho,* showing plenty of high spirit, but remarkable, far
above and beyond his gift of high spirit, for the fine tempering of
his high spirit, for ease, serenity, politeness,—the great virtues, as
Mr Carlyle says, of aristocracy,—in this beautiful and virtuous
mean, there seemed evidently some insufficiency of light; while, on
the other hand, Sir Thomas Bateson,* in whom the high spirit of
aristocracy, its impenetrability, defiant courage, and pride of resistance, were developed even in excess, was manifestly capable, if he
had his way given him, of causing us great danger, and, indeed, of
throwing the whole commonwealth into confusion. Then I reverted
to that old fundamental notion of mine about the grand merit of
our race being really our honesty,* and the very helplessness of our
aristocratic or governing class in dealing with our perturbed social
state gave me a sort of pride and satisfaction, because I saw they
were, as a whole, too honest to try and manage a business for which
they did not feel themselves capable.

Surely, now, it is no inconsiderable boon culture confers upon us,
if in embarrassed times like the present it enables us to look at the

ins and the outs of things in this way, without hatred and without
partiality, and with a disposition to see the good in everybody all
round. And I try to follow just the same course with our middle-class
as with our aristocracy. Mr Lowe talks to us of this strong middle
part of the nation, of the unrivalled deeds of our liberal middle-class
Parliament, of the noble, the heroic work it has performed in the last
thirty years; and I begin to ask myself if we shall not, then, find in
our middle-class the principle of authority we want, and if we had
not better take administration as well as legislation away from the
weak extreme which now administers for us, and commit both to
the strong middle part. I observe, too, that the heroes of middle-class
liberalism, such as we have hitherto known it, speak with a kind of
prophetic anticipation of the great destiny which awaits them, and as
if the future was clearly theirs. The advanced party, the progressive
party, the party in alliance with the future, are the names they like to
give themselves. 'The principles which will obtain recognition in the
future,' says Mr Miall,* a personage of deserved eminence among the
political Dissenters, as they are called, who have been the backbone
of middle-class liberalism—'the principles which will obtain recognition in the future are the principles for which I have long and
zealously laboured. I qualified myself for joining in the work of
harvest by doing to the best of my ability the duties of seedtime.'
These duties, if one is to gather them from the works of the great
liberal party in the last thirty years, are, as I have elsewhere summed
them up, the advocacy of free-trade, of parliamentary reform, of
abolition of church-rates, of voluntaryism in religion and education,
of non-interference of the State between employers and employed,
and of marriage with one's deceased wife's sister.

Now I know, when I object that all this is machinery, the great
liberal middle-class has by this time grown cunning enough to
answer, that it always meant more by these things than meets the eye;
that it has had that within which passes show, and that we are soon
going to see, in a Free Church and all manner of good things, what
it was. But I have learned from Bishop Wilson (if Mr Frederic
Harrison will forgive my again quoting that poor old hierophant of
a decayed superstition): 'If we would really know our heart let us
impartially view our actions;'* and I cannot help thinking that if our
liberals had had so much sweetness and light in their inner minds as
they allege, more of it must have come out in their saying and doings.

An American friend of the English liberals* says, indeed, that their Dissidence of Dissent has been a mere instrument of the political Dissenters for making reason and the will of God prevail (and no doubt he would say the same of marriage with one's deceased wife's sister); and that the abolition of a State Church is merely the Dissenter's means to this end, just as culture is mine. Another American defender of theirs* says just the same of their industrialism and free-trade; indeed, this gentleman, taking the bull by the horns, proposes that we should for the future call industrialism culture, and the industrialists the men of culture, and then of course there can be no longer any misapprehension about their true character; and besides the pleasure of being wealthy and comfortable, they will have authentic recognition as vessels of sweetness and light. All this is undoubtedly specious; but I must remark that the culture of which I talked was an endeavour to come at reason and the will of God by means of reading, observing, and thinking; and that whoever calls anything else culture, may, indeed, call it so if he likes, but then he talks of something quite different from what I talked of. And, again, as culture's way of working for reason and the will of God is by directly trying to know more about them, while the Dissidence of Dissent is evidently in itself no effort of this kind, nor is its Free Church, in fact, a church with worthier conceptions of God and the ordering of the world than the State Church professes, but with mainly the same conceptions of these as the State Church has, only that every man is to comport himself as he likes in professing them,—this being so, I cannot at once accept the Nonconformity any more than the industrialism and the other great works of our liberal middle-class as proof positive that this class is in possession of light, and that here is the true seat of authority for which we are in search; but I must try a little further, and seek for other indications which may enable me to make up my mind.

Why should we not do with the middle-class as we have done with the aristocratic class,—find in it some representative men who may stand for the virtuous mean of this class, for the perfection of its present qualities and mode of being, and also for the excess of them. Such men must clearly not be men of genius like Mr Bright; for, as I have formerly said, so far as a man has genius he tends to take himself out of the category of class altogether, and to become simply a man. Mr Bright's brother, Mr Jacob Bright,* would, perhaps, be more to the purpose; he seems to sum up very well in himself, without disturbing influences, the general liberal force of the middle-class, the force by which it has done its great works of free-trade, parliamentary reform, voluntaryism, and so on, and the spirit in which it has done them. Now it is clear, from what has been already said, that there has been at least an apparent want of light in the force and spirit through which these great works have been done, and that the works have worn in consequence too much a look of machinery. But this will be clearer still if we take, as the happy mean of the middle-class, not Mr Jacob Bright, but his colleague in the representation of Manchester, Mr Bazley.* Mr Bazley sums up for us, in general, the middle-class, its spirit and its works, at least as well as Mr Jacob Bright; and he has given us, moreover, a famous sentence, which bears directly on the resolution of our present question,— whether there is light enough in our middle-class to make it the proper seat of the authority we wish to establish. When there was a talk some little while ago about the state of middle-class education, Mr Bazley, as the representative of that class, spoke some memorable words:—'There had been a cry that middle-class education ought to receive more attention. He confessed himself very much surprised by the clamour that was raised. He did not think that class need excite the sympathy either of the legislature or the public.' Now this satisfaction of Mr Bazley with the mental state of the middle-class was truly representative, and enhances his claim (if that were necessary) to stand as the beautiful and virtuous mean of that class. But it is obviously at variance with our definition of culture, or the pursuit of light and perfection, which made light and perfection consist, not in resting and being, but in growing and becoming, in a perpetual advance in beauty and wisdom. So the middle-class is by its essence, as one may say, by its incomparable self-satisfaction decisively expressed through its beautiful and virtuous mean, self-excluded from wielding an authority of which light is to be the very soul.

Clear as this is, it will be made clearer still if we take some representative man as the excess of the middle-class, and remember that the middle-class, in general, is to be conceived as a body swaying between the qualities of its mean and of its excess, and on the whole, of course, as human nature is constituted, inclining rather towards the excess than the mean. Of its excess no better representative can

possibly be imagined than the Rev. W. Cattle,* a Dissenting minister
from Walsall, who came before the public in connection with the
proceedings at Birmingham of Mr Murphy, already mentioned.
Speaking in the midst of an irritated population of Catholics, the
Rev. W. Cattle exclaimed:—'I say, then, away with the mass! It is from
the bottomless pit; and in the bottomless pit shall all liars have their
part, in the lake that burneth with fire and brimstone.' And again:
'When all the praties were black in Ireland, why didn't the priests say
the hocus-pocus over them, and make them all good again?' He
shared, too, Mr Murphy's fears of some invasion of his domestic
happiness: 'What I wish to say to you as Protestant husbands is, *Take
care of your wives!*' And, finally, in the true vein of an Englishman
doing as he likes, a vein of which I have at some length pointed out
the present dangers, he recommended for imitation the example of
some churchwardens at Dublin, among whom, said he, 'there was a
Luther and also a Melancthon,'* who had made very short work
with some ritualist or other, handed him down from his pulpit,
and kicked him out of church. Now it is manifest, as I said in the
case of Sir Thomas Bateson, that if we let this excess of the sturdy
English middle-class, this conscientious Protestant Dissenter, so
strong, so self-reliant, so fully persuaded in his own mind, have his
way, he would be capable, with his want of light—or, to use the
language of the religious world, with his zeal without knowledge—of
stirring up strife which neither he nor any one else could easily
compose.

And then comes in, as it did also with the aristocracy, the honesty
of our race, and by the voice of another middle-class man, Alderman
Wilson,* Alderman of the City of London and Colonel of the City of
London Militia, proclaims that it has twinges of conscience, and that
it will not attempt to cope with our social disorders, and to deal with
a business which it feels to be too high for it. Every one remembers
how this virtuous Alderman-Colonel, or Colonel-Alderman, led his
militia through the London streets; how the bystanders gathered to
see him pass; how the London roughs, asserting an Englishman's
best and most blissful right of doing what he likes, robbed and beat
the bystanders; and how the blameless warrior-magistrate refused to
let his troops interfere. 'The crowd,' he touchingly said afterwards,
'was mostly composed of fine healthy strong men, bent on mischief;
if he had allowed his soldiers to interfere they might have been

overpowered, their rifles taken from them and used against them by the mob; a riot, in fact, might have ensued, and been attended with bloodshed, compared with which the assaults and loss of property that actually occurred would have been as nothing.' Honest and affecting testimony of the English middle-class to its own inadequacy for the authoritative part one's admiration would sometimes incline one to assign to it! 'Who are we,' they say by the voice of their Alderman-Colonel, 'that we should not be overpowered if we attempt to cope with social anarchy, our rifles taken from us and used against us by the mob, and we, perhaps, robbed and beaten ourselves? Or what light have we, beyond a free-born Englishman's impulse to do as he likes, which could justify us in preventing, at the cost of bloodshed, other free-born Englishmen from doing as they like, and robbing and beating us as much as they please?'

This distrust of themselves as an adequate centre of authority does not mark the working-class, as was shown by their readiness the other day in Hyde Park to take upon themselves all the functions of government. But this comes from the working-class being, as I have often said, still an embryo, of which no one can yet quite foresee the final development; and from its not having the same experience and self-knowledge as the aristocratic and middle classes. Honesty it no doubt has, just like the other classes of Englishmen, but honesty in an inchoate and untrained state; and meanwhile its powers of action, which are, as Mr Frederic Harrison says, exceedingly ready, easily run away with it. That it cannot at present have a sufficiency of light which comes by culture,—that is, by reading, observing, and think-ing,—is clear from the very nature of its condition; and, indeed, we saw that Mr Frederic Harrison, in seeking to make a free stage for its bright powers of sympathy and ready powers of action, had to begin by throwing overboard culture, and flouting it as only fit for a professor of *belles lettres*. Still, to make it perfectly manifest that no more in the working-class than in the aristocratic and middle classes can one find an adequate centre of authority,—that is, as culture teaches us to conceive our required authority, of light,—let us again follow, with this class, the method we have followed with the aristocratic and middle classes, and try to bring before our minds representative men, who may figure to us its virtue and its excess. We must not take, of course, Colonel Dickson or Mr Beales;* because Colonel Dickson, by his martial profession and dashing exterior, seems to belong properly, like Julius Cæsar and Mirabeau* and other great popular leaders, to the aristocratic class, and to be carried into the popular ranks only by his ambition or his genius; while Mr Beales belongs to our solid middle-class, and, perhaps, if he had not been a great popular leader, would have been a Philistine. But Mr Odger,* whose speeches we have all read, and of whom his friends relate, besides, much that is favourable, may very well stand for the beautiful and virtuous mean of our present working-class; and I think everybody will admit that in Mr Odger, as in Lord Elcho, there is manifestly, with all his good points, some insufficiency of light. The excess of the working-class, in its present state of development, is perhaps best shown in Mr Bradlaugh, the iconoclast, who seems to be almost for baptizing us all in blood and fire into his new social dispensation, and to whose reflections, now that I have once been set going on Bishop Wilson's track, I cannot forbear commending this maxim of the good old man: 'Intemperance in talk makes a dreadful havoc in the heart.'* Mr Bradlaugh, like Sir Thomas Bateson and the Rev. W. Cattle, is evidently capable, if he had his head given him, of running us all into great dangers and confusion. I conclude, therefore,—what, indeed, few of those who do me the honour to read this disquisition are likely to dispute,—that we can as little find in the working-class as in the aristocratic or in the middle class our much-wanted source of authority, as culture suggests it to us.

Well, then, what if we tried to rise above the idea of class to the idea of the whole community, *the State*, and to find our centre of light and authority there? Every one of us has the idea of country, as a sentiment; hardly any one of us has the idea of *the State*, as a working power. And why? Because we habitually live in our ordinary selves, which do not carry us beyond the ideas and wishes of the class to which we happen to belong. And we are all afraid of giving to the State too much power, because we only conceive of the State as something equivalent to the class in occupation of the executive government, and are afraid of that class abusing power to its own purposes. If we strengthen the State with the aristocratic class in occupation of the executive government, we imagine we are delivering ourselves up captive to the ideas and wishes of Sir Thomas Bateson; if with the middle-class in occupation of the executive government, to those of the Rev. W. Cattle; if with the working-class, to those of Mr Bradlaugh. And with much justice; owing to the exaggerated notion which we English, as I have said, entertain of the right and blessedness of the mere doing as one likes, of the affirming oneself, and oneself just as it is. People of the aristocratic class want to affirm their ordinary selves, their likings and dislikings; people of the middle-class the same, people of the working-class the same. By our everyday selves, however, we are separate, personal, at war; we are only safe from one another's tyranny when no one has any power, and this safety, in its turn, cannot save us from anarchy. And when, therefore, anarchy presents itself as a danger to us, we know not where to turn.

But by our *best self* we are united, impersonal, at harmony. We are in no peril from giving authority to this, because it is the truest friend we all of us can have; and when anarchy is a danger to us, to this authority we may turn with sure trust. Well, and this is the very self which culture, or the study of perfection, seeks to develop in us; at the expense of our old untransformed self, taking pleasure only in doing what it likes or is used to do, and exposing us to the risk of clashing with every one else who is doing the same! So that our poor culture, which is flouted as so unpractical, leads us to the very ideas capable of meeting the great want of our present embarrassed times! We want an authority, and we find nothing but jealous classes, checks, and a dead-lock; culture suggests the idea of *the State*. We find no basis for a firm State-power in our ordinary selves; culture suggests one to us in our *best self*.

It cannot but acutely try a tender conscience to be accused, in a practical country like ours, of keeping aloof from the work and hope of a multitude of earnest-hearted men, and of merely toying with poetry and aesthetics. So it is with no little sense of relief that I find myself thus in the position of one who makes a contribution in aid of the practical necessities of our times. The great thing, it will be observed, is to find our *best* self, and to seek to affirm nothing but that; not,—as we English with our over-value for merely being free and busy have been so accustomed to do,—resting satisfied with a self which comes uppermost long before our best self, and affirming that with blind energy. In short,—to go back yet once more to Bishop Wilson,—of these two excellent rules of Bishop Wilson's for a man's guidance: 'Firstly, never go against the best light you have; secondly, take care that your light be not darkness,'* we English have

followed with praiseworthy zeal the first rule, but we have not given
so much heed to the second. We have gone manfully, the Rev. W.
Cattle and the rest of us, according to the best light we have; but we
have not taken enough care that this should be really the best light
possible for us, that it should not be darkness. And, our honesty
being very great, conscience has whispered to us that the light we
were following, our ordinary self, was, indeed, perhaps, only an
inferior self, only darkness; and that it would not do to impose this
seriously on all the world.

But our best self inspires faith, and is capable of affording a
serious principle of authority. For example. We are on our way to
what the late Duke of Wellington, with his strong sagacity, foresaw
and admirably described as 'a revolution by due course of law.'* This
is undoubtedly,—if we are still to live and grow, and this famous
nation is not to stagnate and dwindle away on the one hand, or,
on the other, to perish miserably in mere anarchy and confusion,—
what we are on the way to. Great changes there must be, for a
revolution cannot accomplish itself without great changes; yet order
there must be, for without order a revolution cannot accomplish
itself by due course of law. So whatever brings risk of tumult and
disorder, multitudinous processions in the streets of our crowded
towns, multitudinous meetings in their public places and parks,—
demonstrations perfectly unnecessary in the present course of our
affairs,—our best self, or right reason, plainly enjoins us to set our
faces against. It enjoins us to encourage and uphold the occupants
of the executive power, whoever they may be, in firmly prohibiting them. But it does this clearly and resolutely, and is thus a real
principle of authority, because it does it with a free conscience;
because in thus provisionally strengthening the executive power, it
knows that it is not doing this merely to enable Sir Thomas Bateson
to affirm himself as against Mr Bradlaugh, or the Rev. W. Cattle to
affirm himself as against both. It knows that it is stablishing *the
State*, or organ of our collective best self, of our national right reason; and it has the testimony of conscience that it is stablishing the
State on behalf of whatever great changes are needed, just as much
as on behalf of order; stablishing it to deal just as stringently, when
the time comes, with Sir Thomas Bateson's Protestant ascendency,
or with the Rev. W. Cattle's sorry education of his children, as it
deals with Mr Bradlaugh's street-processions.

CHAPTER III

FROM a man without a philosophy no one can expect philosophical completeness. Therefore I may observe without shame, that in trying to get a distinct notion of our aristocratic, our middle, and our working class, with a view of testing the claims of each of these classes to become a centre of authority, I have omitted, I find, to complete the old-fashioned analysis which I had the fancy of applying, and have not shown in these classes, as well as the virtuous mean and the excess, the defect also. I do not know that the omission very much matters; still as clearness is the one merit which a plain, unsystematic writer,* without a philosophy, can hope to have, and as our notion of the three great English classes may perhaps be made clearer if we see their distinctive qualities in the defect, as well as in the excess and in the mean, let us try, before proceeding further, to remedy this omission.

It is manifest, if the perfect and virtuous mean of that fine spirit which is the distinctive quality of aristocracies, is to be found in Lord Elcho's chivalrous style, and its excess in Sir Thomas Bateson's turn for resistance, that its defect must lie in a spirit not bold and high enough, and in an excessive and pusillanimous unaptness for resistance. If, again, the perfect and virtuous mean of that force by which our middle-class has done its great works, and of that self-reliance with which it contemplates itself and them, is to be seen in the performances and speeches of Mr Bazley, and the excess of that force and that self-reliance in the performances and speeches of the Rev. W. Cattle, then it is manifest that their defect must lie in a helpless inaptitude for the great works of the middle-class, and in a poor and despicable lack of its self-satisfaction. To be chosen to exemplify the happy mean of a good quality, or set of good qualities, is evidently a praise to a man; nay, to be chosen to exemplify even their excess, is a kind of praise. Therefore I could have no hesitation in taking Lord Elcho and Mr Bazley, the Rev. W. Cattle and Sir Thomas Bateson, to exemplify, respectively, the mean and the excess of aristocratic and middle-class qualities. But perhaps there might be a want of urbanity in singling out this or that personage as the representative of defect. Therefore I shall leave the defect of aristocracy unillustrated by any representative man. But with oneself one may always, without impropriety, deal quite freely; and, indeed, this sort of plain-dealing with oneself has in it, as all the moralists tell us, something very wholesome. So I will venture to humbly offer myself as an illustration of defect in those forces and qualities which make our middle-class what it is. The too well-founded reproaches of my opponents declare how little I have lent a hand to the great works of the middle-class; for it is evidently these works, and my slackness at them, which are meant, when I am said to 'refuse to lend a hand to the humble operation of uprooting certain definite evils'* (such as church-rates and others), and that therefore 'the believers in action grow impatient' with me. The line, again, of a still unsatisfied seeker which I have followed, the idea of self-transformation, of growing towards some measure of sweetness and light not yet reached, is evidently at clean variance with the perfect self-satisfaction current in my class, the middle-class, and may serve to indicate in me, therefore, the extreme defect of this feeling. But these confessions, though salutary, are bitter and unpleasant.

To pass, then, to the working-class. The defect of this class would be the falling short in what Mr Frederic Harrison calls those 'bright powers of sympathy and ready powers of action,' of which we saw in Mr Odger the virtuous mean, and in Mr Bradlaugh the excess. The working-class is so fast growing and rising at the present time, that instances of this defect cannot well be now very common. Perhaps Canning's 'Needy Knife-grinder'* (who is dead, and therefore cannot be pained at my taking him for an illustration) may serve to give us the notion of defect in the essential quality of a working-class; or I might even cite (since, though he is alive in the flesh, he is dead to all heed of criticism) my poor old poaching friend, Zephaniah Diggs,* who, between his hare-snaring and his gin-drinking, has got his powers of sympathy quite dulled and his powers of action in any great movement of his class hopelessly impaired. But examples of this defect belong, as I have said, to a bygone age rather than to the present.

The same desire for clearness, which has led me thus to extend a little my first analysis of the three great classes of English society, prompts me also to make my nomenclature for them a little fuller, with a view to making it thereby more clear and manageable. It is awkward and tiresome to be always saying the aristocratic class, the middle-class, the working-class. For the middle-class, for that great body which, as we know, 'has done all the great things that have been done in all departments,' and which is to be conceived as chiefly moving between its two cardinal points of Mr Bazley and the Rev. W. Cattle, but inclining, in the mass, rather towards the latter than the former—for this class we have a designation which now has become pretty well known, and which we may as well still keep for them, the designation of Philistines. What this term means I have so often explained that I need not repeat it here. For the aristocratic class, conceived mainly as a body moving between the two cardinal points of Lord Elcho and Sir Thomas Bateson, but as a whole nearer to the latter than the former, we have as yet got no special designation. Almost all my attention has naturally been concentrated on my own class, the middle-class, with which I am in closest sympathy, and which has been, besides, the great power of our day, and has had its praises sung by all speakers and newspapers. Still the aristocratic class is so important in itself, and the weighty functions which Mr Carlyle proposes at the present critical time to commit to it must add so much to its importance, that it seems neglectful, and a strong instance of that want of coherent philosophic method for which Mr Frederic Harrison blames me, to leave the aristocratic class so much without notice and denomination. It may be thought that the characteristic which I have occasionally mentioned as proper to aristocracies,—their natural inaccessibility, as children of the estab-lished fact, to ideas,—points to our extending to this class also the designation of Philistines; the Philistine being, as is well known, the enemy of the children of light, or servants of the idea. Nevertheless, there seems to be an inconvenience in thus giving one and the same designation to two very different classes; and besides, if we look into the thing closely, we shall find that the term Philistine conveys a sense which makes it more peculiarly appropriate to our middle class than to our aristocratic. For *Philistine* gives the notion of something particularly stiff-necked and perverse in the resistance to light and its children, and therein it specially suits our middle-class, who not only do not pursue sweetness and light, but who prefer to them that sort of machinery of business, chapels, tea meetings, and addresses from Mr Murphy and the Rev. W. Cattle, which makes up the dismal and illiberal life on which I have so often touched. But the aristocratic class has actually, as we have seen, in its well-known politeness, a kind of image or shadow of sweetness;* and as for light, if it does not pursue light, it is not that it perversely cherishes some dismal and illiberal existence in preference to light, but it is seduced from following light by those mighty and eternal seducers of our race which weave for this class their most irresistible charms,—by worldly splendour, security, power and pleasure. These seducers are exterior goods, but they are goods; and he who is hindered by them from caring for light and ideas, is not so much doing what is perverse as what is natural.

Keeping this in view, I have in my own mind often indulged myself with the fancy of putting side by side with the idea of our aristocratic class, the idea of *the Barbarians*. The Barbarians, to whom we all owe so much, and who reinvigorated and renewed our worn-out Europe, had, as is well-known, eminent merits; and in this country, where we are for the most part sprung from the Barbarians, we have never had the prejudice against them which prevails among the races of Latin origin. The Barbarians brought with them that staunch individualism, as the modern phrase is, and that passion for doing as one likes, for the assertion of personal liberty, which appears to Mr Bright the central idea of English life, and of which we have, at any rate, a very rich supply. The stronghold and natural seat of this passion was in the nobles of whom our aristocratic class are the inheritors; and this class, accordingly, have signally manifested it, and have done much by their example to recommend it to the body of the nation, who already, indeed, had it in their blood. The Barbarians, again, had the passion for field-sports; and they have handed it on to our aristocratic class, who of this passion too, as of the passion for asserting one's personal liberty, are the great natural stronghold. The care of the Barbarians for the body, and for all manly exercises; the vigour, good looks, and fine complexion which they acquired and perpetuated in their families by these means,— all this may be observed still in our aristocratic class. The chivalry of the Barbarians,* with its characteristics of high spirit, choice manners, and distinguished bearing,—what is this but the beautiful commencement of the politeness of our aristocratic class? In some Barbarian noble, no doubt, one would have admired, if one could have been then alive to see it, the rudiments of Lord Elcho. Only, all this culture (to call it by that name) of the Barbarians was an exterior culture mainly: it consisted principally in outward gifts and graces, in looks, manners, accomplishments, prowess; the chief inward gifts which had part in it were the most exterior, so to speak, of inward gifts, those which come nearest to outward ones: they were courage, a high spirit, self-confidence. Far within, and unawakened, lay a whole range of powers of thought and feeling, to which these interesting productions of nature had, from the circumstances of their life, no access. Making allowances for the difference of the times, surely we can observe precisely the same thing now in our aristocratic class. In general its culture is exterior chiefly; all the exterior graces and accomplishments, and the more external of the inward virtues, seem to be principally its portion. It now, of course, cannot but be often in contact with those studies by which, from the world of thought and feeling, true culture teaches us to fetch sweetness and light; but its hold upon these very studies appears remarkably external, and unable to exert any deep power upon its spirit. Therefore the one insufficiency which we noted in the perfect mean of this class, Lord Elcho, was an insufficiency of light. And owing to the same causes, does not a subtle criticism lead us to make, even on the good looks and politeness of our aristocratic class, the one qualifying remark, that in these charming gifts there should perhaps be, for ideal perfection, a shade more *soul* ?

I often, therefore, when I want to distinguish clearly the aristocratic class from the Philistines proper, or middle-class, name the former, in my own mind, *the Barbarians*: and when I go through the country, and see this and that beautiful and imposing seat of theirs crowning the landscape, 'There,' I say to myself, 'is a great fortified post of the Barbarians.'

It is obvious that that part of the working-class which, working diligently by the light of Mrs Gooch's Golden Rule, looks forward to the happy day when it will sit on thrones with Mr Bazley and other middle-class potentates, to survey, as Mr Bright beautifully says, 'the cities it has built, the railroads it has made, the manufactures it has produced, the cargoes which freight the ships of the greatest mercantile navy the world has ever seen,'*—it is obvious, I say, that this part of the working-class is, or is in a fair way to be, one in spirit with the industrial middle-class. It is notorious that our middle-class liberals have long looked forward to this consummation, when the working-class shall join forces with them, aid them heartily to carry forward their great works, go in a body to their tea-meetings, and, in short, enable them to bring about their millennium. That part of the working-class, therefore, which does really seem to lend itself to these great aims, may, with propriety, be numbered by us among the Philistines. That part of it, again, which so much occupies the attention of philanthropists at present,—the part which gives all its energies to organising itself, through trades' unions and other means, so as to constitute, first, a great working-class power, independent of the middle and aristocratic classes, and then, by dint of numbers, give the law to them, and itself reign absolutely,—this lively and interesting part must also, according to our definition, go with the Philistines; because it is its class and its class-instinct which it seeks to affirm, its ordinary self not its best self; and it is a machinery, an industrial machinery, and power and pre-eminence and other external goods which fill its thoughts, and not an inward perfection. It is wholly occupied, according to Plato's subtle expression,* with the things of itself and not its real self, with the things of the State and not the real State. But that vast portion, lastly, of the working-class which, raw and half-developed, has long lain half-hidden amidst its poverty and squalor, and is now issuing from its hiding-place to assert an Englishman's heaven-born privilege of doing as he likes, and is beginning to perplex us by marching where it likes, meeting where it likes, bawling what it likes, breaking what it likes,—to this vast residuum we may with great propriety give the name of *Populace*.

Thus we have got three distinct terms, *Barbarians*, *Philistines*, *Populace*, to denote roughly the three great classes into which our society is divided; and though this humble attempt at a scientific nomenclature falls, no doubt, very far short in precision of what might be required from a writer equipped with a complete and coherent philosophy, yet, from a notoriously unsystematic and unpretending writer, it will, I trust, be accepted as sufficient.

But in using this new, and, I hope, convenient division of English society, two things are to be borne in mind. The first is, that since, under all our class divisions, there is a common basis of human nature, therefore, in every one of us, whether we be properly Barbarians, Philistines, or Populace, there exists, sometimes only in germ and potentially, sometimes more or less developed, the same tendencies and passions which have made our fellow-citizens of other classes what they are. This consideration is very important, because it has great influence in begetting that spirit of indulgence which is a necessary part of sweetness, and which, indeed, when our culture is complete, is, as I have said, inexhaustible. Thus, an English Barbarian who examines himself, will, in general, find himself to be not so entirely a Barbarian but that he has in him, also, something of the Philistine, and even something of the Populace as well. And the same with Englishmen of the two other classes. This is an experience which we may all verify every day. For instance, I myself (I again take myself as a sort of *corpus vile* to serve for illustration in a matter where serving for illustration may not by every one be thought agreeable), I myself am properly a Philistine,—Mr Swinburne would add, the son of a Philistine,*—and though, through circumstances which will perhaps one day be known, if ever the affecting history of my conversion comes to be written, I have, for the most part, broken with the ideas and the tea-meetings of my own class, yet I have not, on that account, been brought much the nearer to the ideas and works of the Barbarians or of the Populace. Nevertheless, I never take a gun or a fishing-rod in my hands without feeling that I have in the ground of my nature the self-same seeds which, fostered by circumstances, do so much to make the Barbarian; and that, with the Barbarian's advantages, I might have rivalled him. Place me in one of his great fortified posts, with these seeds of a love for field-sports sown in my nature, with all the means of developing them, with all pleasures at my command, with most whom I met deferring to me, every one I met smiling on me, and with every appearance of per- manence and security before me and behind me,—then I too might have grown, I feel, into a very passable child of the established fact, of commendable spirit and politeness, and, at the same time, a little inaccessible to ideas and light; not, of course, with either the eminent fine spirit of Lord Elcho, or the eminent power of resistance of Sir Thomas Bateson, but, according to the measure of the common run of mankind, something between the two. And as to the Populace, who, whether he be Barbarian or Philistine, can look at them without sympathy, when he remembers how often,—every time that we snatch up a vehement opinion in ignorance and passion, every time that we long to crush an adversary by sheer violence, every time that we are envious, every time that we are brutal, every time that we adore mere power or success, every time that we add our voice to swell a blind clamour against some unpopular personage, every time that we trample savagely on the fallen,—he has found in his own bosom the eternal spirit of the Populace, and that there needs only a little help from circumstances to make it triumph in him untameably?

The second thing to be borne in mind I have indicated several times already. It is this. All of us, so far as we are Barbarians, Philistines, or Populace, imagine happiness to consist in doing what one's ordinary self likes. What one's ordinary self likes differs according to the class to which one belongs, and has its severer and its lighter side; always, however, remaining machinery, and nothing more. The graver self of the Barbarian likes honours and consideration; his more relaxed self, field-sports and pleasure. The graver self of one kind of Philistine likes business and money-making; his more relaxed self, comfort and tea-meetings. Of another kind of Philistine, the graver self likes trades' unions,* the relaxed self, deputations, or hearing Mr Odger speak. The sterner self of the Populace likes bawling, hustling, and smashing; the lighter self, beer. But in each class there are born a certain number of natures with a curiosity about their best self, with a bent for seeing things as they are, for disentangling themselves from machinery, for simply concerning themselves with reason and the will of God, and doing their best to make these prevail;—for the pursuit, in a word, of perfection. To certain manifestations of this love for perfection mankind have accustomed themselves to give the name of genius; implying, by this name, something original and heaven-bestowed in the passion. But the passion is to be found far beyond those manifestations of it to which the world usually gives the name of genius, and in which there is, for the most part, a *talent* of some kind or other, a special and striking faculty of execution, informed by the heaven-bestowed ardour, or genius. It is to be found in many manifestations besides these, and may best be called, as we have called it, the love and pursuit of perfection; culture being the true nurse of the pursuing love, and sweetness and light the true character of the pursued perfection. Natures with this bent emerge in all classes,—among the Barbarians, among the Philistines, among the Populace. And this bent always tends, as I have said, to take them out of their class, and to make their distinguishing characteristic not their Barbarianism or their Philistinism, but their *humanity*. They have, in general, a rough time of it in their lives; but they are sown more abundantly than one might think, they appear where and when one least expects it, they set up a fire which enfilades, so to speak, the class with which they are ranked; and, in general, by the extrication of their best self as the self to develope, and by the simplicity of the ends fixed by them as paramount, they hinder the unchecked predominance of that class-life which is the affirmation of our ordinary self, and seasonably disconcert mankind in their worship of machinery.

Therefore, when we speak of ourselves as divided into Barbarians, Philistines, and Populace, we must be understood always to imply that within each of these classes there are a certain number of *aliens*, if we may so call them,—persons who are mainly led, not by their class spirit, but by a general *humane* spirit, by the love of human perfection; and that this number is capable of being diminished or augmented. I mean, the number of those who will succeed in developing this happy instinct will be greater or smaller, in proportion both to the force of the original instinct within them, and to the hindrance or encouragement which it meets with from without. In almost all who have it, it is mixed with some infusion of the spirit of an ordinary self, some quantity of class-instinct, and even, as has been shown, of more than one class-instinct at the same time; so that, in general, the extrication of the best self, the predominance of the *humane* instinct, will very much depend upon its meeting, or not, with what is fitted to help and elicit it. At a moment, therefore, when it is agreed that we want a source of authority, and when it seems probable that the right source is our best self, it becomes of vast importance to see whether or not the things around us are, in general, such as to help and elicit our best self, and if they are not, to see why they are not, and the most promising way of mending them.

Now, it is clear that the very absence of any powerful authority amongst us, and the prevalent doctrine of the duty and happiness of doing as one likes, and asserting our personal liberty, must tend to prevent the erection of any very strict standard of excellence, the belief in any very paramount authority of right reason, the recognition of our best self as anything very recondite and hard to come at. It may be, as I have said, a proof of our honesty that we do not attempt to give to our ordinary self, as we have it in action, predominant authority, and to impose its rule upon other people; but it is evident, also, that it is not easy, with our style of proceeding, to get beyond the notion of an ordinary self at all, or to get the paramount authority of a commanding best self, or right reason, recognised.

The learned Martinus Scriblerus* well says: — 'The taste of the bathos is implanted by nature itself in the soul of man; till, perverted by custom or example, he is taught, or rather compelled, to relish the sublime.' But with us everything seems directed to prevent any such perversion of us by custom or example as might compel us to relish the sublime; by all means we are encouraged to keep our natural taste for the bathos unimpaired. I have formerly pointed out how in literature the absence of any authoritative centre, like an Academy, tends to do this; each section of the public has its own literary organ, and the mass of the public is without any suspicion that the value of these organs is relative to their being nearer a certain ideal centre of correct information, taste, and intelligence, or farther away from it. I have said that within certain limits, which any one who is likely to read this will have no difficulty in drawing for himself, my old adversary, the *Saturday Review*,* may, on matters of literature and taste, be fairly enough regarded, relatively to a great number of newspapers which treat these matters, as a kind of organ of reason. But I remember once conversing with a company of Nonconformist admirers of some lecturer who had let off a great fire-work, which the *Saturday Review* said was all noise and false lights, and feeling my way as tenderly as I could about the effect of this unfavourable judgment upon those with whom I was conversing. 'Oh,' said one who was their spokesman, with the most tranquil air of conviction, 'it is true the *Saturday Review* abuses the lecture, but the *British Banner*'* (I am not quite sure it was the *British Banner*, but it was some newspaper of that stamp) 'says that the *Saturday Review* is quite wrong.' The speaker had evidently no notion that there was a scale of value for judgments on these topics, and that the judgments of the *Saturday Review* ranked high on this scale, and those of the *British Banner* low; the taste of the bathos implanted by nature in the literary judgments of man had never, in my friend's case, encountered any let or hindrance.

Just the same in religion as in literature. We have most of us little idea of a high standard to choose our guides by, of a great and profound spirit, which is an authority, while inferior spirits are none; it is enough to give importance to things that this or that person says them decisively, and has a large following of some strong kind when he says them. This habit of ours is very well shown in that able and interesting work of Mr Hepworth Dixon's,* which we were all reading lately, *The Mormons, by One of Themselves*. Here, again, I am not quite sure that my memory serves me as to the exact title, but I mean the well-known book in which Mr Hepworth Dixon described the Mormons, and other similar religious bodies in America, with so much detail and such warm sympathy. In this work it seems enough for Mr Dixon that this or that doctrine has its Rabbi, who talks big to him, has a staunch body of disciples, and, above all, has plenty of rifles. That there are any further stricter tests to be applied to a doctrine, before it is pronounced important, never seems to occur to him. 'It is easy to say,' he writes of the Mormons, 'that these saints are dupes and fanatics, to laugh at Joe Smith and his church, but what then? *The great facts remain*. Young and his people are at Utah; a church of 200,000 souls; an army of 20,000 rifles.' But if the followers of a doctrine are really dupes, or worse, and its promulgators are really fanatics, or worse, it gives the doctrine no seriousness or authority the more that there should be found 200,000 souls,— 200,000 of the innumerable multitude with a natural taste for the bathos,—to hold it, and 20,000 rifles to defend it. And again, of another religious organisation in America: 'A fair and open field is not to be refused when hosts so mighty throw down wager of battle on behalf of what they hold to be true, however strange their faith may seem.' A fair and open field is not to be refused to any speaker; but this solemn way of heralding him is quite out of place unless he has, for the best reason and spirit of man, some significance. 'Well, but,' says Mr Hepworth Dixon, 'a theory which has been accepted by men like Judge Edmonds, Dr Hare, Elder Frederick, and Professor Bush!'* And again: 'Such are, in brief, the bases of what Newman Weeks, Sarah Horton, Deborah Butler,* and the associated brethren, proclaimed in Rolt's Hall as the new covenant!' If he was summing up an account of the teaching of Plato or St Paul, Mr Hepworth Dixon could not be more earnestly reverential. But the question is, have personages like Judge Edmonds, and Newman Weeks, and Elderess Polly, and Elderess Antoinette,* and the rest of Mr Hepworth Dixon's heroes and heroines, anything of the weight and significance for the best reason and spirit of man that Plato and St Paul have? Evidently they, at present, have not; and a very small taste of them and their doctrines ought to have convinced Mr Hepworth Dixon that they never could have. 'But,' says he, 'the magnetic power which Shakerism* is exercising on American thought would of itself compel us,'—and so on. Now as far as real thought is concerned,—thought which affects the best reason and spirit of man, the scientific thought of the world, the only thought which deserves speaking of in this solemn way,—America has up to the present time been hardly more than a province of England, and even now would not herself claim to be more than abreast of England, and of this only real human thought, English thought itself is not just now, as we must all admit, one of the most significant factors. Neither, then, can American thought be; and the magnetic power which Shakerism exercises on American thought is about as important, for the best reason and spirit of man, as the magnetic power which Mr Murphy exercises on Birmingham Protestantism. And as we shall never get rid of our natural taste for the bathos in religion,—never get access to a best self and right reason which may stand as a serious authority,—by treating Mr Murphy as his own disciples treat him, seriously, and as if he was as much an authority as any one else: so we shall never get rid of it while our able and popular writers treat their Joe Smiths and Deborah Butlers,* with their so many thousand souls and so many thousand rifles, in the like exaggerated and misleading manner, and so do their best to confirm us in a bad mental habit to which we are already too prone.

If our habits make it hard for us to come at the idea of a high best self, of a paramount authority, in literature or religion, how much more do they make this hard in the sphere of politics! In other countries, the governors, not depending so immediately on the favour of the governed, have everything to urge them, if they know anything of right reason (and it is at least supposed that governors should know more of this than the mass of the governed), to set it authoritatively before the community. But our whole scheme of government being representative, every one of our governors has all possible temptation, instead of setting up before the governed who elect him, and on whose favour he depends, a high standard of right reason, to accommodate himself as much as possible to their natural taste for the bathos; and even if he tries to go counter to it, to proceed in this with so much flattering and coaxing, that they shall not suspect their ignorance and prejudices to be anything very unlike right reason, or their natural taste for the bathos to differ much from a relish for the sublime. Every one is thus in every possible way encouraged to trust in his own heart; but 'he that trusteth in his own heart,' says the Wise Man, 'is a fool;'* and at any rate this, which Bishop Wilson says, is undeniably true: 'The number of those who need to be awakened is far greater than that of those who need comfort.'* But in our political system everybody is comforted. Our guides and governors who have to be elected by the influence of the Barbarians, and who depend on their favour, sing the praises of the Barbarians, and say all the smooth things that can be said of them. With Mr Tennyson, they celebrate 'the great broad-shouldered genial Englishman,'* with his 'sense of duty,' his 'reverence for the laws,' and his 'patient force,' who saves us from the 'revolts, republics, revolutions, most no graver than a schoolboy's barring out,' which upset other and less broad-shouldered nations. Our guides who are chosen by the Philistines and who have to look to their favour, tell the Philistines how 'all the world knows that the great middle-class of this country supplies the mind, the will, and the power requisite for all the great and good things that have to be done,' and congratulate them on their 'earnest good sense, which penetrates through sophisms, ignores commonplaces, and gives to conventional illusions their true value.' Our guides who look to the favour of the Populace, tell them that 'theirs are the brightest powers of sympathy, and the readiest powers of action.' Harsh things are said too, no doubt, against all the great classes of the community; but these things so evidently come from a hostile class, and are so manifestly dictated by the passions and prepossessions of a hostile class, and not by right reason, that they make no serious impression on those at whom they are launched, but slide easily off their minds. For instance, when the Reform League orators inveigh against our cruel and bloated aristocracy, these invectives so evidently show the passions and point of view of the Populace, that they do not sink into the minds of those at whom they are addressed, or awaken any thought or self-examination in them. Again, when Sir Thomas Bateson describes* the Philistines and the Populace as influenced with a kind of hideous mania for emasculating the aristocracy, that reproach so clearly comes from the wrath and excited imagination of the Barbarians, that it does not much set the Philistines and the Populace thinking. Or when Mr Lowe calls the Populace drunken and venal,* he so evidently calls them this in an agony of apprehension for his Philistine or middle-class Parliament, which has done so many great and heroic works, and is now threatened with mixture and debasement, that the Populace do not lay his words seriously to heart. So the voice which makes a permanent impression on each of our classes is the voice of its friends, and this is from the nature of things, as I have said, a comforting voice. The Barbarians remain in the belief that the great broad-shouldered genial Englishman may be well satisfied with himself; the Philistines remain in the belief that the great middle-class of this country, with its earnest common-sense penetrating through sophisms and ignoring commonplaces, may be well satisfied with itself: the Populace, that the working-man with his bright powers of sympathy and ready powers of action, may be well satisfied with himself. What hope, at this rate, of extinguishing the taste of the bathos implanted by nature itself in the soul of man, or of inculcating the belief that excellence dwells among high and steep rocks,* and can only be reached by those who sweat blood to reach her?

But it will be said, perhaps, that candidates for political influence and leadership, who thus caress the self-love of those whose suffrages they desire, know quite well that they are not saying the sheer truth as reason sees it, but that they are using a sort of conventional language, or what we call clap-trap, which is essential to the working of representative institutions. And therefore, I suppose, we ought rather to say with Figaro: *Qui est-ce qu'on trompe ici?** Now, I admit that often, but not always, when our governors say smooth things to the self-love of the class whose political support they want, they know very well that they are overstepping, by a long stride, the bounds of truth and soberness; and while they talk, they in a manner, no doubt, put their tongue in their cheek. Not always; because, when a Barbarian appeals to his own class to make him their representative and give him political power, he, when he pleases their self-love by extolling broad-shouldered genial Englishmen with their sense of duty, reverence for the laws, and patient force, pleases his own self-love and extols himself, and is, therefore, himself ensnared by his own smooth words. And so, too, when a Philistine wants to represent his brother Philistines, and extols the earnest good sense which characterises Manchester, and supplies the mind, the will, and the power, as the *Daily News* eloquently says, requisite for all the great and good things that have to be done, he intoxicates and deludes himself as well as his brother Philistines who hear him. But it is true that a Barbarian often wants the political support of the Philistines;

and he unquestionably, when he flatters the self-love of Philistinism, and extols, in the approved fashion, its energy, enterprise, and self-reliance, knows that he is talking clap-trap, and, so to say, puts his tongue in his cheek. On all matters where Nonconformity and its catchwords are concerned, this insincerity of Barbarians needing Nonconformist support, and, therefore, flattering the self-love of Nonconformity and repeating its catchwords without the least real belief in them, is very noticeable. When the Nonconformists, in a transport of blind zeal, threw out Sir James Graham's useful Education Clauses* in 1843, one-half of their parliamentary representatives, no doubt, who cried aloud against 'trampling on the religious liberty of the Dissenters by taking the money of Dissenters to teach the tenets of the Church of England,' put their tongue in their cheek while they so cried out. And perhaps there is even a sort of motion of Mr Frederic Harrison's tongue towards his cheek when he talks of the 'shriek of superstition,'* and tells the working-class that theirs are the brightest powers of sympathy and the readiest powers of action. But the point on which I would insist is, that this involuntary tribute to truth and soberness on the part of certain of our governors and guides never reaches at all the mass of us governed, to serve as a lesson to us, to abate our self-love, and to awaken in us a suspicion that our favourite prejudices may be, to a higher reason, all nonsense. Whatever by-play goes on among the more intelligent of our leaders, we do not see it; and we are left to believe that, not only in our own eyes, but in the eyes of our representative and ruling men, there is nothing more admirable than our ordinary self whatever our ordinary self happens to be,—Barbarian, Philistine, or Populace.

Thus everything in our political life tends to hide from us that there is anything wiser than our ordinary selves, and to prevent our getting the notion of a paramount right reason. Royalty itself, in its idea the expression of the collective nation, and a sort of constituted witness to its best mind, we try to turn into a kind of grand advertising van, to give publicity and credit to the inventions, sound or unsound, of the ordinary self of individuals. I remember, when I was in North Germany, having this very strongly brought to my mind in the matter of schools and their institution. In Prussia, the best schools are Crown patronage schools,* as they are called; schools which have been established and endowed (and new ones are to this day being established and endowed) by the Sovereign himself out of his own revenues, to be under the direct control and management of him or of those representing him, and to serve as types of what schools should be. The Sovereign, as his position raises him above many prejudices and littlenesses, and as he can always have at his disposal the best advice, has evident advantages over private founders in well planning and directing a school; while at the same time his great means and his great influence secure, to a well-planned school of his, credit and authority. This is what, in North Germany, the governors do, in the matter of education, for the governed; and one may say that they thus give the governed a lesson, and draw out in them the idea of a right reason higher than the suggestions of an ordinary man's ordinary self. But in England how different is the part which in this matter our governors are accustomed to play! The Licensed Victuallers or the Commercial Travellers* propose to make a school for their children; and I suppose, in the matter of schools, one may call the Licensed Victuallers or the Commercial Travellers ordinary men, with their natural taste for the bathos still strong; and a Sovereign with the advice of men like Wilhelm von Humboldt* or Schleiermacher* may, in this matter, be a better judge, and nearer to right reason. And it will be allowed, probably, that right reason would suggest that, to have a sheer school of Licensed Victuallers' children, or a sheer school of Commercial Travellers' children, and to bring them all up, not only at home but at school too, in a kind of odour of licensed victualism or of bagmanism, is not a wise training to give to these children. And in Germany, I have said, the action of the national guides or governors is to suggest and provide a better. But, in England, the action of the national guides or governors is, for a Royal Prince or a great Minister to go down to the opening of the Licensed Victuallers' or of the Commercial Travellers' school, to take the chair, to extol the energy and self-reliance of the Licensed Victuallers or the Commercial Travellers, to be all of their way of thinking, to predict full success to their schools, and never so much as to hint to them that they are doing a very foolish thing, and that the right way to go to work with their children's education is quite different. And it is the same in almost every department of affairs. While, on the Continent, the idea prevails that it is the business of the heads and representatives of the nation, by virtue of their superior means, power, and information, to set an example and to provide suggestions of right reason, among us the idea is that the business of the heads and representatives of the nation is to do nothing of the kind, but to applaud the natural taste for the bathos showing itself vigorously in any part of the community, and to encourage its works.

Now I do not say that the political system of foreign countries has not inconveniences which may outweigh the inconveniences of our own political system; nor am I the least proposing to get rid of our own political system and to adopt theirs. But a sound centre of authority being what, in this disquisition, we have been led to seek, and right reason, or our best self, appearing alone to offer such a sound centre of authority, it is necessary to take note of the chief impediments which hinder, in this country, the extrication or recognition of this right reason as a paramount authority, with a view to afterwards trying in what way they can best be removed.

This being borne in mind, I proceed to remark how not only do we get no suggestions of right reason, and no rebukes of our ordinary self, from our governors, but a kind of philosophical theory is widely spread among us to the effect that there is no such thing at all as a best self and a right reason having claim to paramount authority, or, at any rate, no such thing ascertainable and capable of being made use of; and that there is nothing but an infinite number of ideas and works of our ordinary selves, and suggestions of our natural taste for the bathos, pretty equal in value, which are doomed either to an irreconcileable conflict, or else to a perpetual give and take; and that wisdom consists in choosing the give and take rather than the conflict, and in sticking to our choice with patience and good humour. And, on the other hand, we have another philosophical theory rife among us, to the effect that without the labour of perverting ourselves by custom or example to relish right reason, but by continuing all of us to follow freely our natural taste for the bathos, we shall, by the mercy of Providence, and by a kind of natural tendency of things, come in due time to relish and follow right reason. The great promoters of these philosophical theories are our newspapers, which, no less than our parliamentary representatives, may be said to act the part of guides and governors to us; and these favourite doctrines of theirs I call,—or should call, if the doctrines were not preached by authorities I so much respect,—the first, a peculiarly British form of Atheism, the second, a peculiarly British form of Quietism.* The first-named melancholy doctrine is preached in *The*

*Times** with great clearness and force of style; indeed, it is well known, from the example of the poet Lucretius and others, what great masters of style the atheistic doctrine has always counted among its promulgators. 'It is of no use,' says *The Times*, 'for us to attempt to force upon our neighbours our several likings and dislikings. We must take things as they are. Everybody has his own little vision of religious or civil perfection. Under the evident impossibility of satisfying everybody, we agree to take our stand on equal laws and on a system as open and liberal as is possible. The result is that everybody has more liberty of action and of speaking here than anywhere else in the Old World.' We come again here upon Mr Roebuck's celebrated definition of happiness,* on which I have so often commented: 'I look around me and ask what is the state of England? Is not every man able to say what he likes? I ask you whether the world over, or in past history, there is anything like it? Nothing. I pray that our unrivalled happiness may last.' This is the old story of our system of checks and every Englishman doing as he likes, which we have already seen to have been convenient enough so long as there were only Barbarians and the Philistines to do what they liked, but to be getting inconvenient, and productive of anarchy, now that the Populace wants to do what it likes too. But for all that, I will not at once dismiss this famous doctrine, but will first quote another passage from *The Times*,* applying the doctrine to a matter of which we have just been speaking,—education. 'The difficulty here' (in providing a national system of education), says *The Times*, 'does not reside in any removeable arrangements. It is inherent and native in the actual and inveterate state of things in this country. All these powers and personages, all these conflicting influences and varieties of character, exist, and have long existed among us; they are fighting it out, and will long continue to fight it out, without coming to that happy consummation when some one element of the British character is to destroy or to absorb all the rest.' There it is; the various promptings of the natural taste for the bathos in this man and that amongst us are fighting it out; and the day will never come (and, indeed, why should we wish it to come?) when one man's particular sort of taste for the bathos shall tyrannise over another man's; nor when right reason (if that may be called an element of the British character) shall absorb and rule them all. 'The whole system of this country, like the constitution we boast to inherit, and are glad to uphold, is made up of established facts, prescriptive authorities, existing usages, powers that be, persons in possession, and communities or classes that have won dominion for themselves, and will hold it against all comers.' Every force in the world, evidently, except the one reconciling force, right reason! Sir Thomas Bateson here, the Rev. W. Cattle on this side, Mr Bradlaugh on that!—pull devil, pull baker! Really, presented with the mastery of style of our leading journal, the sad picture, as one gazes upon it, assumes the iron and inexorable solemnity of tragic Destiny.

After this, the milder doctrine of our other philosophical teacher, the *Daily News*,* has, at first, something very attractive and assuaging. The *Daily News* begins, indeed, in appearance, to weave the iron web of necessity round us like *The Times*. 'The alternative is between a man's doing what he likes and his doing what some one else, probably not one whit wiser than himself, likes.' This points to the tacit compact, mentioned in my last paper, between the Barbarians and the Philistines, and into which it is hoped that the Populace will one day enter; the compact, so creditable to English honesty, that no class, if it exercise power, having only the ideas and aims of its ordinary self to give effect to, shall treat its ordinary self too seriously, or attempt to impose it on others; but shall let these others,—the Rev. W. Cattle, for instance, in his Papist-baiting, and Mr Bradlaugh in his Hyde Park anarchy-mongering,—have their fling. But then the *Daily News* suddenly lights up the gloom of necessitarianism with bright beams of hope. 'No doubt,' it says, 'the common reason of society ought to check the aberrations of individual eccentricity.' This common reason of society looks very like our best self or right reason, to which we want to give authority, by making the action of the *State*, or nation in its collective character, the expression of it. But of this project of ours, the *Daily News*, with its subtle dialectics, makes havoc. 'Make the State the organ of the common reason?'—it says. 'You may make it the organ of something or other, but how can you be certain that reason will be the quality which will be embodied in it?' You cannot be certain of it, undoubtedly, if you never try to bring the thing about; but the question is, the action of the State being the action of the collective nation, and the action of the collective nation carrying naturally great publicity, weight, and force of example with it, whether we should not try to put into the action of the State as much as possible of right reason, or our best self, which may, in this manner, come back to us with new force and authority, may have visibility, form, and influence, and help to confirm us, in the many moments when we are tempted to be our ordinary selves merely, in resisting our natural taste of the bathos rather than in giving way to it?

But no! says our teacher: 'it is better there should be an infinite variety of experiments in human action, because, as the explorers multiply, the true track is more likely to be discovered. The common reason of society can check the aberrations of individual eccentricity only by acting on the individual reason; and it will do so in the main sufficiently, if left to this natural operation.' This is what I call the specially British form of Quietism, or a devout, but excessive, reliance on an over-ruling Providence.* Providence, as the moralists are careful to tell us, generally works in human affairs by human means; so when we want to make right reason act on individual reason, our best self on our ordinary self, we seek to give it more power of doing so by giving it public recognition and authority, and embodying it, so far as we can, in the State. It seems too much to ask of Providence, that while we, on our part, leave our congenital taste for the bathos to its natural operation and its infinite variety of experiments, Providence should mysteriously guide it into the true track, and compel it to relish the sublime. At any rate, great men and great institutions have hitherto seemed necessary for producing any considerable effect of this kind. No doubt we have an infinite variety of experiments, and an ever-multiplying multitude of explorers; even in this short paper I have enumerated many: the *British Banner*, Judge Edmonds, Newman Weeks, Deborah Butler, Elderess Polly, Brother Noyes, the Rev. W. Cattle, the Licensed Victuallers, the Commercial Travellers, and I know not how many more; and the numbers of this noble army are swelling every day. But what a depth of Quietism, or rather, what an over-bold call on the direct inter-position of Providence, to believe that these interesting explorers will discover the true track, or at any rate, 'will do so in the main sufficiently' (whatever that may mean) if left to their natural oper-ation; that is, by going on as they are! Philosophers say, indeed, that we learn virtue by performing acts of virtue; but to say that we shall learn virtue by performing any acts to which our natural taste for the bathos carries us, that the Rev. W. Cattle comes at his best self by Papist-baiting, or Newman Weeks and Deborah Butler at right reason by following their noses, this certainly does appear over-sanguine.

It is true, what we want is to make right reason act on individual reason, the reason of individuals; all our search for authority has that for its end and aim. The *Daily News* says, I observe, that all my argument for authority 'has a non-intellectual root;' and from what I know of my own mind and its inertness, I think this so probable, that I should be inclined easily to admit it, if it were not that, in the first place, nothing of this kind, perhaps, should be admitted without examination; and, in the second, a way of accounting for this charge being made, in this particular instance, without full grounds, appears to present itself. What seems to me to account here, perhaps, for the charge, is the want of flexibility of our race, on which I have so often remarked. I mean, it being admitted that the conformity of the individual reason of the Rev. W. Cattle or Mr Bradlaugh with right reason is our true object, and not the mere restraining them, by the strong arm of the State, from Papist-baiting or railing-breaking,— admitting this, we have so little flexibility that we cannot readily perceive that the State's restraining them from these indulgences may yet fix clearly in their minds that, to the collective nation, these indulgences appear irrational and unallowable, may make them pause and reflect, and may contribute to bringing, with time, their individual reason into harmony with right reason. But in no country, owing to the want of intellectual flexibility above mentioned, is the leaning which is our natural one, and, therefore, needs no recommending to us, so sedulously recommended, and the leaning which is not our natural one, and, therefore, does not need dispraising to us, so sedulously dispraised, as in ours. To rely on the individual being, with us, the natural leaning, we will hear of nothing but the good of relying on the individual; to act through the collective nation on the individual being not our natural leaning, we will hear nothing in recommendation of it. But the wise know that we often need to hear most of that to which we are least inclined, and even to learn to employ, in certain circumstances, that which is capable, if employed amiss, of being a danger to us.

Elsewhere this is certainly better understood than here. In a recent number of the *Westminster Review*,* an able writer, but with precisely our national want of flexibility of which I have been speaking, has unearthed, I see, for our present needs, an English translation, published some years ago, of Wilhelm von Humboldt's book, *The Sphere and Duties of Government*. Humboldt's object in this book is to show that the operation of government ought to be severely limited to what directly and immediately relates to the security of person and property. Wilhelm von Humboldt, one of the most beautiful and perfect souls that have ever existed, used to say that one's business in life was, first, to perfect oneself by all the means in one's power, and, secondly, to try and create in the world around one an aristocracy, the most numerous that one possibly could, of talents and characters. He saw, of course, that, in the end, everything comes to this,—that the individual must act for himself, and must be perfect in himself; and he lived in a country, Germany, where people were disposed to act too little for themselves, and to rely too much on the Government. But even thus, such was his flexibility, so little was he in bondage to a mere abstract maxim, that he saw very well that for his purpose itself, of enabling the individual to stand perfect on his own foundations and to do without the State, the action of the State would for long, long years be necessary; and soon after he wrote his book on *The Sphere and Duties of Government*, Wilhelm von Humboldt became Minister of Education in Prussia, and from his ministry all the great reforms which give the control of Prussian education to the State,—the transference of the management of public schools from their old boards of trustees to the State, the obligatory State-examination for schools, the obligatory State-examination for schoolmasters, and the foundation of the great State University of Berlin,—take their origin. This his English reviewer says not a word of. But, writing for a people whose dangers lie, as we have seen, on the side of their unchecked and unguided individual action, whose dangers none of them lie on the side of an over-reliance on the State, he quotes just so much of Wilhelm von Humboldt's example as can flatter them in their propensities, and do them no good; and just what might make them think, and be of use to them, he leaves on one side. This precisely recalls the manner, it will be observed, in which we have seen that our royal and noble personages proceed with the Licensed Victuallers.

In France the action of the State on individuals is yet more preponderant than in Germany; and the need which friends of human perfection feel to enable the individual to stand perfect on his own foundations is all the stronger. But what says one of the staunchest of these friends, Monsieur Renan, on State action,* and even State action in that very sphere where in France it is most excessive, the sphere of education? Here are his words:—'A liberal believes in liberty, and liberty signifies the non-intervention of the State. *But such an ideal is still a long way off from us, and the very means to remove it to an indefinite distance would be precisely the State's withdrawing its action too soon.*' And this, he adds, is even truer of education than of any other department of public affairs.

We see, then, how indispensable to that human perfection which we seek is, in the opinion of good judges, some public recognition and establishment of our best self, or right reason. We see how our habits and practice oppose themselves to such a recognition, and the many inconveniences which we therefore suffer. But now let us try to go a little deeper, and to find, beneath our actual habits and practice, the very ground and cause out of which they spring.

CHAPTER IV

THIS fundamental ground is our preference of doing to thinking. Now this preference is a main element in our nature, and as we study it we find ourselves opening up a number of large questions on every side.

Let me go back for a moment to what I have already quoted from Bishop Wilson:—'First, never go against the best light you have; secondly, take care that your light be not darkness.'* I said we show, as a nation, laudable energy and persistence in walking according to the best light we have, but are not quite careful enough, perhaps, to see that our light be not darkness. This is only another version of the old story that energy is our strong point and favourable characteristic, rather than intelligence. But we may give to this idea a more general form still, in which it will have a yet larger range of application. We may regard this energy driving at practice, this paramount sense of the obligation of duty, self-control, and work, this earnestness in going manfully with the best light we have as one force. And we may regard the intelligence driving at those ideas which are, after all, the basis of right practice, the ardent sense for all the new and changing combinations of them which man's development brings with it, the indomitable impulse to know and adjust them perfectly, as another force. And these two forces we may regard as in some sense rivals,—rivals not by the necessity of their own nature, but as exhibited in man and his history,—and rivals dividing the empire of the world between them. And to give these forces names from the two races of men who have supplied the most signal and splendid manifestations of them, we may call them respectively the forces of Hebraism and Hellenism. Hebraism and Hellenism,—between these two points of influence moves our world. At one time it feels more powerfully the attraction of one of them, at another time of the other; and it ought to be, though it never is, evenly and happily balanced between them.

The final aim of both Hellenism and Hebraism, as of all great spiritual disciplines, is no doubt the same: man's perfection or salvation. The very language which they both of them use in schooling us to reach this aim is often identical. Even when their language indicates by variation,—sometimes a broad variation, often a but slight and subtle variation,—the different courses of thought which are uppermost in each discipline, even then the unity of the final end and aim is still apparent. To employ the actual words of that discipline with which we ourselves are all of us most familiar, and the words of which, therefore, come most home to us, that final end and aim is 'that we might be partakers of the divine nature.'* These are the words of a Hebrew apostle, but of Hellenism and Hebraism alike this is, I say, the aim. When the two are confronted, as they very often are confronted, it is nearly always with what I may call a rhetorical purpose; the speaker's whole design is to exalt and enthrone one of the two, and he uses the other only as a foil and to enable him the better to give effect to his purpose. Obviously, with us, it is usually Hellenism which is thus reduced to minister to the triumph of Hebraism. There is a sermon on Greece and the Greek spirit by a man never to be mentioned without interest and respect, Frederick Robertson,* in which this rhetorical use of Greece and the Greek spirit, and the inadequate exhibition of them necessarily consequent upon this, is almost ludicrous, and would be censurable if it were not to be explained by the exigences of a sermon. On the other hand, Heinrich Heine,* and other writers of his sort, give us the spectacle of the tables completely turned, and of Hebraism brought in just as a foil and contrast to Hellenism, and to make the superiority of Hellenism more manifest. In both these cases there is injustice and misrepresentation. The aim and end of both Hebraism and Hellenism is, as I have said, one and the same, and this aim and end is august and admirable.

Still, they pursue this aim by very different courses. The uppermost idea with Hellenism is to see things as they really are; the uppermost idea with Hebraism is conduct and obedience. Nothing can do away with this ineffaceable difference; the Greek quarrel with the body and its desires is, that they hinder right thinking, the Hebrew quarrel with them is that they hinder right acting. 'He that keepeth the law, happy is he;'* 'There is nothing sweeter than to take heed unto the commandments of the Lord;'*—that is the Hebrew notion of felicity; and, pursued with passion and tenacity, this notion would not let the Hebrew rest till, as is well known, he had, at last, got out of the law a network of prescriptions to enwrap his whole life, to govern every moment of it, every impulse, every action. The Greek notion of felicity, on the other hand, is perfectly conveyed in these words of a great French moralist: '*C'est le bonheur des hommes*'—when? when they abhor that which is evil?*—no; when they exercise themselves in the law of the Lord day and night?*—no; when they die daily?*—no; when they walk about the New Jerusalem with palms in their hands?*—no; but when they think aright, when their thought hits,—'*quand ils pensent juste.*'* At the bottom of both the Greek and the Hebrew notion is the desire, native in man, for reason and the will of God, the feeling after the universal order,—in a word, the love of God. But, while Hebraism seizes upon certain plain, capital intimations of the universal order, and rivets itself, one may say, with unequalled grandeur of earnestness and intensity on the study and observance of them, the bent of Hellenism is to follow, with flexible activity, the whole play of the universal order, to be apprehensive of missing any part of it, of sacrificing one part to another, to slip away from resting in this or that intimation of it, however capital. An unclouded clearness of mind, an unimpeded play of thought, is what this bent drives at. The governing idea of Hellenism is *spontaneity of consciousness*; that of Hebraism, *strictness of conscience.**

Christianity changed nothing in this essential bent of Hebraism to set doing above knowing. Self-conquest, self-devotion,* the following not our own individual will, but the will of God, *obedience*, is the fundamental idea of this form, also, of the discipline to which we

have attached the general name of Hebraism. Only, as the old law
and the network of prescriptions with which it enveloped human life
were evidently a motive power not driving and searching enough
to produce the result aimed at,—patient continuance in well doing,
self-conquest,—Christianity substituted for them boundless devotion to that inspiring and affecting pattern of self-conquest offered
by Christ; and by the new motive power, of which the essence was
this, though the love and admiration of Christian churches have for
centuries been employed in varying, amplifying, and adorning the
plain description of it, Christianity, as St Paul truly says, 'establishes
the law,'* and in the strength of the ampler power which she has thus
supplied to fulfil it, has accomplished the miracles, which we all see,
of her history.

So long as we do not forget that both Hellenism and Hebraism are
profound and admirable manifestations of man's life, tendencies, and
powers, and that both of them aim at a like final result, we can hardly
insist too strongly on the divergence of line and of operation with
which they proceed. It is a divergence so great that it most truly, as
the prophet Zechariah* says, 'has raised up thy sons, O Zion, against
thy sons, O Greece!' The difference whether it is by doing or by
knowing that we set most store, and the practical consequences
which follow from this difference, leave their mark on all the history
of our race and of its development. Language may be abundantly
quoted from both Hellenism and Hebraism to make it seem that one
follows the same current as the other towards the same goal. They
are, truly, borne towards the same goal; but the currents which bear
them are infinitely different. It is true, Solomon will praise knowing:*
'Understanding is a well-spring of life unto him that hath it.' And in
the New Testament, again, Christ is a 'light,' and 'truth makes us
free.'* It is true, Aristotle will undervalue knowing. 'In what concerns
virtue,' says he, 'three things are necessary,—knowledge, deliberate
will, and perseverance; but, whereas the two last are all important,
the first is a matter of little importance.'* It is true that with the same
impatience with which St James enjoins a man to be not a forgetful
hearer, but a *doer of the work*,* Epictetus exhorts us to *do* what we
have demonstrated to ourselves we ought to do;* or he taunts us with
futility, for being armed at all points to prove that lying is wrong, yet
all the time continuing to lie. It is true, Plato, in words which are
almost the words of the New Testament or the Imitation, calls life

a learning to die.* But underneath the superficial agreement the fundamental divergence still subsists. The understanding of Solomon* is 'the walking in the way of the commandments;' this is 'the way of peace,' and it is of this that blessedness comes. In the New Testament,* the truth which gives us the peace of God and makes us free, is the love of Christ constraining us to crucify, as he did, and with a like purpose of moral regeneration, the flesh with its affections and lusts, and thus establishing, as we have seen, the law. To St Paul it appears possible to 'hold the truth in unrighteousness,' which is just what Socrates judged impossible. The moral virtues, on the other hand, are with Aristotle but the porch and access to the intellectual,* and with these last is blessedness. That partaking of the divine life, which both Hellenism and Hebraism, as we have said, fix as their crowning aim, Plato expressly denies to the man of practical virtue merely,* of self-conquest with any other motive than that of perfect intellectual vision; he reserves it for the lover of pure knowledge, of seeing things as they really are, the φιλομαθής.

Both Hellenism and Hebraism arise out of the wants of human nature and address themselves to satisfying those wants. But their methods are so different, they lay stress on such different points, and call into being by their respective disciplines such different activities, that the face which human nature presents when it passes from the hands of one of them to those of the other, is no longer the same. To get rid of one's ignorance, to see things as they are, and by seeing them as they are to see them in their beauty, is the simple and attractive ideal which Hellenism holds out before human nature; and from the simplicity and charm of this ideal, Hellenism, and human life in the hands of Hellenism, is invested with a kind of aerial ease, clearness, and radiancy; they are full of what we call sweetness and light. Difficulties are kept out of view, and the beauty and rationalness of the ideal have all our thoughts. 'The best man is he who most tries to perfect himself, and the happiest man is he who most feels that he *is* perfecting himself,'—this account of the matter by Socrates, the true Socrates of the *Memorabilia*,* has something so simple, spontaneous, and unsophisticated about it, that it seems to fill us with clearness and hope when we hear it. But there is a saying which I have heard attributed to Mr Carlyle about Socrates,*—a very happy saying, whether it is really Mr Carlyle's or not,—which excellently marks the essential point in which Hebraism differs from

Hellenism. 'Socrates,' this saying goes, 'is terribly *at ease in Zion*.'
Hebraism,—and here is the source of its wonderful strength,—has
always been severely preoccupied with an awful sense of the impossibility of being at ease in Zion; of the difficulties which oppose
themselves to man's pursuit or attainment of that perfection of
which Socrates talks so hopefully, and, as from this point of view one
might almost say, so glibly. It is all very well to talk of getting rid of
one's ignorance, of seeing things in their reality, seeing them in their
beauty; but how is this to be done when there is something which
thwarts and spoils all our efforts? This something is *sin*; and the
space which sin fills in Hebraism, as compared with Hellenism, is
indeed prodigious. This obstacle to perfection fills the whole scene,
and perfection appears remote and rising away from earth, in the
background. Under the name of sin, the difficulties of knowing
oneself and conquering oneself which impede man's passage to perfection, become, for Hebraism, a positive, active entity hostile to
man, a mysterious power which I heard Dr Pusey* the other day, in
one of his impressive sermons, compare to a hideous hunchback
seated on our shoulders, and which it is the main business of our
lives to hate and oppose. The discipline of the Old Testament may
be summed up as a discipline teaching us to abhor and flee from sin;
the discipline of the New Testament, as a discipline teaching us to die
to it. As Hellenism speaks of thinking clearly, seeing things in their
essence and beauty, as a grand and precious feat for man to achieve,
so Hebraism speaks of becoming conscious of sin, of awakening to
a sense of sin, as a feat of this kind. It is obvious to what wide
divergence these differing tendencies, actively followed, must lead.
As one passes and repasses from Hellenism to Hebraism, from Plato
to St Paul, one feels inclined to rub one's eyes and ask oneself
whether man is indeed a gentle and simple being, showing the traces
of a noble and divine nature; or an unhappy chained captive,* labouring with groanings that cannot be uttered to free himself from the
body of this death.

Apparently it was the Hellenic conception of human nature which
was unsound, for the world could not live by it. Absolutely to call it
unsound, however, is to fall into the common error of its Hebraising
enemies; but it was unsound at that particular moment of man's
development, it was premature. The indispensable basis of conduct
and self-control, the platform upon which alone the perfection

aimed at by Greece can come into bloom, was not to be reached by
our race so easily; centuries of probation and discipline were needed
to bring us to it. Therefore the bright promise of Hellenism faded,
and Hebraism ruled the world. Then was seen that astonishing
spectacle, so well marked by the often quoted words of the prophet
Zechariah,* when men of all languages of the nations took hold of the
skirt of him that was a Jew, saying:—'*We will go with you, for we have
heard that God is with you.*' And the Hebraism which thus received
and ruled a world all gone out of the way and altogether become
unprofitable, was, and could not but be, the later, the more spiritual,
the more attractive development of Hebraism. It was Christianity;
that is to say, Hebraism aiming at self-conquest and rescue from the
thrall of vile affections, not by obedience to the letter of a law, but
by conformity to the image of a self-sacrificing example. To a world
stricken with moral enervation Christianity offered its spectacle of
an inspired self-sacrifice; to men who refused themselves nothing, it
showed one who refused himself everything:—'*my Saviour banished
joy!*' says George Herbert.* When the *alma Venus,** the life-giving and
joy-giving power of nature, so fondly cherished by the Pagan world,
could not save her followers from self-dissatisfaction and ennui, the
severe words of the apostle came bracingly and refreshingly: 'Let no
man deceive you with vain words, for because of these things cometh
the wrath of God upon the children of disobedience.'* Throughout
age after age, and generation after generation, our race, or all that
part of our race which was most living and progressive, was *baptized
into a death*; and endeavoured, by suffering in the flesh, to cease from
sin. Of this endeavour, the animating labours and afflictions of early
Christianity, the touching asceticism of mediæval Christianity, are
the great historical manifestations. Literary monuments of it, each,
in its own way, incomparable, remain in the Epistles of St Paul, in
St Augustine's Confessions, and in the two original and simplest
books of the Imitation.[1]

Of two disciplines laying their main stress, the one, on clear
intelligence, the other, on firm obedience; the one, on comprehen-
sively knowing the grounds of one's duty, the other, on diligently
practising it; the one on taking all possible care (to use Bishop
Wilson's words again) that the light we have be not darkness, the

---

[1] The two first books.

other, that according to the best light we have we diligently walk,—
the priority naturally belongs to that discipline which braces man's
moral powers, and founds for him an indispensable basis of character.
And, therefore, it is justly said of the Jewish people, who were
charged with setting powerfully forth that side of the divine order to
which the words *conscience* and *self-conquest* point, that they were
'entrusted with the oracles of God:'* as it is justly said of Christianity,
which followed Judaism and which set forth this side with a much
deeper effectiveness and a much wider influence, that the wisdom of
the old Pagan world was foolishness compared to it. No words of
devotion and admiration can be too strong to render thanks to these
beneficent forces which have so borne forward humanity in its
appointed work of coming to the knowledge and possession of
itself; above all, in those great moments when their action was the
wholesomest and the most necessary.

But the evolution of these forces, separately and in themselves, is
not the whole evolution of humanity,—their single history is not the
whole history of man; whereas their admirers are always apt to make
it stand for the whole history. Hebraism and Hellenism are, neither
of them, the *law* of human development, as their admirers are
prone to make them; they are, each of them, *contributions* to human
development,—august contributions, invaluable contributions; and
each showing itself to us more august, more invaluable, more preponderant over the other, according to the moment in which we take
them, and the relation in which we stand to them. The nations of
our modern world, children of that immense and salutary movement
which broke up the Pagan world, inevitably stand to Hellenism in a
relation which dwarfs it, and to Hebraism in a relation which magni-
fies it. They are inevitably prone to take Hebraism as the law of
human development, and not as simply a contribution to it, however
precious. And yet the lesson must perforce be learned, that the
human spirit is wider than the most priceless of the forces which
bear it onward, and that to the whole development of man Hebraism
itself is, like Hellenism, but a contribution.

Perhaps we may help ourselves to see this clearer by an illustration
drawn from the treatment of a single great idea which has profoundly
engaged the human spirit, and has given it eminent opportunities for
showing its nobleness and energy. It surely must be perceived that the
idea of the immortality of the soul, as this idea rises in its generality

before the human spirit, is something grander, truer, and more satisfying, than it is in the particular forms by which St Paul, in the famous fifteenth chapter of the Epistle to the Corinthians, and Plato, in the *Phædo*, endeavour to develope and establish it. Surely we cannot but feel, that the argumentation with which the Hebrew apostle goes about to expound this great idea is, after all, confused and inconclusive; and that the reasoning, drawn from analogies of likeness and equality, which is employed upon it by the Greek philosopher, is over-subtle and sterile? Above and beyond the inadequate solutions which Hebraism and Hellenism here attempt, extends the immense and august problem itself, and the human spirit which gave birth to it. And this single illustration may suggest to us how the same thing happens in other cases also.

But meanwhile, by alternations of Hebraism and Hellenism, of man's intellectual and moral impulses, of the effort to see things as they really are, and the effort to win peace by self-conquest, the human spirit proceeds, and each of these two forces has its appointed hours of culmination and seasons of rule. As the great movement of Christianity was a triumph of Hebraism and man's moral impulses, so the great movement which goes by the name of the Renascence[1] was an uprising and re-instatement of man's intellectual impulses and of Hellenism. We in England, the devoted children of Protestantism, chiefly know the Renascence by its subordinate and secondary side of the Reformation. The Reformation has been often called a Hebraising revival, a return to the ardour and sincereness of primitive Christianity. No one, however, can study the development of Protestantism and of Protestant churches without feeling that into the Reformation too,—Hebraising child of the Renascence and offspring of its fervour, rather than its intelligence, as it undoubtedly was,—the subtle Hellenic leaven of the Renascence found its way, and that the exact respective parts in the Reformation, of Hebraism and of Hellenism, are not easy to separate. But what we may with truth say is, that all which Protestantism was to itself clearly conscious of, all which it succeeded in clearly setting forth in words, had the characters of Hebraism rather than of Hellenism. The Reformation was strong, in that it was an earnest return to the Bible and to

---

[1] I have ventured to give to the foreign word *Renaissance*, destined to become of more common use amongst us as the movement which it denotes comes, as it will come, increasingly to interest us, an English form.

doing from the heart the will of God as there written; it was weak, in that it never consciously grasped or applied the central idea of the Renascence,—the Hellenic idea of pursuing, in all lines of activity, the law and science, to use Plato's words, of things as they really are. Whatever direct superiority, therefore, Protestantism had over Catholicism was a moral superiority, a superiority arising out of its greater sincerity and earnestness,—at the moment of its apparition at any rate,—in dealing with the heart and conscience; its pretensions to an intellectual superiority are in general quite illusory. For Hellenism, for the thinking side in man as distinguished from the acting side, the attitude of mind of Protestantism towards the Bible in no respect differs from the attitude of mind of Catholicism towards the Church.* The mental habit of him who imagines that Balaam's ass spoke, in no respect differs from the mental habit of him who imagines that a Madonna of wood or stone winked; and the one, who says that God's Church makes him believe what he believes, and the other, who says that God's Word makes him believe what he believes, are for the philosopher perfectly alike in not really and truly knowing, when they say *God's Church* and *God's Word*, what it is they say, or whereof they affirm.

In the sixteenth century, therefore, Hellenism re-entered the world, and again stood in presence of Hebraism,—a Hebraism renewed and purged. Now, it has not been enough observed, how, in the seventeenth century, a fate befell Hellenism in some respects analogous to that which befell it at the commencement of our era. The Renascence, that great reawakening of Hellenism, that irresistible return of humanity to nature and to seeing things as they are, which in art, in literature, and in physics, produced such splendid fruits, had, like the anterior Hellenism of the Pagan world, a side of moral weakness, and of relaxation or insensibility of the moral fibre, which in Italy showed itself with the most startling plainness, but which in France, England, and other countries was very apparent too. Again this loss of spiritual balance, this exclusive preponderance given to man's perceiving and knowing side, this unnatural defect of his feeling and acting side, provoked a reaction. Let us trace that reaction where it most nearly concerns us.

Science has now made visible to everybody the great and pregnant elements of difference which lie in race, and in how signal a manner they make the genius and history of an Indo-European people* vary from those of a Semitic people. Hellenism is of Indo-European growth, Hebraism is of Semitic growth; and we English, a nation of Indo-European stock, seem to belong naturally to the movement of Hellenism. But nothing more strongly marks the essential unity of man than the affinities we can perceive, in this point or that, between members of one family of peoples and members of another; and no affinity of this kind is more strongly marked than that likeness in the strength and prominence of the moral fibre, which, notwithstanding immense elements of difference, knits in some special sort the genius and history of us English, and of our American descendants across the Atlantic, to the genius and history of the Hebrew people. Puritanism, which has been so great a power in the English nation, and in the strongest part of the English nation, was originally the reaction, in the seventeenth century, of the conscience and moral sense of our race, against the moral indifference and lax rule of conduct which in the sixteenth century came in with the Renascence. It was a reaction of Hebraism against Hellenism; and it powerfully manifested itself, as was natural, in a people with much of what we call a Hebraising turn, with a signal affinity for the bent which was the master-bent of Hebrew life. Eminently Indo-European by its *humour*, by the power it shows, through this gift, of imaginatively acknowledging the multiform aspects of the problem of life, and of thus getting itself unfixed from its own over-certainty, of smiling at its own over-tenacity, our race has yet (and a great part of its strength lies here), in matters of practical life and moral conduct, a strong share of the assuredness, the tenacity, the intensity of the Hebrews. This turn manifested itself in Puritanism, and has had a great part in shaping our history for the last two hundred years. Undoubtedly it checked and changed amongst us that movement of the Renascence which we see producing in the reign of Elizabeth such wonderful fruits; undoubtedly it stopped the prominent rule and direct development of that order of ideas which we call by the name of Hellenism, and gave the first rank to a different order of ideas. Apparently, too, as we said of the former defeat of Hellenism, if Hellenism was defeated, this shows that Hellenism was imperfect, and that its ascendency at that moment would not have been for the world's good.

Yet there is a very important difference between the defeat inflicted on Hellenism by Christianity eighteen hundred years ago,

and the check given to the Renascence by Puritanism. The greatness
of the difference is well measured by the difference in force, beauty,
significance and usefulness, between primitive Christianity and
Protestantism. Eighteen hundred years ago it was altogether the hour
of Hebraism; primitive Christianity was legitimately and truly the
ascendent force in the world at that time, and the way of mankind's
progress lay through its full development. Another hour in man's
development began in the fifteenth century, and the main road of
his progress then lay for a time through Hellenism. Puritanism was
no longer the central current of the world's progress, it was a side
stream crossing the central current and checking it. The cross and
the check may have been necessary and salutary, but that does not do
away with the essential difference between the main stream of man's
advance and a cross or side stream. For more than two hundred
years the main stream of man's advance has moved towards knowing
himself and the world, seeing things as they are, spontaneity of
consciousness; the main impulse of a great part, and that the strongest part, of our nation, has been towards strictness of conscience.
They have made the secondary the principal at the wrong moment,
and the principal they have at the wrong moment treated as secondary. This contravention of the natural order has produced, as such
contravention always must produce, a certain confusion and false
movement, of which we are now beginning to feel, in almost every
direction, the inconvenience. In all directions our habitual courses of
action seem to be losing efficaciousness, credit, and control, both
with others and even with ourselves; everywhere we see the beginnings of confusion, and we want a clue to some sound order and
authority. This we can only get by going back upon the actual
instincts and forces which rule our life, seeing them as they really
are, connecting them with other instincts and forces, and enlarging
our whole view and rule of life.

CHAPTER V

THE matter here opened is so large, and the trains of thought to
which it gives rise are so manifold, that we must be careful to limit
ourselves scrupulously to what has a direct bearing upon our actual
discussion. We have found that at the bottom of our present unsettled

state, so full of the seeds of trouble, lies the notion of its being the prime right and happiness, for each of us, to affirm himself, and his ordinary self; to be doing, and to be doing freely and as he likes. We have found at the bottom of it the disbelief in right reason as a lawful authority. It was easy to show from our practice and current history that this is so; but it was impossible to show why it is so without taking a somewhat wider sweep and going into things a little more deeply. Why, in fact, should good, well-meaning, energetic, sensible people, like the bulk of our countrymen, come to have such light belief in right reason, and such an exaggerated value for their own independent doing, however crude? The answer is: because of an exclusive and excessive development in them, without due allowance for time, place, and circumstance, of that side of human nature, and that group of human forces, to which we have given the general name of Hebraism. Because they have thought their real and only important homage was owed to a power concerned with their obedience rather than with their intelligence, a power interested in the moral side of their nature almost exclusively. Thus they have been led to regard in themselves, as the one thing needful, *strictness of conscience*, the staunch adherence to some fixed law of doing we have got already, instead of *spontaneity of consciousness*, which tends continually to enlarge our whole law of doing. They have fancied themselves to have in their religion a sufficient basis for the whole of their life fixed and certain for ever, a full law of conduct and a full law of thought, so far as thought is needed, as well; whereas what they really have is a law of conduct, a law of unexampled power for enabling them to war against the law of sin in their members and not to serve it in the lusts thereof. The book which contains this invaluable law they call the Word of God,* and attribute to it, as I have said, and as, indeed, is perfectly well known, a reach and sufficiency co-extensive with all the wants of human nature. This might, no doubt, be so, if humanity were not the composite thing it is, if it had only, or in quite overpowering eminence, a moral side, and the group of instincts and powers which we call moral. But it has besides, and in notable eminence, an intellectual side, and the group of instincts and powers which we call intellectual. No doubt, mankind makes in general its progress in a fashion which gives at one time full swing to one of these groups of instincts, at another time to the other; and man's faculties are so intertwined, that when his moral side, and the current of force which we call Hebraism, is uppermost, this side will manage somehow to provide, or appear to provide, satisfaction for his intellectual needs; and when his moral side, and the current of force which we call Hellenism, is uppermost, this, again, will provide, or appear to provide, satisfaction for men's moral needs. But sooner or later it becomes manifest that when the two sides of humanity proceed in this fashion of alternate preponderance, and not of mutual understanding and balance, the side which is uppermost does not really provide in a satisfactory manner for the needs of the side which is undermost, and a state of confusion is, sooner or later, the result. The Hellenic half of our nature, bearing rule, makes a sort of provision for the Hebrew half, but it turns out to be an inadequate provision; and again the Hebrew half of our nature bearing rule makes a sort of provision for the Hellenic half, but this, too, turns out to be an inadequate provision. The true and smooth order of humanity's development is not reached in either way. And therefore, while we willingly admit with the Christian apostle that the world by wisdom,—that is, by the isolated preponderance of its intellectual impulses,—knew not God, or the true order of things, it is yet necessary, also, to set up a sort of converse to this proposition, and to say likewise (what is equally true) that the world by Puritanism knew not God. And it is on this converse of the apostle's proposition that it is particularly needful to insist in our own country just at present.

Here, indeed, is the answer to many criticisms which have been addressed to all that we have said in praise of sweetness and light. Sweetness and light evidently have to do with the bent or side in humanity which we call Hellenic. Greek intelligence has obviously for its essence the instinct for what Plato calls the true, firm, intelligible law of things; the love of light, of seeing things as they are. Even in the natural sciences, where the Greeks had not time and means adequately to apply this instinct, and where we have gone a great deal further than they did, it is this instinct which is the root of the whole matter and the ground of all our success; and this instinct the world has mainly learnt of the Greeks, inasmuch as they are humanity's most signal manifestation of it. Greek art, again, Greek beauty, have their root in the same impulse to see things as they really are, inasmuch as Greek art and beauty rest on fidelity to nature,—the *best* nature,—and on a delicate discrimination of what this best nature is. To say we work for sweetness and light, then, is only another way of saying that we work for Hellenism. But, oh! cry many people, sweetness and light are not enough; you must put strength or energy along with them, and make a kind of trinity of strength, sweetness and light, and then, perhaps, you may do some good. That is to say, we are to join Hebraism, strictness of the moral conscience, and manful walking by the best light we have, together with Hellenism, inculcate both, and rehearse the praises of both.

Or, rather, we may praise both in conjunction, but we must be careful to praise Hebraism most. 'Culture,' says an acute, though somewhat rigid critic, Mr Sidgwick,* 'diffuses sweetness and light. I do not undervalue these blessings, but religion gives fire and strength, and the world wants fire and strength even more than sweetness and light.' By religion, let me explain, Mr Sidgwick here means particularly that Puritanism on the insufficiency of which I have been commenting and to which he says I am unfair. Now, no doubt, it is possible to be a fanatical partisan of light and the instincts which push us to it, a fanatical enemy of strictness of moral con- science and the instincts which push us to it. A fanaticism of this sort deforms and vulgarises the well-known work, in some respects so remarkable, of the late Mr Buckle.* Such a fanaticism carries its own mark with it, in lacking sweetness; and its own penalty, in that, lacking sweetness, it comes in the end to lack light too. And the Greeks,—the great exponents of humanity's bent for sweetness and light united, of its perception that the truth of things must be at the same time beauty,—singularly escaped the fanaticism which we moderns, whether we Hellenise or whether we Hebraise, are so apt to show, and arrived,—though failing, as has been said, to give adequate practical satisfaction to the claims of man's moral side,—at the idea of a comprehensive adjustment of the claims of both the sides in man, the moral as well as the intellectual, of a full estimate of both, and of a reconciliation of both; an idea which is philosophically of the greatest value, and the best of lessons for us moderns. So we ought to have no difficulty in conceding to Mr Sidgwick that manful walking by the best light one has,—fire and strength as he calls it,— has its high value as well as culture, the endeavour to see things in their truth and beauty, the pursuit of sweetness and light. But whether at this or that time, and to this or that set of persons, one ought to insist most on the praises of fire and strength, or on the praises of sweetness and light, must depend, one would think, on the circumstances and needs of that particular time and those particular persons. And all that we have been saying, and indeed any glance at the world around us, shows that with us, with the most respectable and strongest part of us, the ruling force is now, and long has been, a Puritan force, the care for fire and strength, strictness of conscience, Hebraism, rather than the care for sweetness and light, spontaneity of consciousness, Hellenism.

Well, then, what is the good of our now rehearsing the praises of fire and strength to ourselves, who dwell too exclusively on them already? When Mr Sidgwick says so broadly, that the world wants fire and strength even more than sweetness and light, is he not carried away by a turn from powerful generalisation? does he not forget that the world is not all of one piece, and every piece with the same needs at the same time? It may be true that the Roman world at the beginning of our era, or Leo the Tenth's Court at the time of the Reformation, or French society in the eighteenth century, needed fire and strength even more than sweetness and light. But can it be said that the Barbarians who overran the empire, needed fire and strength even more than sweetness and light; or that the Puritans needed them more; or that Mr Murphy, the Birmingham lecturer, and the Rev. W. Cattle and his friends, need them more?

The Puritan's great danger is that he imagines himself in possession of a rule telling him the *unum necessarium*, or one thing needful,* and that he then remains satisfied with a very crude conception of what this rule really is and what it tells him, thinks he has now knowledge and henceforth needs only to act, and, in this dangerous state of assurance and self-satisfaction, proceeds to give full swing to a number of the instincts of his ordinary self. Some of the instincts of his ordinary self he has, by the help of his rule of life, conquered; but others which he has not conquered by this help he is so far from perceiving to need subjugation, and to be instincts of an inferior self, that he even fancies it to be his right and duty, in virtue of having conquered a limited part of himself, to give unchecked swing to the remainder. He is, I say, a victim of Hebraism, of the tendency to cultivate strictness of conscience rather than spontaneity of consciousness. And what he wants is a larger conception of human nature, showing him the number of other points at which his nature must come to its best, besides the points which he himself knows and thinks of. There is no *unum necessarium*, or one thing needful, which can free human nature from the obligation of trying to come to its best at all these points. The real *unum necessarium* for us is to come to our best at all points. Instead of our 'one thing needful,' justifying in us vulgarity, hideousness, ignorance, violence,—our vulgarity, hideousness, ignorance, violence, are really so many touchstones which try our one thing needful, and which prove that in the state, at any rate, in which we ourselves have it, it is not all we want. And as the force which encourages us to stand staunch and fast by the rule and ground we have is Hebraism, so the force which encourages us to go back upon this rule, and to try the very ground on which we appear to stand, is Hellenism,—a turn for giving our consciousness free play and enlarging its range. And what I say is, not that Hellenism is always for everybody more wanted than Hebraism, but that for the Rev. W. Cattle at this particular moment, and for the great majority of us his fellow-countrymen, it is more wanted.

Nothing is more striking than to observe in how many ways a limited conception of human nature, the notion of a one thing needful, a one side in us to be made uppermost, the disregard of a full and harmonious development of ourselves, tells injuriously on our thinking and acting. In the first place, our hold upon the rule or standard to which we look for our one thing needful, tends to become less and less near and vital, our conception of it more and more mechanical, and unlike the thing itself as it was conceived in the mind where it originated. The dealings of Puritanism with the writings of St Paul afford a noteworthy illustration of this. Nowhere so much as in the writings of St Paul, and in that great apostle's greatest work, the Epistle to the Romans, has Puritanism found what seemed to furnish it with the one thing needful, and to give it canons of truth absolute and final. Now all writings, as has been already said, even the most precious writings and the most fruitful, must inevitably, from the very nature of things, be but contributions to human thought and human development, which extend wider than they do. Indeed, St Paul, in the very Epistle of which we are speaking,* shows, when he asks, 'Who hath known the mind of the Lord?'—who hath known, that is, the true and divine order of things in its entirety,— that he himself acknowledges this fully. And we have already pointed out in another Epistle of St Paul a great and vital idea of the human spirit,—the idea of the immortality of the soul,—transcending and overlapping, so to speak, the expositor's power to give it adequate definition and expression. But quite distinct from the question whether St Paul's expression, or any man's expression, can be a perfect and final expression of truth, comes the question whether we rightly seize and understand his expression as it exists. Now, perfectly to seize another man's meaning, as it stood in his own mind, is not easy; especially when the man is separated from us by such differences of race, training, time, and circumstances as St Paul. But there are degrees of nearness in getting at a man's meaning; and though we cannot arrive quite at what St Paul had in his mind, yet we may come near it. And who, that comes thus near it, must not feel how terms which St Paul employs in trying to follow, with his analysis of such profound power and originality, some of the most delicate, intricate, obscure, and contradictory workings and states of the human spirit, are detached and employed by Puritanism, not in the connected and fluid way in which St Paul employs them, and for which alone words are really meant, but in an isolated, fixed, mechanical way,* as if they were talismans; and how all trace and sense of St Paul's true movement of ideas, and sustained masterly analysis, is thus lost? Who, I say, that has watched Puritanism,—the force which so strongly Hebraises, which so takes St Paul's writings as something absolute and final, containing the one thing needful,—handle such terms as *grace, faith, election, righteousness*, but must feel, not only that these terms have for the mind of Puritanism a sense false and misleading, but also that this sense is the most monstrous, and grotesque caricature of the sense of St Paul, and that his true meaning is by these worshippers of his words altogether lost?

Or to take another eminent example, in which not Puritanism only, but, one may say, the whole religious world, by their mechanical use of St Paul's writings, can be shown to miss or change his real meaning. The whole religious world, one may say, use now the word *resurrection*,—a word which is so often in their thoughts and on their lips, and which they find so often in St Paul's writings,—in one sense only. They use it to mean a rising again after the physical death of the body. Now it is quite true that St Paul speaks of resurrection in this sense, that he tries to describe and explain it, and that he condemns those who doubt and deny it. But it is true, also, that in nine cases out of ten where St Paul thinks and speaks of resurrection, he thinks and speaks of it in a sense different from this; in the sense of a rising to a new life before the physical death of the body, and not after it. The idea on which we have already touched, the profound idea of being baptized into the death of the great exemplar of self-devotion and self-annulment, of repeating in our own person, by virtue of identification with our exemplar, his course of self-devotion and self-annulment, and of thus coming, within the limits of our present life, to a new life, in which, as in the death going before it, we are identified with our exemplar,—this is the fruitful and original conception of being *risen with Christ* which possesses the mind of St Paul, and this is the central point around which, with such incomparable emotion and eloquence, all his teaching moves. For him, the life after our physical death is really in the main but a consequence and continuation of the inexhaustible energy of the new life thus originated on this side the grave. This grand Pauline idea of Christian resurrection is worthily rehearsed in one of the noblest collects of the Prayer-Book,* and is destined, no doubt, to fill a more and more important place in the Christianity of the future; but almost as signal as is the essentialness of this characteristic idea in St Paul's teaching, is the completeness with which the worshippers of St Paul's words, as an absolute final expression of saving truth, have lost it, and have substituted for the apostle's living and near conception of a resurrection now, their mechanical and remote conception of a resurrection hereafter!

In short, so fatal is the notion of possessing, even in the most precious words or standards, the one thing needful, of having in them, once for all, a full and sufficient measure of light to guide us, and of there being no duty left for us except to make our practice square exactly with them,—so fatal, I say, is this notion to the right knowledge and comprehension of the very words or standards we thus adopt, and to such strange distortions and perversions of them does it inevitably lead, that whenever we hear that commonplace which Hebraism, if we venture to inquire what a man knows, is so apt to bring out against us in disparagement of what we call culture, and in praise of a man's sticking to the one thing needful,—*he knows*, says Hebraism, *his Bible!*—whenever we hear this said, we may, without any elaborate defence of culture, content ourselves with answering simply: 'No man, who knows nothing else, knows even his Bible.'*

Now the force which we have so much neglected, Hellenism, may be liable to fail in moral force and earnestness, but by the law of its nature,—the very same law which makes it sometimes deficient in intensity when intensity is required,—it opposes itself to the notion of cutting our being in two, of attributing to one part the dignity of dealing with the one thing needful, and leaving the other part to take its chance, which is the bane of Hebraism. Essential in Hellenism is the impulse to the development of the whole man, to connecting and harmonising all parts of him, perfecting all, leaving none to take their chance; because the characteristic bent of Hellenism, as has been said, is to find the intelligible law of things, and there is no intelligible law of things, things cannot really appear intelligible, unless they are also beautiful. The body is not intelligible, is not seen in its true nature and as it really is, unless it is seen as beautiful; behaviour is not intelligible, does not account for itself to the mind and show the reason for its existing, unless it is beautiful. The same with discourse, the same with song, the same with worship, the same with all the modes in which man proves his activity and expresses himself. To think that when one shows what is mean, or vulgar, or hideous, one can be permitted to plead that one has that within which passes show; to suppose that the possession of what benefits and satisfies one part of our being can make allowable either discourse like Mr Murphy's and the Rev. W. Cattle's, or poetry like the hymns we all hear, or places of worship like the chapels we all see,—this it is abhorrent to the nature of Hellenism to concede. And to be, like our honoured and justly honoured Faraday,* a great natural philosopher with one side of his being and a Sandemanian with the other, would to Archimedes* have been impossible. It is evident to what a many-sided perfecting of man's powers and activities this demand of Hellenism for satisfaction to be given to the mind by everything which we do, is calculated to impel our race. It has its dangers, as has been fully granted; the notion of this sort of equipollency in man's modes of activity may lead to moral relaxation, what we do not make our one thing needful we may come to treat not enough as if it were needful, though it is indeed very needful and at the same time very hard. Still, what side in us has not its dangers, and which of our impulses can be a talisman to give us perfection outright, and not merely a help to bring us towards it? Has not Hebraism, as we have shown, its dangers as well as Hellenism; and have we used so exces- sively the tendencies in ourselves to which Hellenism makes appeal, that we are now suffering from it? Are we not, on the contrary, now suffering because we have not enough used these tendencies as a help towards perfection?

For we see whither it has brought us, the long exclusive predominance of Hebraism,—the insisting on perfection in one part of our nature and not in all; the singling out the moral side, the side of obedience and action, for such intent regard; making strictness of the moral conscience so far the principal thing, and putting off for hereafter and for another world the care for being complete at all points, the full and harmonious development of our humanity. Instead of watching and following on its ways the desire which, as Plato says, 'for ever through all the universe tends towards that which is lovely,'* we think that the world has settled its accounts with this desire, knows what this desire wants of it, and that all the impulses of our ordinary self which do not conflict with the terms of this settlement, in our narrow view of it, we may follow unrestrainedly, under the sanction of some such text as 'Not slothful in business,' or 'Whatsoever thy hand findeth to do, do it with all thy might,'* or something else of the same kind. And to any of these impulses we soon come to give that same character of a mechanical, absolute law, which we give to our religion; we regard it, as we do our religion, as an object for strictness of conscience, not for spontaneity of consciousness; for unremitting adherence on its own account, not for going back upon, viewing in its connection with other things, and adjusting to a number of changing circumstances; we treat it, in short, just as we treat our religion,—as machinery. It is in this way that the Barbarians treat their bodily exercises, the Philistines their business, Mr Spurgeon his voluntaryism, Mr Bright the assertion of personal liberty, Mr Beales the right of meeting in Hyde Park. In all those cases what is needed is a freer play of consciousness upon the object of pursuit; and in all of them Hebraism, the valuing staunchness and earnestness more than this free play, the entire subordination of thinking to doing, has led to a mistaken and misleading treatment of things.

The newspapers a short time ago contained an account of the suicide of a Mr Smith,* secretary to some insurance company, who, it was said, 'laboured under the apprehension that he would come to poverty, and that he was eternally lost.' And when I read these words, it occurred to me that the poor man who came to such a

mournful end was, in truth, a kind of type, by the selection of his
two grand objects of concern, by their isolation from everything else,
and their juxtaposition to one another, of all the strongest, most
respectable, and most representative part of our nation. 'He laboured
under the apprehension that he would come to poverty, and that he
was eternally lost.' The whole middle-class have a conception of
things,—a conception which makes us call them Philistines,—just
like that of this poor man; though we are seldom, of course, shocked
by seeing it take the distressing, violently morbid, and fatal turn,
which it took with him. But how generally, with how many of us, are
the main concerns of life limited to these two,—the concern for
making money, and the concern for saving our souls! And how
entirely does the narrow and mechanical conception of our secular
business proceed from a narrow and mechanical conception of our
religious business! What havoc do the united conceptions make of
our lives! It is because the second-named of these two master-
concerns presents to us the one thing needful in so fixed, narrow,
and mechanical a way, that so ignoble a fellow master-concern to it as
the first-named becomes possible; and, having been once admitted,
takes the same rigid and absolute character as the other. Poor
Mr Smith had sincerely the nobler master-concern as well as the
meaner,—the concern for saving his soul (according to the narrow
and mechanical conception which Puritanism has of what the salvation of the soul is), and the concern for making money. But let us
remark how many people there are, especially outside the limits of
the serious and conscientious middle-class to which Mr Smith
belonged, who take up with a meaner master-concern,—whether it
be pleasure, or field-sports, or bodily exercises, or business, or popular agitation,—who take up with one of these exclusively, and neglect
Mr Smith's nobler master-concern, because of the mechanical form
which Hebraism has given to this nobler master-concern, making it
stand, as we have said, as something talismanic, isolated, and all-
sufficient, justifying our giving our ordinary selves free play in
amusement, or business, or popular agitation, if we have made our
accounts square with this master-concern; and, if we have not,
rendering other things indifferent, and our ordinary self all we have
to follow, and to follow with all the energy that is in us, till we do.
Whereas the idea of perfection at all points, the encouraging in
ourselves spontaneity of consciousness, the letting a free play of

thought live and flow around all our activity, the indisposition to allow one side of our activity to stand as so all-important and all-sufficing that it makes other sides indifferent,—this bent of mind in us may not only check us in following unreservedly a mean master-concern of any kind, but may even, also, bring new life and movement into that side of us with which alone Hebraism concerns itself, and awaken a healthier and less mechanical activity there. Hellenism may thus actually serve to further the designs of Hebraism.

Undoubtedly it thus served in the first days of Christianity. Christianity, as has been said, occupied itself, like Hebraism, with the moral side of man exclusively, with his moral affections and moral conduct; and so far it was but a continuation of Hebraism. But it transformed and renewed Hebraism* by going back upon a fixed rule, which had become mechanical, and had thus lost its vital motive-power; by letting the thought play freely around this old rule, and perceive its inadequacy; by developing a new motive-power, which men's moral consciousness could take living hold of, and could move in sympathy with. What was this but an importation of Hellenism, as we have defined it, into Hebraism? And as St Paul used the contradiction between the Jew's profession and practice,* his shortcomings on that very side of moral affection and moral conduct which the Jew and St Paul, both of them, regarded as all in all— ('Thou that sayest a man should not steal, dost thou steal? thou that sayest a man should not commit adultery, dost thou commit adultery?')—for a proof of the inadequacy of the old rule of life, in the Jew's mechanical conception of it, and tried to rescue him by making his consciousness play freely around this rule,—that is, by a, so far, Hellenic treatment of it,—even so, when we hear so much said of the growth of commercial immorality in our serious middle-class,* of the melting away of habits of strict probity before the temptation to get quickly rich and to cut a figure in the world; when we see, at any rate, so much confusion of thought and of practice in this great representative class of our nation, may we not be disposed to say that this confusion shows that his new motive-power of grace and imputed righteousness has become to the Puritan as mechanical, and with as ineffective a hold upon his practice, as the old motive-power of the law was to the Jew? and that the remedy is the same as that which St Paul employed,—an importation of what we have called Hellenism into his Hebraism, a making his consciousness flow freely round his petrified rule of life and renew it? Only with this difference: that whereas St Paul imported Hellenism within the limits of our moral part only, this part being still treated by him as all in all; and whereas he exhausted, one may say, and used to the very uttermost, the possibilities of fruitfully importing it on that side exclusively; we ought to try and import it,—guiding ourselves by the ideal of a human nature harmoniously perfect at all points,—into all the lines of our activity, and only by so doing can we rightly quicken, refresh, and renew those very instincts, now so much baffled, to which Hebraism makes appeal.

But if we will not be warned by the confusion visible enough at present in our thinking and acting, that we are in a false line in having developed our Hebrew side so exclusively, and our Hellenic side so feebly and at random, in loving fixed rules of action so much more than the intelligible law of things, let us listen to a remarkable testimony which the opinion of the world around us offers. All the world now sets great and increasing value on three objects which have long been very dear to us, and pursues them in its own way, or tries to pursue them. These three objects are industrial enterprise, bodily exercises, and freedom. Certainly we have, before and beyond our neighbours, given ourselves to these three things with ardent passion and with high success. And this our neighbours cannot but acknowledge; and they must needs, when they themselves turn to these things, have an eye to our example, and take something of our practice. Now, generally, when people are interested in an object of pursuit, they cannot help feeling an enthusiasm for those who have already laboured successfully at it, and for their success; not only do they study them, they also love and admire them. In this way a man who is interested in the art of war not only acquaints himself with the performance of great generals, but he has an admiration and enthusiasm for them. So, too, one who wants to be a painter or a poet cannot help loving and admiring the great painters or poets who have gone before him and shown him the way. But it is strange with how little of love, admiration, or enthusiasm, the world regards us and our freedom, our bodily exercises, and our industrial prowess, much as these things themselves are beginning to interest it. And is not the reason because we follow each of these things in a mechanical manner, as an end in and for itself, and not in reference to a general end of human perfection? and this makes our pursuit of them uninteresting to humanity, and not what the world truly wants? It seems to them mere machinery that we can, knowingly, teach them to worship,—a mere fetish. British freedom, British industry, British muscularity, we work for each of these three things blindly, with no notion of giving each its due proportion and prominence, because we have no ideal of harmonious human perfection before our minds, to set our work in motion, and to guide it. So the rest of the world, desiring industry, or freedom, or bodily strength, yet desiring these not, as we do, absolutely, but as means to something else, imitate, indeed, of our practice what seems useful for them, but us, whose practice they imitate, they seem to entertain neither love nor admiration for. Let us observe, on the other hand, the love and enthusiasm excited by others who have laboured for these very things. Perhaps of what we call industrial enterprise it is not easy to find examples in former times; but let us consider how Greek freedom and Greek gymnastics have attracted the love and praise of mankind, who give so little love and praise to ours. And what can be the reason of this difference? Surely because the Greeks pursued freedom and pursued gymnastics not mechanically, but with constant reference to some ideal of complete human perfection and happiness. And therefore, in spite of faults and failures, they interest and delight by their pursuit of them all the rest of mankind, who instinctively feel that only as things are pursued with reference to this ideal are they valuable.

Here again, therefore, as in the confusion into which the thought and action of even the steadiest class amongst us is beginning to fall, we seem to have an admonition that we have fostered our Hebraising instincts, our preference of earnestness of doing to delicacy and flexibility of thinking, too exclusively, and have been landed by them in a mechanical and unfruitful routine. And again we seem taught that the development of our Hellenising instincts, seeking skilfully the intelligible law of things, and making a stream of fresh thought play freely about our stock notions and habits, is what is most wanted by us at present.

Well, then, from all sides, the more we go into the matter, the currents seem to converge, and together to bear us along towards culture. If we look at the world outside us we find a disquieting absence of sure authority; we discover that only in right reason can we get a source of sure authority, and culture brings us towards right reason. If we look at our own inner world, we find all manner of confusion arising out of the habits of unintelligent routine and one-sided growth, to which a too exclusive worship of fire, strength, earnestness, and action has brought us. What we want is a fuller harmonious development of our humanity, a free play of thought upon our routine notions, spontaneity of consciousness, sweetness and light; and these are just what culture generates and fosters. Proceeding from this idea of the harmonious perfection of our humanity, and seeking to help itself up towards this perfection by knowing and spreading the best which has been reached in the world—an object not to be gained without books and reading—culture has got its name touched, in the fancies of men, with a sort of air of bookishness and pedantry, cast upon it from the follies of the many bookmen who forget the end in the means, and use their books with no real aim at perfection. We will not stickle for a name, and the name of culture one might easily give up, if only those who decry the frivolous and pedantic sort of culture, but wish at bottom for the same things as we do, would be careful on their part, not, in disparaging and discrediting the false culture, to unwittingly disparage and discredit, among a people with little natural reverence for it, the true also. But what we are concerned for is the thing, not the name; and the thing, call it by what name we will, is simply the enabling ourselves, whether by reading, observing, or thinking, to come as near as we can to the firm intelligible law of things, and thus to get a basis for a less confused action and a more complete perfection than we have at present.

And now, therefore, when we are accused of preaching up a spirit of cultivated inaction, of provoking the earnest lovers of action, of refusing to lend a hand at uprooting certain definite evils, of despairing to find any lasting truth to minister to the diseased spirit of our time, we shall not be so much confounded and embarrassed what to answer for ourselves. We shall say boldly that we do not at all despair of finding some lasting truth to minister to the diseased spirit of our time; but that we have discovered the best way of finding this to be, not so much by lending a hand to our friends and countrymen in their actual operations for the removal of certain definite evils, but rather in getting our friends and countrymen to seek culture, to let their consciousness play freely round their present operations and the stock notions on which they are founded, show what these are like, and how related to the intelligible law of things, and auxiliary to true human perfection.

CHAPTER VI

But an unpretending writer,* without a philosophy based on inter-dependent, subordinate, and coherent principles, must not presume to indulge himself too much in generalities, but he must keep close to the level ground of common fact, the only safe ground for under-standings without a scientific equipment. Therefore I am bound to take, before concluding, some of the practical operations in which my friends and countrymen are at this moment engaged, and to make these, if I can, show the truth of what I have advanced. Probably I could hardly give a greater proof of my confessed inexpertness in reasoning and arguing, than by taking, for my first example of an operation of this kind, the proceedings for the disestablishment of the Irish Church, which we are now witnessing. It seems so clear that this is surely one of those operations for the uprooting of a certain definite evil in which one's Liberal friends engage, and have a right to complain and to get impatient and to reproach one with delicate Conservative scepticism and cultivated inaction if one does not lend a hand to help them. This does, indeed, seem evident; and yet this operation comes so prominently before us just at this moment,—it so challenges everybody's regard,—that one seems cowardly in blinking it. So let us venture to try and see whether this conspicuous operation is one of those round which we need to let our conscious-ness play freely and reveal what manner of spirit we are of in doing it; or whether it is one which by no means admits the application of this doctrine of ours, and one to which we ought to lend a hand immediately.

Now it seems plain that the present Church establishment in Ireland is contrary to reason and justice, in so far as the Church of a very small minority of the people there takes for itself all the Church property of the Irish people. And one would think, that property assigned for the purpose of providing for a people's religious worship when that worship was one, the State should, when that worship is split into several forms, apportion between those several forms, with due regard to circumstances, taking account only of great differences, which are likely to be lasting, and of considerable com-munions, which are likely to represent profound and widespread

religious characteristics; and overlooking petty differences, which
have no serious reason for lasting, and inconsiderable communions,
which can hardly be taken to express any broad and necessary
religious lineaments of our common nature. This is just in accordance with that maxim about the State which we have more than once
used: *The State is of the religion of all its citizens, without the fanaticism
of any of them.** Those who deny this, either think so poorly of the
State that they do not like to see religion condescend to touch the
State, or they think so poorly of religion that they do not like to see
the State condescend to touch religion; but no good statesman will
easily think thus unworthily either of the State or of religion, and
our statesmen of both parties were inclined, one may say, to follow
the natural line of the State's duty, and to make in Ireland some
fair apportionment of Church property between large and radically
divided religious communions in that country. But then it was discovered that in Great Britain the national mind, as it is called, is
grown averse to endowments for religion* and will make no new ones;
and though this in itself looks general and solemn enough, yet there
were found political philosophers, like Mr Baxter and Mr Charles
Buxton, to give it a look of more generality and more solemnity still,
and to elevate, by their dexterous command of powerful and beautiful
language, this supposed edict of the British national mind into a
sort of formula for expressing a great law of religious transition
and progress for all the world. But we, who, having no coherent
philosophy, must not let ourselves philosophise, only see that the
English and Scotch Nonconformists have a great horror of establishments and endowments for religion, which, they assert, were
forbidden by Christ when he said: 'My kingdom is not of this world;'*
and that the Nonconformists will be delighted to aid statesmen in
disestablishing any church, but will suffer none to be established or
endowed if they can help it. Then we see that the Nonconformists
make the strength of the Liberal majority in the House of Commons,
and that, therefore, the leading Liberal statesmen, to get the support
of the Nonconformists, forsake the notion of fairly apportioning
Church property in Ireland among the chief religious communions,
declare that the national mind has decided against new endowments,
and propose simply to disestablish and disendow the present establishment in Ireland without establishing or endowing any other. The
actual power, in short, by virtue of which the Liberal party in the

House of Commons is now trying to disestablish the Irish Church, is not the power of reason and justice, it is the power of the Non-conformists' antipathy to Church establishments. Clearly it is this; because Liberal statesmen, relying on the power of reason and justice to help them, proposed something quite different from what they now propose; and they proposed what they now propose, and talked of the decision of the national mind, because they had to rely on the English and Scotch Nonconformists. And clearly the Nonconformists are actuated by antipathy to establishments, not by antipathy to the injustice and irrationality of the present appropriation of Church property in Ireland; because Mr Spurgeon, in his eloquent and memorable letter,* expressly avowed that he would sooner leave things as they are in Ireland, that is, he would sooner let the injustice and irrationality of the present appropriation continue, than do any-thing to set up the Roman image, that is, than give the Catholics their fair and reasonable share of Church property. Most indisput-ably, therefore, we may affirm that the real moving power by which the Liberal party are now operating the overthrow of the Irish establishment is the antipathy of the Nonconformists to Church establishments, and not the sense of reason or justice, except so far as reason and justice may be contained in this antipathy. And thus the matter stands at present.

Now surely we must all see many inconveniences in performing the operation of uprooting this evil, the Irish Church establishment, in this particular way. As was said about industry and freedom and gymnastics, we shall never awaken love and gratitude by this mode of operation; for it is pursued, not in view of reason and justice and human perfection and all that enkindles the enthusiasm of men, but it is pursued in view of a certain stock notion, or fetish, of the Nonconformists, which proscribes Church establishments. And yet, evidently, one of the main benefits to be got by operating on the Irish Church is to win the affections of the Irish people. Besides this, an operation performed in virtue of a mechanical rule, or fetish, like the supposed decision of the English national mind against new endow-ments, does not easily inspire respect in its adversaries, and make their opposition feeble and hardly to be persisted in, as an operation evidently done in virtue of reason and justice might. For reason and justice have in them something persuasive and irresistible; but a fetish or mechanical maxim, like this of the Nonconformists, has in it nothing at all to conciliate either the affections or the understanding; nay, it provokes the counter-employment of other fetishes or mechanical maxims on the opposite side, by which the confusion and hostility already prevalent are heightened. Only in this way can be explained the apparition of such fetishes as are beginning to be set up on the Conservative side against the fetish of the Nonconformists:— *The Constitution in danger! The bulwarks of British freedom menaced! The lamp of the Reformation put out! No Popery!**— and so on. To elevate these against an operation relying on reason and justice to back it is not so easy, or so tempting to human infirmity, as to elevate them against an operation relying on the Nonconformists' antipathy to Church establishments to back it; for after all, *No Popery!* is a rallying cry which touches the human spirit quite as vitally as *No Church establishments!*—that is to say, neither the one nor the other, in themselves, touch the human spirit vitally at all.

Ought the believers in action, then, to be so impatient with us, if we say, that even for the sake of this operation of theirs itself and its satisfactory accomplishment, it is more important to make our consciousness play freely round the stock notion or habit on which their operation relies for aid, than to lend a hand to it straight away? Clearly they ought not; because nothing is so effectual for operating as reason and justice, and a free play of thought will either disengage the reason and justice lying hid in the Nonconformist fetish, and make them effectual, or else it will help to get this fetish out of the way, and to let statesmen go freely where reason and justice take them.

So, suppose we take this absolute rule, this mechanical maxim of Mr Spurgeon and the Nonconformists, that Church establishments are bad things because Christ said: 'My kingdom is not of this world.' Suppose we try and make our consciousness bathe and float this piece of petrifaction,—for such it now is,—and bring it within the stream of the vital movement of our thought, and into relation with the whole intelligible law of things. An enemy and a disputant might probably say that much machinery which Nonconformists themselves employ, the Liberation Society,* which exists already, and the Nonconformist Union which Mr Spurgeon desires to see existing, come within the scope of Christ's words as well as Church establishments. This, however, is merely a negative and contentious way of dealing with the Nonconformist maxim; whereas what we desire is to bring this maxim within the positive and vital movement of our thought. We say, therefore, that Christ's words mean that his religion is a force of inward persuasion acting on the soul, and not a force of outward constraint acting on the body; and if the Nonconformist maxim against Church establishments and Church endowments has warrant given to it from what Christ thus meant, then their maxim is good, even though their own practice in the matter of the Liberation Society may be at variance with it.

And here we cannot but remember what we have formerly said about religion, Miss Cobbe, and the British College of Health in the New Road.* In religion there are two parts, the part of thought and speculation, and the part of worship and devotion. Christ certainly meant his religion, as a force of inward persuasion acting on the soul, to employ both parts as perfectly as possible. Now thought and speculation is eminently an individual matter, and worship and devotion is eminently a collective matter. It does not help me to think a thing more clearly that thousands of other people are thinking the same; but it does help me to worship with more emotion that thousands of other people are worshipping with me. The consecration of common consent, antiquity, public establishment, long-used rites, national edifices, is everything for religious worship. 'Just what makes worship impressive,' says Joubert, 'is its publicity, its external manifestation, its sound, its splendour, its observance universally and visibly holding its way through all the details both of our outward and of our inward life.' Worship, therefore, should have in it as little as possible of what divides us, and should be as much as possible a common and public act; as Joubert says again:* 'The best prayers are those which have nothing distinct about them, and which are thus of the nature of simple adoration.' For, 'The same devotion,' as he says in another place, 'unites men far more than the same thought and knowledge.' Thought and knowledge, as we have said before, is eminently something individual, and of our own; the more we possess it as strictly of our own, the more power it has on us. Man worships best, therefore, with the community; he philosophises best alone. So it seems that whoever would truly give effect to Christ's declaration that his religion is a force of inward persuasion acting on the soul, would leave our thought on the intellectual aspects of Christianity as individual as possible, but would make Christian worship as collective as possible. Worship, then, appears to be eminently a matter for public and national establishment; for even Mr Bright, who, when he stands in Mr Spurgeon's great Tabernacle is so ravished with admiration, will hardly say that the great Tabernacle and its worship are in themselves, as a temple and service of religion, so impressive and affecting as the public and national Westminster Abbey, or Notre Dame, with their worship. And when, very soon after the great Tabernacle, one comes plump down to the mass of private and individual establishments of religious worship, establishments falling, like the British College of Health in the New Road, conspicuously short of what a public and national establishment might be, then one cannot but feel that Christ's command to make his religion a force of persuasion to the soul, is, so far as one main source of persuasion is concerned, altogether set at nought.

But perhaps the Nonconformists worship so unimpressively because they philosophise so keenly; and one part of religion, the part of public national worship, they have subordinated to the other part, the part of individual thought and knowledge? This, however, their organisation in congregations forbids us to admit. They are members of congregations, not isolated thinkers; and a true play of individual thought is at least as much impeded by membership of a small congregation as by membership of a great church; thinking by batches of fifties is to the full as fatal to free thought as thinking by batches of thousands. Accordingly, we have had occasion already to notice that Nonconformity does not at all differ from the Established Church by having worthier or more philosophical ideas about God* and the ordering of the world than the Established Church has; it has very much the same ideas about these as the Established Church has, but it differs from the Established Church in that its worship is a much less collective and national affair. So Mr Spurgeon and the Nonconformists seem to have misapprehended the true meaning of Christ's words, *My kingdom is not of this world;* because, by these words, Christ meant that his religion was to work on the soul; and of the two parts of the soul on which religion works,—the thinking and speculative part, and the feeling and imaginative part,—Nonconformity satisfies the first no better than the Established Churches, which Christ by these words is supposed to have condemned, satisfy it; and the second part it satisfies much worse than the Established Churches. And thus the balance of advantage seems to rest with the Established Churches; and they seem to have apprehended and applied Christ's words, if not with perfect adequacy, at least less inadequately than the Nonconformists.

Might it not, then, be urged with great force that the way to do good, in presence of this operation for uprooting the Church establishment in Ireland by the power of the Nonconformists' antipathy to publicly establishing or endowing religious worship, is not by lending a hand straight away to the operation, and Hebraising,—that is, in this case, taking an uncritical interpretation of certain Bible words as our absolute rule of conduct,—with the Nonconformists. It may be very well for born Hebraisers, like Mr Spurgeon, to Hebraise; but for Liberal statesmen to Hebraise is surely unsafe, and to see poor old Liberal hacks Hebraising, whose real self belongs to a kind of negative Hellenism,—a state of moral indifferency without intellectual ardour,—is even painful. And when, by our Hebraising, we neither do what the better mind of statesmen prompted them to do, nor win the affections of the people we want to conciliate, nor yet reduce the opposition of our adversaries but rather heighten it, surely it may be not unreasonable to Hellenise a little, to let our thought and consciousness play freely about our proposed operation and its motives, dissolve these motives if they are unsound, which certainly they have some appearance, at any rate, of being, and create in their stead, if they are, a set of sounder and more persuasive motives conducting to a more solid operation. May not the man who promotes this be giving the best help towards finding some lasting truth to minister to the diseased spirit of his time, and does he really deserve that the believers in action should grow impatient with him?

But now to take another operation which does not at this moment so excite people's feelings as the disestablishment of the Irish Church, but which, I suppose, would also be called exactly one of those operations of simple, practical, common-sense reform, aiming at the removal of some particular abuse, and rigidly restricted to that object, to which a Liberal ought to lend a hand, and deserves that other Liberals should grow impatient with him if he does not. This operation I had the great advantage of with my own ears hearing discussed in the House of Commons, and recommended by a powerful speech from that famous speaker, Mr Bright; so that the effeminate horror* which, it is alleged, I have of practical reforms of this kind, was put to a searching test; and if it survived, it must have, one would think, some reason or other to support it, and can hardly

quite merit the stigma of its present name. The operation I mean was
that which the Real Estate Intestacy Bill* aimed at accomplishing,
and the discussion on this bill I heard in the House of Commons.
The bill proposed, as every one knows, to prevent the land of a
man who dies intestate from going, as it goes now, to his eldest son,
and was thought, by its friends and by its enemies, to be a step
towards abating the now almost exclusive possession of the land of
this country by the people whom we call the Barbarians. Mr Bright,
and other speakers on his side, seemed to hold that there is a kind of
natural law or fitness of things which assigns to all a man's children
a right to equal shares in the enjoyment of his property after his
death; and that if, without depriving a man of an Englishman's
prime privilege of doing what he likes by making what will he
chooses, you provide that when he makes none his land shall be
divided among his family, then you give the sanction of the law to the
natural fitness of things, and inflict a sort of check on the present
violation of this by the Barbarians. It occurred to me, when I saw
Mr Bright and his friends proceeding in this way, to ask myself a
question. If the almost exclusive possession of the land of this country by the Barbarians is a bad thing, is this practical operation of the
Liberals, and the stock notion, on which it seems to rest, about the
right of children to share equally in the enjoyment of their father's
property after his death, the best and most effective means of dealing
with it? Or is it best dealt with by letting one's thought and consciousness play freely and naturally upon the Barbarians, this Liberal
operation, and the stock notion at the bottom of it, and trying to get
as near as we can to the intelligible law of things as to each of them?

Now does any one, if he simply and naturally reads his consciousness, discover that he has any rights at all? For my part, the deeper I
go in my own consciousness, and the more simply I abandon myself
to it, the more it seems to tell me that I have no rights at all, only
duties; and that men get this notion of rights from a process of
abstract reasoning, inferring that the obligations they are conscious
of towards others, others must be conscious of towards them, and
not from any direct witness of consciousness at all. But it is obvious
that the notion of a right, arrived at in this way, is likely to stand as a
formal and petrified thing, deceiving and misleading us; and that the
notions got directly from our consciousness ought to be brought to
bear upon it, and to control it. So it is unsafe and misleading to say

that our children have rights against us; what is true and safe to say is, that we have duties towards our children. But who will find among these natural duties, set forth to us by our consciousness, the obligation to leave to all our children an equal share in the enjoyment of our property? or, though consciousness tells us we ought to provide for our children's welfare, whose consciousness tells him that the enjoyment of property is in itself welfare? Whether our children's welfare is best served by their all sharing equally in our property depends on circumstances and on the state of the community in which we live. With this equal sharing, society could not, for example, have organised itself afresh out of the chaos left by the fall of the Roman Empire, and to have an organised society to live in is more for a child's welfare than to have an equal share of his father's property. So we see how little convincing force the stock notion on which the Real Estate Intestacy Bill was based,—the notion that in the nature and fitness of things all a man's children have a right to an equal share in the enjoyment of what he leaves,—really has; and how powerless, therefore, it must of necessity be to persuade and win any one who has habits and interests which disincline him to it. On the other hand, the practical operation proposed relies entirely, if it is to be effectual in altering the present practice of the Barbarians, on the power of truth and persuasiveness in the notion which it seeks to consecrate; for it leaves to the Barbarians full liberty to continue their present practice, to which all their habits and interests incline them, unless the promulgation of a notion, which we have seen to have no vital efficacy and hold upon our consciousness, shall hinder them.

Are we really to adorn an operation of this kind, merely because it proposes to do something, with all the favourable epithets of simple, practical, common-sense, definite; to enlist on its side all the zeal of the believers in action, and to call indifference to it a really effeminate horror of useful reforms? It seems to me quite easy to show that a free disinterested play of thought on the Barbarians and their land-holding is a thousand times more really practical, a thousand times more likely to lead to some effective result, than an operation such as that of which we have been now speaking. For if, casting aside the impediments of stock notions and mechanical action, we try to find the intelligible law of things respecting a great land-owning class such as we have in this country, does not our consciousness readily tell us that whether the perpetuation of such a class is for its own real welfare and for the real welfare of the community, depends on the actual circumstances of this class and of the community? Does it not readily tell us that wealth, power, and consideration are, and above all when inherited and not earned, in themselves trying and dangerous things? as Bishop Wilson excellently says: 'Riches are almost always abused without a very extraordinary grace.'* But this extraordinary grace was in great measure supplied by the circumstances of the feudal epoch, out of which our landholding class, with its rules of inheritance, sprang. The labour and contentions of a rude, nascent, and struggling society supplied it; these perpetually were trying, chastising, and forming the class whose predominance was then needed by society to give it points of cohesion, and was not so harmful to themselves because they were thus sharply tried and exercised. But in a luxurious, settled, and easy society, where wealth offers the means of enjoyment a thousand times more, and the temptation to abuse them is thus made a thousand times greater, the exercising discipline is at the same time taken away, and the feudal class is left exposed to the full operation of the natural law well put by the French moralist: *Pouvoir sans savoir est fort dangereux.** And, for my part, when I regard the young people of this class, it is above all by the trial and shipwreck made of their own welfare by the circumstances in which they live that I am struck; how far better it would have been for nine out of every ten among them, if they had had their own way to make in the world, and not been tried by a condition for which they had not the extraordinary grace requisite!

This, I say, seems to be what a man's consciousness, simply consulted, would tell him about the actual welfare of our Barbarians themselves. Then, as to their actual effect upon the welfare of the community, how can this be salutary, if a class which, by the very possession of wealth, power and consideration, becomes a kind of ideal or standard for the rest of the community, is tried by ease and pleasure more than it can well bear, and almost irresistibly carried away from excellence and strenuous virtue? This must certainly be what Solomon meant when he said: 'As he who putteth a stone in a sling, so is he that giveth honour to a fool.'* For any one can perceive how this honouring of a false ideal, not of intelligence and strenuous virtue, but of wealth and station, pleasure and ease, is as a stone from a sling to kill in our great middle-class, in us who are called

Philistines, the desire before spoken of, which by nature for ever carries all men towards that which is lovely; and to leave instead of it only a blind deteriorating pursuit, for ourselves also, of the false ideal. And in those among us Philistines whom this desire does not wholly abandon, yet, having no excellent ideal set forth to nourish and to steady it, it meets with that natural bent for the bathos which together with this desire itself is implanted at birth in the breast of man, and is by that force twisted awry, and borne at random hither and thither, and at last flung upon those grotesque and hideous forms of popular religion which the more respectable part among us Philistines mistake for the true goal of man's desire after all that is lovely. And for the Populace this false idea is a stone which kills the desire before it can even arise; so impossible and unattainable for them do the conditions of that which is lovely appear according to this ideal to be made, so necessary to the reaching of them by the few seems the falling short of them by the many. So that, perhaps, of the actual vulgarity of our Philistines and brutality of our Populace, the Barbarians and their feudal habits of succession, enduring out of their due time and place, are involuntarily the cause in a great degree; and they hurt the welfare of the rest of the community at the same time that, as we have seen, they hurt their own.

But must not, now, the working in our minds of considerations like these, to which culture, that is, the disinterested and active use of reading, reflection, and observation, carries us, be really much more effectual to the dissolution of feudal habits and rules of succession in land than an operation like the Real Estate Intestacy Bill, and a stock notion like that of the natural right of all a man's children to an equal share in the enjoyment of his property; since we have seen that this mechanical maxim is unsound, and that, if it is unsound, the operation relying upon it cannot possibly be effective? If truth and reason have, as we believe, any natural irresistible effect on the mind of man, it must. These considerations, when culture has called them forth and given them free course in our minds, will live and work. They will work gradually, no doubt, and will not bring us ourselves to the front to sit in high place and put them into effect; but so they will be all the more beneficial. Everything teaches us how gradually nature would have all profound changes brought about; and we can even see, too, where the absolute abrupt stoppage of feudal habits has worked harm. And appealing to the sense of truth and reason, these considerations will, without doubt, touch and move all those of even the Barbarians themselves, who are (as are some of us Philistines also, and some of the Populace) beyond their fellows quick of feeling for truth and reason. For indeed this is just one of the advantages of sweetness and light over fire and strength, that sweetness and light make a feudal class quietly and gradually drop its feudal habits because it sees them at variance with truth and reason, while fire and strength tear them passionately off it because it applauded Mr Lowe when he called, or was supposed to call, the working-class drunken and venal.*

But when once we have begun to recount the practical operations by which our Liberal friends work for the removal of definite evils, and in which if we do not join them they are apt to grow impatient with us, how can we pass over that very interesting operation of this kind,—the attempt to enable a man to marry his deceased wife's sister? This operation, too, like that for abating the feudal customs of succession in land, I have had the advantage of myself seeing and hearing my Liberal friends labour at. I was lucky enough to be present when Mr Chambers, I think, brought forward in the House of Commons his bill for enabling a man to marry his deceased wife's sister, and I heard the speech which Mr Chambers then made in support of his bill.* His first point was that God's law,—the name he always gave to the Book of Leviticus,—did not really forbid a man to marry his deceased wife's sister. God's law not forbidding it, the Liberal maxim that a man's prime right and happiness is to do as he likes ought at once to come into force, and to annul any such check upon the assertion of personal liberty as the prohibition to marry one's deceased wife's sister. A distinguished Liberal supporter of Mr Chambers, in the debate which followed the introduction of the bill, produced a formula of much beauty and neatness for conveying in brief the Liberal notions on this head: 'Liberty,' said he, 'is the law of human life.' And, therefore, the moment it is ascertained that God's law, the Book of Leviticus, does not stop the way, man's law, the law of liberty, asserts its right, and makes us free to marry our deceased wife's sister.

And this exactly falls in with what Mr Hepworth Dixon, who may almost be called the Colenso of love and marriage,*—such a revolution does he make in our ideas on these matters, just as Dr Colenso does in our ideas on religion,—tells us of the notions and proceedings of our kinsmen in America. With that affinity of genius to the Hebrew genius which we have already noticed, and with the strong belief of our race that liberty is the law of human life, so far as a fixed, perfect, and paramount rule of conscience, the Bible, does not expressly control it, our American kinsmen go again, Mr Hepworth Dixon tells us, to their Bible, the Mormons to the patriarchs and the Old Testament, Brother Noyes to St Paul and the New, and having never before read anything else but their Bible, they now read their Bible over again, and make all manner of great discoveries there. All these discoveries are favourable to liberty, and in this way is satisfied that double craving so characteristic of the Philistine, and so eminently exemplified in that crowned Philistine, Henry the Eighth,*—the craving for forbidden fruit and the craving for legality. Mr Hepworth Dixon's eloquent writings give currency, over here, to these important discoveries; so that now, as regards love and marriage, we seem to be entering, with all our sails spread, upon what Mr Hepworth Dixon, its apostle and evangelist, calls a Gothic Revival, but what one of the many newspapers that so greatly admire Mr Hepworth Dixon's lithe and sinewy style and form their own style upon it, calls, by a yet bolder and more striking figure, 'a great sexual insurrection of our Anglo-Teutonic race.' For this end we have to avert our eyes from everything Hellenic and fanciful, and to keep them steadily fixed upon the two cardinal points of the Bible and liberty. And one of those practical operations in which the Liberal party engage, and in which we are summoned to join them, directs itself entirely, as we have seen, to these cardinal points, and may almost be regarded, perhaps, as a kind of first instalment or public and parliamentary pledge of the great sexual insurrection of our Anglo-Teutonic race.

But here, as elsewhere, what we seek is the Philistine's perfection, the development of his best self, not mere liberty for his ordinary self. And we no more allow absolute validity to his stock maxim, *Liberty is the law of human life*, than we allow it to the opposite maxim,* which is just as true, *Renouncement is the law of human life*. For we know that the only perfect freedom is, as our religion says, a service;* not a service to any stock maxim, but an elevation of our best self, and a harmonising in subordination to this, and to the idea of a perfected humanity, all the multitudinous, turbulent, and blind impulses of our ordinary selves. Now, the Philistine's great defect being a defect in delicacy of perception, to cultivate in him this delicacy, to render it independent of external and mechanical rule, and a law to itself, is what seems to make most for his perfection, his true humanity. And his true humanity, and therefore his happiness, appears to lie much more, so far as the relations of love and marriage are concerned, in becoming alive to the finer shades of feeling which arise within these relations, in being able to enter with tact and sympathy into the subtle instinctive propensions and repugnances of the person with whose life his own life is bound up, to make them his own, to direct and govern, in harmony with them, the arbitrary range of his personal action, and thus to enlarge his spiritual and intellectual life and liberty, than in remaining insensible to these finer shades of feeling, this delicate sympathy, in giving unchecked range, so far as he can, to his mere personal action, in allowing no limits or government to this except such as a mechanical external law imposes, and in thus really narrowing, for the satisfaction of his ordinary self, his spiritual and intellectual life and liberty.

Still more must this be so when his fixed eternal rule, his God's law, is supplied to him from a source which is less fit, perhaps, to supply final and absolute instructions on this particular topic of love and marriage than on any other relation of human life. Bishop Wilson, who is full of examples of that fruitful Hellenising within the limits of Hebraism itself, of that renewing of the stiff and stark notions of Hebraism by turning upon them a stream of fresh thought and consciousness, which we have already noticed in St Paul,—Bishop Wilson gives an admirable lesson to rigid Hebraisers,* like Mr Chambers, asking themselves: Does God's law (that is, the Book of Leviticus) forbid us to marry our wife's sister?—Does God's law (that is, again, the Book of Leviticus) allow us to marry our wife's sister?—when he says: 'Christian duties are founded on reason, not on the sovereign authority of God commanding what he pleases; God cannot command us what is not fit to be believed or done, all his commands being founded in the necessities of our nature.' And, immense as is our debt to the Hebrew race and its genius, incomparable as is its authority on certain profoundly important sides of our human nature, worthy as it is to be described as having uttered, for those sides, the voice of the deepest necessities of our nature, the statutes of the divine and eternal order of things, the law of God,—who, that is not manacled and hoodwinked by his

Hebraism, can believe that, as to love and marriage, our reason and the necessities of our humanity have their true, sufficient, and divine law expressed for them by the voice of any Oriental and polygamous nation like the Hebrews? Who, I say, will believe, when he really considers the matter, that where the feminine nature, the feminine ideal,* and our relations to them, are brought into question, the delicate and apprehensive genius of the Indo-European race, the race which invented the Muses, and chivalry, and the Madonna, is to find its last word on this question in the institutions of a Semitic people, whose wisest king had seven hundred wives and three hundred concubines?*

If here again, therefore, we seem to minister better to the diseased spirit of our time by leading it to think about the operation our Liberal friends have in hand, than by lending a hand to this operation ourselves, let us see, before we dismiss from our view the practical operations of our Liberal friends, whether the same thing does not hold good as to their celebrated industrial and economical labours also. Their great work of this kind is, of course, their free-trade policy. This policy, as having enabled the poor man to eat untaxed bread, and as having wonderfully augmented trade, we are accustomed to speak of with a kind of solemnity; it is chiefly on their having been our leaders in this policy that Mr Bright founds for himself and his friends the claim, so often asserted by him, to be considered guides of the blind, teachers of the ignorant, benefactors slowly and laboriously developing in the Conservative party and in the country that which Mr Bright is fond of calling *the growth of intelligence*,—the object, as is well known, of all the friends of culture also, and the great end and aim of the culture that we preach. Now, having first saluted free-trade and its doctors with all respect, let us see whether even here, too, our Liberal friends do not pursue their operations in a mechanical way, without reference to any firm intelligible law of things, to human life as a whole, and human happiness; and whether it is not more for our good, at this particular moment at any rate, if, instead of worshipping free-trade with them Hebraistically, as a kind of fetish, and helping them to pursue it as an end in and for itself, we turn the free stream of our thought upon their treatment of it, and see how this is related to the intelligible law of human life, and to national well-being and happiness. In short, suppose we Hellenise a little with free-trade, as we Hellenised with the Real Estate Intestacy Bill, and with the disestablishment of the Irish Church by the power of the Nonconformists' antipathy to religious establishments and endowments, and see whether what our reprovers beautifully call ministering to the diseased spirit of our time is best done by the Hellenising method of proceeding, or by the other.

But first let us understand how the policy of free-trade really shapes itself for our Liberal friends, and how they practically employ it as an instrument of national happiness and salvation. For as we said that it seemed clearly right to prevent the Church property of Ireland from being all taken for the benefit of the Church of a small minority, so it seems clearly right that the poor man should eat untaxed bread, and, generally, that restrictions and regulations which, for the supposed benefit of some particular person or class of persons, make the price of things artificially high here, or artificially low there, and interfere with the natural flow of trade and commerce, should be done away with. But in the policy of our Liberal friends free-trade means more than this, and is specially valued as a stimulant to the production of wealth, as they call it, and to the increase of the trade, business, and population of the country. We have already seen how these things,—trade, business, and population,—are mechanically pursued by us as ends precious in themselves, and are worshipped as what we call fetishes; and Mr Bright, I have already said, when he wishes to give the working-class a true sense of what makes glory and greatness, tells it to look at the cities it has built, the railroads it has made, the manufactures it has produced.* So to this idea of glory and greatness the free-trade which our Liberal friends extol so solemnly and devoutly has served,—to the increase of trade, business, and population; and for this it is prized. Therefore, the untaxing of the poor man's bread has, with this view of national happiness, been used, not so much to make the existing poor man's bread cheaper or more abundant, but rather to create more poor men to eat it; so that we cannot precisely say that we have fewer poor men than we had before free-trade, but we can say with truth that we have many more centres of industry, as they are called, and much more business, population, and manufactures. And if we are sometimes a little troubled by our multitude of poor men, yet we know the increase of manufactures and population to be such a salutary thing in itself, and our free-trade policy begets such an admirable movement, creating fresh centres of industry and fresh poor men here, while we were thinking about our poor men there, that we are quite dazzled and borne away, and more and more industrial movement is called for, and our social progress seems to become one triumphant and enjoyable course of what is sometimes called, vulgarly, outrunning the constable.*

If, however, taking some other criterion of man's well-being than the cities he has built and the manufactures he has produced, we persist in thinking that our social progress would be happier if there were not so many of us so very poor, and in busying ourselves with notions of in some way or other adjusting the poor man and business one to the other, and not multiplying the one and the other mechanically and blindly, then our Liberal friends, the appointed doctors of free-trade, take us up very sharply. 'Art is long,' says *The Times*, 'and life is short;* for the most part we settle things first and understand them afterwards. Let us have as few theories as possible; what is wanted is not the light of speculation. If nothing worked well of which the theory was not perfectly understood, we should be in sad confusion. The relations of labour and capital, we are told, are not understood, yet trade and commerce, on the whole, work satisfactorily.' I quote from *The Times* of only the other day. But thoughts like these, as I have often pointed out, are thoroughly British thoughts, and we have been familiar with them for years.

Or, if we want more of a philosophy of the matter than this, our free-trade friends have two axioms for us, axioms laid down by their justly esteemed doctors, which they think ought to satisfy us entirely. One is, that, other things being equal, the more population increases, the more does production increase to keep pace with it; because men by their numbers and contact call forth all manner of activities and resources in one another and in nature, which, when men are few and sparse, are never developed. The other is, that, although population always tends to equal the means of subsistence, yet people's notions of what subsistence is enlarge as civilisation advances, and take in a number of things beyond the bare necessaries of life; and thus, therefore, is supplied whatever check on population is needed. But the error of our friends is just, perhaps, that they apply axioms of this sort as if they were self-acting laws which will put themselves into operation without trouble or planning on our part, if we will only pursue free-trade, business, and population zealously and staunchly. Whereas the real truth is, that, however the case might be under other circumstances, yet in fact, as we now manage the matter, the enlarged conception of what is included in *subsistence* does not operate to prevent the bringing into the world of numbers of people who but just attain to the barest necessaries of life or who even fail to attain to them; while, again, though production may increase as population increases, yet it seems that the production may be of such a kind, and so related, or rather non-related, to population, that the population may be little the better for it. For instance, with the increase of population since Queen Elizabeth's time the production of silk-stockings has wonderfully increased, and silk-stockings have become much cheaper and procurable in much greater abundance by many more people, and tend perhaps, as population and manufactures increase, to get cheaper and cheaper and at last to become, according to Bastiat's favourite image,* a common free property of the human race, like light and air. But bread and bacon have not become much cheaper with the increase of population since Queen Elizabeth's time, nor procurable in much greater abundance by many more people; neither do they seem at all to promise to become, like light and air, a common free property of the human race. And if bread and bacon have not kept pace with our population, and we have many more people in want of them now than in Queen Elizabeth's time, it seems vain to tell us that silk-stockings have kept pace with our population, or even more than kept pace with it, and that we are to get our comfort out of that. In short, it turns out that our pursuit of free-trade, as of so many other things, has been too mechanical. We fix upon some object, which in this case is the production of wealth, and the increase of manu-factures, population, and commerce through free-trade, as a kind of one thing needful, or end in itself, and then we pursue it staunchly and mechanically, and say that it is our duty to pursue it staunchly and mechanically, not to see how it is related to the whole intelligible law of things and to full human perfection, or to treat it as the piece of machinery, of varying value as its relations to the intelligible law of things vary, which it really is.

So it is of no use to say to *The Times*, and to our Liberal friends rejoicing in the possession of their talisman of free-trade, that about one in nineteen of our population is a pauper, and that, this being so, trade and commerce can hardly be said to prove by their satisfactory working that it matters nothing whether the relations between labour and capital are understood or not; nay, that we can hardly be said not to be in sad confusion. For here comes in our faith in the staunch mechanical pursuit of a fixed object, and covers itself with that imposing and colossal necessitarianism of *The Times* which we have before noticed. And this necessitarianism, taking for granted that an increase in trade and population is a good in itself, one of the chiefest of goods, tells us that disturbances of human happiness caused by ebbs and flows in the tide of trade and business, which, on the whole, steadily mounts, are inevitable and not to be quarrelled with. This firm philosophy I seek to call to mind when I am in the East of London, whither my avocations often lead me; and, indeed, to fortify myself against the depressing sights which on these occasions assail us, I have transcribed from *The Times* one strain of this kind, full of the finest economical doctrine, and always carry it about with me. The passage is this:—

'The East End* is the most commercial, the most industrial, the most fluctuating region of the metropolis. It is always the first to suffer; for it is the creature of prosperity, and falls to the ground the instant there is no wind to bear it up. The whole of that region is covered with huge docks, shipyards, manufactories, and a wilderness of small houses, all full of life and happiness in brisk times, but in dull times withered and lifeless, like the deserts we read of in the East. Now their brief spring is over. There is no one to blame for this; it is the result of Nature's simplest laws!' We must all agree that it is impossible that anything can be firmer than this, or show a surer faith in the working of free-trade, as our Liberal friends understand and employ it.

But, if we still at all doubt whether the indefinite multiplication of manufactories and small houses can be such an absolute good in itself as to counter-balance the indefinite multiplication of poor people, we shall learn that this multiplication of poor people, too, is an absolute good in itself, and the result of divine and beautiful laws. This is indeed a favourite thesis with our Philistine friends, and I have already noticed the pride and gratitude with which they receive certain articles in *The Times*, dilating in thankful and solemn language on the majestic growth of our population. But I prefer to quote now, on this topic, the words of an ingenious young Scotch writer, Mr Robert Buchanan,* because he invests with so much imagination and poetry this current idea of the blessed and even divine character which the multiplying of population is supposed in itself to have. 'We move to multiplicity,' says Mr Robert Buchanan. 'If there is one quality which seems God's, and his exclusively, it seems that divine philoprogenitiveness, that passionate love of distribution and expansion into living forms. Every animal added seems a new ecstasy to the Maker; every life added, a new embodiment of his love. He would *swarm* the earth with beings. There are never enough. Life, life, life,—faces gleaming, hearts beating, must fill every cranny. Not a corner is suffered to remain empty. The whole earth breeds and God glories.'

It is a little unjust, perhaps, to attribute to the Divinity exclusively this philoprogenitiveness, which the British Philistine, and the poorer class of Irish, may certainly claim to share with him; yet how inspiriting is here the whole strain of thought! and these beautiful words, too, I carry about with me in the East of London, and often read them there. They are quite in agreement with the popular language one is accustomed to hear about children and large families, which describes children as *sent*. And a line of poetry which Mr Robert Buchanan throws in presently after the poetical prose I have quoted:—

'Tis the old story of the fig-leaf time—

this fine line, too, naturally connects itself, when one is in the East of London, with the idea of God's desire to *swarm* the earth with beings; because the swarming of the earth with beings does indeed, in the East of London, so seem to revive

. . . the old story of the fig-leaf time—

such a number of the people one meets there having hardly a rag to cover them; and the more the swarming goes on, the more it promises to revive this old story. And when the story is perfectly revived, the swarming quite completed, and every cranny choke-full, then, too, no doubt, the faces in the East of London will be gleaming faces, which Mr Robert Buchanan says it is God's desire they should be, and which every one must perceive they are not at present, but, on the contrary, very miserable.

But to prevent all this philosophy and poetry from quite running away with us, and making us think with *The Times*, and our practical

Liberal free-traders, and the British Philistines generally, that the increase of small houses and manufactories, or the increase of population, are absolute goods in themselves, to be mechanically pursued, and to be worshipped like fetishes,—to prevent this, we have got that notion of ours immoveably fixed, of which I have long ago spoken, the notion that culture, or the study of perfection, leads us to conceive of no perfection as being real which is not a *general* perfection, embracing all our fellow-men with whom we have to do. Such is the sympathy which binds humanity together, that we are indeed, as our religion says, members of one body,* and if one member suffer, all the members suffer with it; individual perfection is impossible so long as the rest of mankind are not perfected along with us. 'The *multitude* of the wise is the welfare of the world,'* says the wise man. And to this effect that excellent and often quoted guide of ours, Bishop Wilson, has some striking words:—'It is not,' says he, 'so much our neighbour's interest as our own that we love him,' And again he says: 'Our salvation does in some measure depend upon that of others.'* And the author of the *Imitation* puts the same thing admirably when he says:—'*Obscurior etiam via ad cœlum videbatur quando tam pauci regnum cœlorum quærere curabant,*'—the fewer there are who follow the way to perfection, the harder that way is to find.* So all our fellow-men, in the East of London and elsewhere, we must take along with us in the progress towards perfection, if we ourselves really, as we profess, want to be perfect; and we must not let the worship of any fetish, any machinery, such as manufactures or population,—which are not, like perfection, absolute goods in themselves, though we think them so,—create for us such a multitude of miserable, sunken, and ignorant human beings, that to carry them all along with us is impossible, and perforce they must for the most part be left by us in their degradation and wretchedness. But evidently the conception of free-trade, on which our Liberal friends vaunt themselves, and in which they think they have found the secret of national prosperity,—evidently, I say, the mere unfettered pursuit of the production of wealth, and the mere mechanical multiplying, for this end, of manufactures and population, threatens to create for us, if it has not created already, those vast, miserable, unmanageable masses of sunken people,—one pauper, at the present moment, for every nineteen of us,—to the existence of which we are, as we have seen, absolutely forbidden to reconcile ourselves, in spite of all that the philosophy of *The Times* and the poetry of Mr Robert Buchanan may say to persuade us.

And though Hebraism, following its best and highest instinct,— identical, as we have seen, with that of Hellenism in its final aim, the aim of perfection,—teaches us this very clearly; and though from Hebraising counsellors,—the Bible, Bishop Wilson, the author of the *Imitation*,—I have preferred (as well I may, for from this rock of Hebraism we are all hewn!) to draw the texts which we use to bring home to our minds this teaching; yet Hebraism seems powerless, almost as powerless as our free-trading Liberal friends, to deal effi- caciously with our ever-accumulating masses of pauperism, and to prevent their accumulating still more.* Hebraism builds churches, indeed, for these masses, and sends missionaries among them; above all, it sets itself against the social necessitarianism of *The Times*, and refuses to accept their degradation as inevitable; but with regard to their ever-increasing accumulation, it seems to be led to the very same conclusions, though from a point of view of its own, as our free-trading Liberal friends. Hebraism, with that mechanical and misleading use of the letter of Scripture on which we have already commented, is governed by such texts as: *Be fruitful and multiply*;*— the edict of God's law, as Mr Chambers would say; or by the declar- ation of what he would call God's words in the Psalms,* that the man who has a great number of children is thereby made happy. And in conjunction with such texts as these it is apt to place another text: *The poor shall never cease out of the land*.* Thus Hebraism is conducted to nearly the same notion as the popular mind and as Mr Robert Buchanan, that children are *sent*, and that the divine nature takes a delight in swarming the East End of London with paupers. Only, when they are perishing in their helplessness and wretchedness, it asserts the Christian duty of succouring them, instead of saying, like *The Times*: 'Now their brief spring is over; there is nobody to blame for this; it is the result of Nature's simplest laws!' But, like *The Times*, Hebraism despairs of any help from knowledge and says that 'what is wanted is not the light of specula- tion.' I remember, only the other day, a good man,* looking with me upon a multitude of children who were gathered before us in one of the most miserable regions of London,—children eaten up with disease, half-sized, half-fed, half-clothed, neglected by their parents, without health, without home, without hope,—said to me: 'The one thing really needful is to teach these little ones to succour one another, if only with a cup of cold water; but now, from one end of the country to the other, one hears nothing but the cry for knowledge, knowledge, knowledge!' And yet surely, so long as these children are there in these festering masses, without health, without home, without hope, and so long as their multitude is perpetually swelling, charged with misery they must still be for themselves, charged with misery they must still be for us, whether they help one another with a cup of cold water or no; and the knowledge how to prevent their accumulating is necessary, even to give their moral life and growth a fair chance!

May we not, therefore, say, that neither the true Hebraism of this good man, willing to spend and be spent for these sunken multitudes, nor what I may call the spurious Hebraism of our free-trading Liberal friends,—mechanically worshipping their fetish of the production of wealth and of the increase of manufactures and population, and looking neither to the right nor left so long as this increase goes on,—avail us much here; and that here, again, what we want is Hellenism, the letting our consciousness play freely and simply upon the facts before us, and listening to what it tells us of the intelligible law of things as concerns them? And surely what it tells us is, that a man's children are not really *sent*, any more than the pictures upon his wall, or the horses in his stable, are *sent*; and that to bring people into the world, when one cannot afford to keep them and oneself decently and not too precariously, or to bring more of them into the world than one can afford to keep thus, is, whatever *The Times* and Mr Robert Buchanan may say, by no means an accomplishment of the divine will or a fulfilment of Nature's simplest laws, but is just as wrong, just as contrary to reason and the will of God, as for a man to have horses, or carriages, or pictures, when he cannot afford them, or to have more of them than he can afford; and that, in the one case as in the other, the larger the scale on which the violation of reason's laws is practised, and the longer it is persisted in, the greater must be the confusion and final trouble. Surely no laudations of free-trade, no meetings of bishops and clergy in the East End of London, no reading of papers and reports, can tell us anything about our social condition which it more concerns us to know than that! and not only to know, but habitually to have the knowledge present, and to act upon it as one acts upon the knowledge that water wets and fire burns! And not only the sunken populace of our great cities are concerned to know it, and the pauper twentieth of our population; we Philistines of the middle-class, too, are concerned to know it, and all who have to set themselves to make progress in perfection.

But we all know it already! some one will say; it is the simplest law of prudence. But how little reality must there be in our knowledge of it; how little can we be putting it in practice; how little is it likely to penetrate among the poor and struggling masses of our population, and to better our condition, so long as an unintelligent Hebraism of one sort keeps repeating as an absolute eternal word of God the psalm-verse* which says that the man who has a great many children is happy, or an unintelligent Hebraism of another sort keeps assigning as an absolute proof of national prosperity the multiplying of manufactures and population! Surely, the one set of Hebraisers have to learn that their psalm-verse was composed at the resettlement of Jerusalem after the Captivity, when the Jews of Jerusalem were a handful, an under-manned garrison, and every child was a blessing; and that the word of God, or the voice of the divine order of things, declares the possession of a great many children to be a blessing only when it really is so! And the other set of Hebraisers, have they not to learn that if they call their private acquaintances imprudent and unlucky, when, with no means of support for them or with precarious means, they have a large family of children, then they ought not to call the State well managed and prosperous merely because its manufactures and its citizens multiply, if the manufactures, which bring new citizens into existence just as much as if they had actually begotten them, bring more of them into existence than they can maintain, or are too precarious to go on maintaining those whom for a while they maintained? Hellenism, surely, or the habit of fixing our mind upon the intelligible law of things, is most salutary if it makes us see that the only absolute good, the only absolute and eternal object prescribed to us by God's law, or the divine order of things, is the progress towards perfection,—our own progress towards it and the progress of humanity. And therefore, for every individual man, and for every society of men, the possession and multiplication of children, like the possession and multiplication of horses and pictures, is to be accounted good or bad, not in itself, but with reference to this object and the progress towards it. And as no man is to be excused in having horses or pictures, if his having them hinders his own or others' progress towards perfection and makes them lead a servile and ignoble life, so is no man to be excused for having children if his having them makes him or others lead this. Plain thoughts of this kind are surely the spontaneous product of our consciousness, when it is allowed to play freely and disinterestedly upon the actual facts of our social condition, and upon our stock notions and stock habits in respect to it. Firmly grasped and simply uttered, they are more likely, one cannot but think, to better that condition, and to diminish our formidable rate of one pauper to every nineteen of us, than is the Hebraising and mechanical pursuit of free-trade by our Liberal friends.

So that, here as elsewhere, the practical operations of our Liberal friends, by which they set so much store, and in which they invite us to join them and to show what Mr Bright calls a commendable interest, do not seem to us so practical for real good as they think; and our Liberal friends seem to us themselves to need to Hellenise, as we say, a little,—that is, to examine into the nature of real good, and to listen to what their consciousness tells them about it,—rather than to pursue with such heat and confidence their present practical operations. And it is clear that they have no just cause, so far as regards several operations of theirs which we have canvassed, to reproach us with delicate Conservative scepticism; for often by Hellenising we seem to subvert stock Conservative notions and usages more effectually than they subvert them by Hebraising. But, in truth, the free spontaneous play of consciousness with which culture tries to float our stock habits of thinking and acting, is by its very nature, as has been said, disinterested. Sometimes the result of floating them may be agreeable to this party, sometimes to that; now it may be unwelcome to our so-called Liberals, now to our so-called Conservatives; but what culture seeks is, above all, to *float* them, to prevent their being stiff and stark pieces of petrifaction any longer. It is mere Hebraising, if we stop short, and refuse to let our consciousness play freely, whenever we or our friends do not happen to like what it discovers to us. This is to make the Liberal party, or the Conservative party, our one thing needful, instead of human perfection; and we have seen what mischief arises from making an even greater thing than the Liberal or the Conservative party,—the predominance of the moral side in man,—our one thing needful. But wherever the free play of our consciousness leads us, we shall follow;

believing that in this way we shall tend to make good at all points what is wanting to us, and so shall be brought nearer to our complete human perfection.

Thus we may often, perhaps, praise much that a so-called Liberal thinks himself forbidden to praise, and yet blame much that a so-called Conservative thinks himself forbidden to blame, because these are both of them partisans, and no partisan can afford to be thus disinterested. But we who are not partisans can afford it; and so, after we have seen what Nonconformists lose by being locked up in their New Road forms of religious institution, we can let ourselves see, on the other hand, how their ministers, in a time of movement of ideas like our present time, are apt to be more exempt than the ministers of a great Church establishment from that self-confidence, and sense of superiority to such a movement, which are natural to a powerful hierarchy; and which in Archdeacon Denison,* for instance, seem almost carried to such a pitch that they may become, one cannot but fear, his spiritual ruin. But seeing this does not dispose us, therefore, to lock up all the nation in forms of worship of the New Road type; but it points us to the quite new ideal, of combining grand and national forms of worship with an openness and movement of mind not yet found in any hierarchy. So, again, if we see what is called ritualism* making conquests in our Puritan middle-class, we may rejoice that portions of this class should have become alive to the æsthetical weakness of their position, even although they have not yet become alive to the intellectual weakness of it. In Puritanism, on the other hand, we can respect that idea of dealing sincerely with oneself, which is at once the great force of Puritanism,— Puritanism's great superiority over all products, like ritualism, of our Catholicising tendencies,—and also an idea rich in the latent seeds of intellectual promise. But we do this, without on that account hiding from ourselves that Puritanism has by Hebraising misapplied that idea, has as yet developed none or hardly one of those seeds, and that its triumph at its present stage of development would be baneful.

Everything, in short, confirms us in the doctrine, so unpalatable to the believers in action, that our main business at the present moment is not so much to work away at certain crude reforms of which we have already the scheme in our own mind, as to create, through the help of that culture which at the very outset we began by praising and recommending, a frame of mind out of which really fruitful reforms may with time grow. At any rate, we ourselves must put up with our friends' impatience, and with their reproaches against cultivated inaction, and must still decline to lend a hand to their practical operations, until we, for our own part at least, have grown a little clearer about the nature of real good, and have arrived nearer to a condition of mind out of which really fruitful and solid operations may spring.

  In the meanwhile, since our Liberal friends keep loudly and resolutely assuring us that their actual operations at present are fruitful and solid, let us in each case keep testing these operations in the simple way we have indicated, by letting the natural stream of our consciousness flow over them freely; and if they stand this test successfully, then let us give them our commendable interest, but not else. For example. Our Liberal friends assure us, at the very top of their voices, that their present actual operation for the disestablishment of the Irish Church is fruitful and solid. But what if, on testing it, the truth appears to be, that the statesmen and reasonable people of both parties wished for much the same thing,—the fair apportionment of the church property of Ireland among the principal religious bodies there; but that, behind the statesmen and reasonable people, there was, on one side, a mass of Tory prejudice, and, on the other, a mass of Nonconformist prejudice, to which such an arrangement was unpalatable? Well, the natural way, one thinks, would have been for the statesmen and reasonable people of both sides to have united, and to have allayed and dissipated, so far as they could, the resistance of their respective extremes, and where they could not, to have confronted it in concert. But we see that, instead of this, Liberal statesmen waited to trip up their rivals, if they proposed the arrangement which both knew to be reasonable, by means of the prejudice of their own Nonconformist extreme; and then, themselves proposing an arrangement to flatter this prejudice, made the other arrangement, which they themselves knew to be reasonable, out of the question; and drove their rivals in their turn to blow up with all their might, in the hope of baffling them, a great fire, among their own Tory extreme, of fierce prejudice and religious bigotry,—a fire which, once kindled, may always very easily spread further? If, I say, on testing the present operation of our Liberal friends for the disestablishment of the Irish Church, the truth about it appears to be very much this, then, I think,—even with a triumphant

Liberal majority, and with our Liberal friends making impassioned
appeals to us to take a commendable interest in their operation
and them, and to rally round what Sir Henry Hoare* (who may be
described, perhaps, as a Barbarian converted to Philistinism, as I, on
the other hand, seem to be a Philistine converted to culture) finely
calls the conscientiousness of a Gladstone and the intellect of a
Bright,—it is rather our duty to abstain, and, instead of lending a
hand to the operation of our Liberal friends, to do what we can to
abate and dissolve the mass of prejudice, Tory or Nonconformist,
which makes so doubtfully begotten and equivocal an operation as
the present, producible and possible.

CONCLUSION

AND so we bring to an end what we had to say in praise of culture,
and in evidence of its special utility for the circumstances in which
we find ourselves, and the confusion which environs us. Through
culture seems to lie our way, not only to perfection, but even to
safety. Resolutely refusing to lend a hand to the imperfect operations
of our Liberal friends, disregarding their impatience, taunts, and
reproaches, firmly bent on trying to find in the intelligible law of
things a firmer and sounder basis for future practice than any which
we have at present, and believing this search and discovery to be, for
our generation and circumstances, of yet more vital and pressing
importance than practice itself, we nevertheless may do more, perhaps, we poor disparaged followers of culture, to make the actual
present, and the frame of society in which we live, solid and sea-
worthy, than all which our bustling politicians can do. For we have
seen how much of our disorders and perplexities is due to the disbelief, among the classes and combinations of men, Barbarian or
Philistine, which have hitherto governed our society, in right reason,
in a paramount best self; to the inevitable decay and break-up of the
organisations by which, asserting and expressing in these organisations their ordinary self only, they have so long ruled us; and to their
irresolution, when the society, which their conscience tells them
they have made and still manage not with right reason but with their
ordinary self, is rudely shaken, in offering resistance to its sub-
verters. But for us,—who believe in right reason, in the duty and

possibility of extricating and elevating our best self, in the progress of humanity towards perfection,—for us the framework of society, that theatre on which this august drama has to unroll itself, is sacred; and whoever administers it, and however we may seek to remove them from the tenure of administration, yet, while they administer, we steadily and with undivided heart support them in repressing anarchy and disorder; because without order there can be no society, and without society there can be no human perfection.*

With me, indeed, this rule of conduct is hereditary. I remember my father, in one of his unpublished letters written more than forty years ago, when the political and social state of the country was gloomy and troubled, and there were riots in many places, goes on, after strongly insisting on the badness and foolishness of the government, and on the harm and dangerousness of our feudal and aristocratical constitution of society, and ends thus: 'As for rioting, the old Roman way of dealing with *that* is always the right one: flog the rank and file, and fling the ringleaders from the Tarpeian Rock!'* And this opinion we can never forsake, however our Liberal friends may think a little rioting, and what they call popular demonstrations, useful sometimes to their own interests and to the interests of the valuable practical operations they have in hand, and however they may preach the right of an Englishman to be left to do as far as possible what he likes, and the duty of his government to indulge him and connive as much as possible and abstain from all harshness of repression. And even when they artfully show us operations which are undoubtedly precious, such as the abolition of the slave-trade, and ask us if, for their sake, foolish and obstinate governments may not wholesomely be frightened by a little disturbance, the good design in view and the difficulty of overcoming opposition to it being considered,—still we say no, and that monster processions in the streets and forcible irruptions into the parks, even in professed support of this good design, ought to be unflinchingly forbidden and repressed; and that far more is lost than is gained by permitting them. Because a State in which law is authoritative and sovereign, a firm and settled course of public order, is requisite if man is to bring to maturity anything precious and lasting now, or to found anything precious and lasting for the future.

Thus, in our eyes, the very framework and exterior order of the State, whoever may administer the State, is sacred; and culture is the most resolute enemy of anarchy, because of the great hopes and designs for the State which culture teaches us to nourish. But as believing in right reason, and having faith in the progress of humanity towards perfection, and ever labouring for this end, we grow to have clearer sight of the ideas of right reason, and of the elements and helps of perfection, and come gradually to fill the framework of the State with them, to fashion its internal composition and all its laws and institutions conformably to them, and to make the State more and more the expression, as we say, of our best self, which is not manifold, and vulgar, and unstable, and contentious, and ever-varying, but one, and noble, and secure, and peaceful, and the same for all mankind,—with what aversion shall we not *then* regard anarchy, with what firmness shall we not check it, when there is so much that is so precious which it will endanger! So that, for the sake of the present, but far more for the sake of the future, the lovers of culture are unswervingly and with a good conscience the opposers of anarchy. And not as the Barbarians and Philistines, whose honesty and whose sense of humour make them shrink, as we have seen, from treating the State as too serious a thing, and from giving it too much power;—for indeed the only State they know of, and think they administer, is the expression of their ordinary self; and though the headstrong and violent extreme among them might gladly arm this with full authority, yet their virtuous mean is, as we have said, pricked in conscience at doing this, and so our Barbarian Secretaries of State let the Park railings be broken down, and our Philistine Alderman-Colonels let the London roughs rob and beat the bystanders. But we, beholding in the State no expression of our ordinary self, but even already, as it were, the appointed frame and prepared vessel of our best self, and, for the future, our best self's powerful, beneficent, and sacred expression and organ,—we are willing and resolved, even now, to strengthen against anarchy the trembling hands of our Barbarian Home Secretaries, and the feeble knees of our Philistine Alderman-Colonels; and to tell them, that it is not really in behalf of their own ordinary self that they are called to protect the Park railings, and to suppress the London roughs, but in behalf of the best self both of themselves and of all of us in the future.

Nevertheless, though for resisting anarchy the lovers of culture may prize and employ fire and strength,* yet they must, at the same time, bear constantly in mind that it is not at this moment true, what the majority of people tell us, that the world wants fire and strength more than sweetness and light, and that things are for the most part to be settled first and understood afterwards. We have seen how much of our present perplexities and confusion this untrue notion of the majority of people amongst us has caused, and tends to perpetuate. Therefore the true business of the friends of culture now is, to dissipate this false notion, to spread the belief in right reason and in a firm intelligible law of things, and to get men to allow their thought and consciousness to play on their stock notions and habits disinterestedly and freely; to get men to try, in preference to staunchly acting with imperfect knowledge, to obtain some sounder basis of knowledge on which to act. This is what the friends and lovers of culture have to do, however the believers in action may grow impatient with us for saying so, and may insist on our lending a hand to their practical operations, and showing a commendable interest in them.

To this insistence we must indeed turn a deaf ear. But neither, on the other hand, must the friends of culture expect to take the believers in action by storm, or to be visibly and speedily important, and to rule and cut a figure in the world. Aristotle says* that those for whom ideas and the pursuit of the intelligible law of things can have much attraction, are principally the young, filled with generous spirit and with a passion for perfection; but the mass of mankind, he says, follow seeming goods for real, bestowing hardly a thought upon true sweetness and light;—'and to *their* lives,' he adds mournfully, 'who can give another and a better rhythm?' But, although those chiefly attracted by sweetness and light will probably always be the young and enthusiastic, and culture must not hope to take the mass of mankind by storm, yet we will not therefore, for our own day and for our own people, admit and rest in the desponding sentence of Aristotle. For is not this the right crown of the long discipline of Hebraism, and the due fruit of mankind's centuries of painful schooling in self-conquest, and the just reward, above all, of the strenuous energy of our own nation and kindred in dealing honestly with itself and walking steadfastly according to the best light it knows,—that, when in the fulness of time it has reason and beauty offered to it, and the law of things as they really are, it should at last walk by this true light with the same staunchness and zeal with which it formerly walked by its imperfect light; and thus man's two great natural forces, Hebraism and Hellenism, should no longer be dissociated and rival, but should be a joint force of right thinking and strong doing to carry him on towards perfection? This is what the lovers of culture may perhaps dare to augur for such a nation as ours. Therefore, however great the changes to be accomplished, and however dense the array of Barbarians, Philistines, and Populace, we will neither despair on the one hand, nor, on the other, threaten violent revolution and change. But we will look forward cheerfully and hopefully to 'a revolution,' as the Duke of Wellington said, 'by due course of law;' though not exactly such laws as our Liberal friends are now, with their actual lights, fond of offering us.

But if despondency and violence are both of them forbidden to the believer in culture, yet neither, on the other hand, is public life and direct political action much permitted to him. For it is his business, as we have seen, to get the present believers in action, and lovers of political talking and doing, to make a return upon their own minds, scrutinise their stock notions and habits much more, value their present talking and doing much less; in order that, by learning to think more clearly, they may come at last to act less confusedly. But how shall we persuade our Barbarian to hold lightly to his feudal usages; how shall we persuade our Nonconformist that his time spent in agitating for the abolition of church-rates* would have been better spent in getting worthier ideas than churchmen have of God and the ordering of the world, or his time spent in battling for voluntaryism in education better spent in learning to value and found a public and national culture; how shall we persuade, finally, our Alderman-Colonel not to be content with sitting in the hall of judgment or marching at the head of his men of war, without some knowledge how to perform judgment and how to direct men of war,—how, I say, shall we persuade all these of this, if our Alderman-Colonel sees that we want to get his leading-staff and his scales of justice for our own hands; or the Nonconformist, that we want for ourselves his platform; or the Barbarian, that we want for ourselves his pre-eminence and function? Certainly they will be less slow to believe, as we want them to believe, that the intelligible law of things has in itself something desirable and precious, and that all place, function, and bustle are hollow goods without it, if they see that we can content ourselves with it, and find in it our satisfaction, without making it an instrument to give us for ourselves place, function, and bustle.

And although Mr Sidgwick says that social usefulness really means 'losing oneself in a mass of disagreeable, hard, mechanical details,'* and though all the believers in action are fond of asserting the same thing, yet, as to lose ourselves is not what we want, but to find the intelligible law of things, this assertion too we shall not blindly accept, but shall sift and try it a little first. And if we see that because the believers in action, forgetting Goethe's maxim, 'to act is easy, to think is hard,'* imagine there is some wonderful virtue in losing oneself in a mass of mechanical details, therefore they excuse themselves from much thought about the clear ideas which ought to govern these details, then we shall give our chief care and pains to seeking out those ideas and to setting them forth; being persuaded, that, if we have the ideas firm and clear, the mechanical details for their execution will come a great deal more simply and easily than we now suppose. And even in education, where our Liberal friends are now with much zeal, bringing out their train of practical operations and inviting all men to lend them a hand; and where, since education is the road to culture, we might gladly lend them a hand with their practical operations if we could lend them one anywhere; yet, if we see that any German or Swiss or French law for education rests on very clear ideas about the citizen's claim, in this matter, upon the State, and the State's duty towards the citizen, but has its mechanical details comparatively few and simple, while an English law for the same concern is ruled by no clear idea about the citizen's claim and the State's duty, but has, in compensation, a mass of minute mechanical details about the number of members on a school-committee, and how many shall be a quorum, and how they shall be summoned, and how often they shall meet,—then we must conclude that our nation stands in more need of clear ideas on the main matter than of laboured details about the accessories of the matter, and that we do more service by trying to help it to the ideas than by lending it a hand with the details. So while Mr Samuel Morley* and his friends talk of changing their policy on education, not for the sake of modelling it on more sound ideas, but 'for fear the management of education should be taken out of their hands,' we shall not much care for taking the management out of their hands and getting it into ours; but rather we shall try and make them perceive, that to model education on sound ideas is of more importance than to have the management of it in one's own hands ever so fully.

At this exciting juncture, then, while so many of the lovers of new ideas, somewhat weary, as we too are, of the stock performances of our Liberal friends upon the political stage, are disposed to rush valiantly upon this public stage themselves, we cannot at all think that for a wise lover of new ideas this stage is the right one. Plenty of people there will be without us,—country gentlemen in search of a club, demagogues in search of a tub, lawyers in search of a place, industrialists in search of gentility,—who will come from the east and from the west, and will sit down at that Thyestean banquet* of clap-trap, which English public life for these many years past has been. Because, so long as those old organisations, of which we have seen the insufficiency,—those expressions of our ordinary self, Barbarian or Philistine,—have force anywhere, they will have force in Parliament. There, the man whom the Barbarians send, cannot but be impelled to please the Barbarians' ordinary self, and their natural taste for the bathos; and the man whom the Philistines send, cannot but be impelled to please those of the Philistines. Parliamentary Conservatism will and must long mean this, that the Barbarians should keep their heritage; and Parliamentary Liberalism, that the Barbarians should pass away, as they will pass away, and that into their heritage the Philistines should enter. This seems, indeed, to be the true and authentic promise of which our Liberal friends and Mr Bright believe themselves the heirs, and the goal of that great man's labours. Presently, perhaps, Mr Odger and Mr Bradlaugh will be there with their mission to oust both Barbarians and Philistines, and to get the heritage for the Populace. We, on the other hand, are for giving the heritage neither to the Barbarians nor to the Philistines, nor yet to the Populace; but we are for the transformation of each and all of these according to the law of perfection. Through the length and breadth of our nation a sense,— vague and obscure as yet,—of weariness with the old organisations, of desire for this transformation, works and grows. In the House of Commons the old organisations must inevitably be most enduring and strongest, the transformation must inevitably be longest in showing itself; and it may truly be averred, therefore, that at the present juncture the centre of movement is not in the House of Commons. It is in the fermenting mind of the nation; and his is for the next twenty years the real influence who can address himself to this.

Pericles was perhaps the most perfect public speaker who ever lived, for he was the man who most perfectly combined thought and wisdom with feeling and eloquence. Yet Plato brings in Alcibiades declaring, that men went away from the oratory of Pericles,* saying it was very fine, it was very good, and afterwards thinking no more about it; but they went away from hearing Socrates talk, he says, with the point of what he had said sticking fast in their minds, and they could not get rid of it. Socrates is poisoned and dead; but in his own breast does not every man carry about with him a possible Socrates, in that power of a disinterested play of consciousness upon his stock notions and habits, of which this wise and admirable man gave all through his lifetime the great example, and which was the secret of his incomparable influence? And he who leads men to call forth and exercise in themselves this power, and who busily calls it forth and exercises it in himself, is at the present moment, perhaps, as Socrates was in his time, more in concert with the vital working of men's minds, and more effectually significant, than any House of Commons' orator, or practical operator in politics.

Every one is now boasting of what he has done to educate men's minds and to give things the course they are taking. Mr Disraeli educates,* Mr Bright educates, Mr Beales educates. We, indeed, pretend to educate no one, for we are still engaged in trying to clear and educate ourselves. But we are sure that the endeavour to reach, through culture, the firm intelligible law of things, we are sure that the detaching ourselves from our stock notions and habits, that a more free play of consciousness, an increased desire for sweetness and light, and all the bent which we call Hellenising, is the master-impulse now of the life of our nation and of humanity,—somewhat obscurely perhaps for this moment, but decisively for the immediate future; and that those who work for this are the sovereign educators. Docile echoes of the eternal voice, pliant organs of the infinite will, they are going along with the essential movement of the world; and this is their strength, and their happy and divine fortune. For if the believers in action, who are so impatient with us and call us effeminate, had had the same fortune, they would, no doubt, have surpassed us in this sphere of vital influence by all the superiority of their genius and energy over ours. But now we go the way the world is going, while they abolish the Irish Church by the power of the Nonconformists' antipathy to establishments, or they enable a man to marry his deceased wife's sister.

APPENDIX

HENRY SIDGWICK, 'THE PROPHET OF CULTURE'

[This review of 'Culture and its Enemies' by the Cambridge moral philosopher Henry Sidgwick, published in *Macmillan's Magazine* 16 (1867), 271–80, was in many ways the most penetrating of the critiques to which Arnold had to respond, and the questions which Sidgwick raised have a continued resonance.]

THE movement against anonymous writing, in which this journal some years ago took a part, has received, I think, an undeniable accession of strength from the development (then unexpected) of Mr Matthew Arnold. Some persons who sympathised on the whole with that movement yet felt that the case was balanced, and that if it succeeded we should have sacrificed something that we could not sacrifice without regret. One felt the evils that 'irresponsible reviewers' were continually inflicting on the progress of thought and society: and yet one felt that, in form and expression, anonymous writing tended to be good writing. The buoyant confidence of youth was invigorated and yet sobered by having to sustain the *prestige* of a well-earned reputation: while the practised weapon of age, relieved from the restraints of responsibility, was wielded with almost the elasticity of youth. It was thought we should miss the freedom, the boldness, the reckless vivacity with which one talented writer after another had discharged his missiles from behind the common shield of a coterie of unknown extent, or at least half veiled by a pseudonym. It was thought that periodical literature would gain in carefulness, in earnestness, in sincerity, in real moral influence: but that possibly it might become just a trifle dull. We did not foresee that the dashing insolences of 'we-dom' that we should lose would be more than compensated by the delicate impertinences of egotism that we should gain. We did not imagine the new and exquisite literary enjoyment that would be created when a man of genius and ripe thought, perhaps even elevated by a position of academic dignity, should deliver profound truths and subtle observations with all the dogmatic authority and self-confidence of a prophet: at the same time titillating the public by something like the airs and graces, the playful affectations of a favourite comedian. We did not, in short, foresee a Matthew Arnold: and I think it must be allowed that our apprehensions have been much removed, and our cause much strengthened, by this new phenomenon.

I have called Mr Arnold the prophet of culture: I will not call him an 'elegant Jeremiah,' because he seems to have been a little annoyed (he who is never annoyed) by that phrase of the *Daily Telegraph*. 'Jeremiah!' he exclaims, 'the very Hebrew prophet whose style I admire the least.' I confess I thought the phrase tolerably felicitous for a Philistine, from whom one would not expect any very subtle discrimination of the differentiæ of prophets. Nor can I quite determine which Hebrew prophet Mr Arnold does most resemble. But it is certainly hard to compare him to Jeremiah, for Jeremiah is our type of the lugubrious; whereas there is nothing more striking than the imperturbable cheerfulness with which Mr Arnold seems to sustain himself on the fragment of culture that is left him, amid the deluge of Philistinism that he sees submerging our age and country. A prophet however, I gather, Mr Arnold does not object to be called; as such I wish to consider and weigh him; and thus I am led to examine the lecture with which he has closed his connexion with Oxford,— the most full, distinct, and complete of the various utterances in which he has set forth the Gospel of Culture.

As it will clearly appear in the course of this article, how highly I admire Mr Arnold as a writer, I may say at once, without reserve or qualification, that this utterance has disappointed me very much. It is not even so good in style as former essays; it has more of the mannerism of repeating his own phrases, which, though very effective up to a certain point, may be carried too far. But this is a small point: and Mr Arnold's style, when most faulty, is very charming. My complaint is, that though there is much in it beautifully and subtly said, and many fine glimpses of great truths, it is, as a whole, ambitious, vague, and perverse. It seems to me over-ambitious, because it treats of the most profound and difficult problems of individual and social life with an airy dogmatism that ignores their depth and difficulty. And though dogmatic, Mr Arnold is yet vague; because when he employs indefinite terms he does not attempt to limit their indefiniteness, but rather avails himself of it. Thus he speaks of the relation of culture and religion, and sums it up by saying, that the idea of culture is destined to 'transform and govern' the idea of religion. Now I do not wish to be pedantic; and I think that we may discuss culture and religion, and feel that we are talking about the same social and intellectual facts, without attempting any rigorous definition of our terms. But there is one indefiniteness that ought to be avoided. When we speak of culture and religion in common conversation, we sometimes refer to an ideal state of things and sometimes to an actual. But if we are appraising, weighing, as it were, these two, one with the other, it is necessary to know whether it is the ideal or the actual that we are weighing. When I say ideal, I do not mean something that is not realized at all by individuals at present, but something not realized sufficiently to be much called to mind by the term denoting the general social fact. I think it clear that Mr Arnold, when he speaks of culture, is speaking sometimes of an ideal, sometimes of an actual culture, and does not always know which. He describes it in one page as 'a study of perfection, moving by the force, not merely or primarily of the scientific passion for pure knowledge, but of the moral and social passion for doing good.' A study of this vast aim, moving with the impetus of this double passion, is something that does, I hope, exist among us, but to a limited extent: it is hardly that which has got itself stamped and recognised as culture. And Mr Arnold afterwards admits as much. For we might have thought, from the words I have quoted, that we had in culture, thus possessed by the passion of doing good, a mighty social power, continually tending to make 'reason and the will of God prevail.' But we find that this power only acts in fine weather. 'It needs times of faith and ardour to flourish in.' Exactly; it is not itself a spring and source of faith and ardour. Culture 'believes' in making reason and the will of God prevail, and will even 'endeavour' to make them prevail, but it must be under very favourable circumstances. This is rather a languid form of the passion of doing good; and we feel that we have passed from the ideal culture, towards which Mr Arnold aspires, to the actual culture in which he lives and moves.

Mr Arnold afterwards explains to us a little further how much of the passion for doing good culture involves, and how it involves it. 'Men are all members of one great whole, and the sympathy which is in human nature will not allow one member to be indifferent to the rest, or to have a perfect welfare independent of the rest. . . . . The individual is obliged, under pain of being stunted and enfeebled in his own development if he disobeys, to carry others along with him in his march towards perfection.' These phrases are true of culture as we know it. In using them Mr Arnold assumes implicitly what, perhaps, should have been expressly avowed—that the study of perfection, as it forms itself in members of the human race, is naturally and primarily a study of the individual's perfection, and only incidentally and secondarily a study of the general perfection of humanity. It is so incidentally and secondarily for the two reasons Mr Arnold gives, one internal, and the other external: first, because it finds sympathy as one element of the human nature that it desires harmoniously to develop; and secondly, because the development of one individual is bound up by the laws of the universe with the development of at least some other individuals. Still the root of culture, when examined ethically, is found to be a refined eudæmonism: in it the social impulse springs out of and re-enters into the self-regarding, which remains predominant. That is, I think, the way in which the love of culture is generally developed: an exquisite pleasure is experienced in refined states of thought and feeling, and a desire for this pleasure is generated, which may amount to a passion, and lead to the utmost intellectual and moral effort. Mr Arnold may, perhaps, urge (and I would allow it true in certain cases) that the direct impulse towards perfection, whether realized in a man's self or in the world around, may inspire and impassion some minds, without any consideration of the enjoyment connected with it. In any case, it must be admitted that the impulse toward perfection in a man of culture is not practically limited to himself, but tends to expand in infinitely increasing circles. It is the wish of culture, taking ever wider and wider sweeps, to carry the whole race, the whole universe, harmoniously towards perfection.

And, if it were possible that all men, under all circumstances, should feel what some men, in some fortunate spheres, may truly feel—that there is no conflict, no antagonism, between the full development of the individual and the progress of the world—I should be loth to hint at any jar or discord in this harmonious movement. But this paradisaical state of culture is rare. We dwell in it a little space, and then it vanishes into the ideal. Life shows us the conflict and the discord: on one side are the claims of harmonious self-development, on the other the cries of struggling humanity: we have hitherto let our sympathies expand along with our other refined instincts, but now they threaten to sweep us into regions from which those refined instincts shrink. Not that harmonious self-development calls on us to *crush* our sympathies; it asks only that they should be a little repressed, a little kept under: we may become (as Mr Arnold delicately words it) philanthropists 'tempered by renouncement.' There is much useful and important work to be done, which may be done harmoniously: still we cannot honestly say that this seems to us the most useful, the most important work, or what in the interests of the world is most pressingly entreated and demanded. This latter, if done at all, must be done as self-sacrifice, not as self-development. And so we are brought face to face with the most momentous and profound problem of ethics.

It is at this point, I think, that the relation of culture and religion is clearly tested and defined. Culture (if I have understood and analysed it rightly) inevitably takes one course. It recognises with a sigh the limits of self-development, and its first enthusiasm becomes 'tempered by renouncement.' Religion, of which the essence is self-sacrifice, inevitably takes the other course. We see this daily realized in practice: we see those we know and love, we see the *élite* of humanity in history and literature, coming to this question, and after a struggle answering it: going, if they are strong clear souls, some one way and some the other; if they are irresolute, vacillating and 'moving in a strange diagonal' between the two. It is because he ignores this antagonism, which seems to me so clear and undeniable if stated without the needless and perilous exaggerations which preachers have used about it, that I have called Mr Arnold perverse. A philosopher[1] with whom he is more familiar than I am speaks, I think, of 'the reconciliation of antagonisms' as the essential feature of the most important steps in the progress of humanity. I seem to see profound truth in this conception, and perhaps Mr Arnold has intended to realize it. But, in order to reconcile antagonisms, it is needful to probe them to the bottom; whereas Mr Arnold skims over them with a lightly-won tranquillity that irritates instead of soothing.

Of course we are all continually trying to reconcile this and other antagonisms, and many persuade themselves that they have found a reconciliation. The religious man tells himself that in obeying the instinct of self-sacrifice he has chosen true culture, and the man of culture tells himself that by seeking self-development he is really

[1] Hegel.*

taking the best course to 'make reason and the will of God prevail.'
But I do not think either is quite convinced. I think each dimly feels
that it is necessary for the world that the other line of life should be
chosen by some, and each and all look forward with yearning to a
time when circumstances shall have become kinder and more pliable
to our desires, and when the complex impulses of humanity that we
share shall have been chastened and purified into something more
easy to harmonize. And sometimes the human race seems to the eye
of enthusiasm so very near this consummation: it seems that if just a
few simple things were done it would reach it. But these simple
things prove mountains of difficulty; and the end is far off. I remember saying to a friend once—a man of deep culture—that his was a
'fair-weather theory of life.' He answered with much earnestness,
'We mean it to be fair weather henceforth.' And I hope the skies are
growing clearer every century; but meanwhile there is much storm
and darkness yet, and we want—the world wants—all the self-
sacrifice that religion can stimulate. Culture diffuses 'sweetness and
light;' I do not undervalue these blessings: but religion gives fire and
strength, and the world wants fire and strength even more than
sweetness and light. Mr Arnold feels this when he says that culture
must 'borrow a devout energy' from religion; but devout energy, as
Dr Newman somewhere says, is not to be borrowed. At the same
time, I trust that the ideal of culture and the ideal of religion will
continually approach one another: that culture will keep developing
its sympathy, and gain in fire and strength; that religion will teach
that unnecessary self-sacrifice is folly, and that whatever tends to
make life harsh and gloomy cometh of evil. And if we may allow that
the progress of culture is clearly in this direction, surely we may
say the same of religion. Indeed the exegetic artifices by which the
Hellenic view of life is introduced and allowed a place in Christian
preaching would sometimes be almost ludicrous, if they were not
touching, and if they were not, on the whole, such a sign of a hopeful
progress; of progress not as yet, perhaps, very great or very satisfactory, but still very distinct. I wish Mr Arnold had recognised this. I
do not think he would then have said that culture would transform
and absorb religion, any more than religion transform and absorb
culture. To me the ultimate and ideal relation of culture and religion
is imaged like the union of the golden and silver sides of the famous
shield—each leading to the same 'orbed perfection' of actions and

results, but shining with a diverse splendour in the light of its different principle.

Into the difficulties of this question I have barely entered; but I hope I have shown the inadequacy of Mr Arnold's treatment of it. I think we shall be more persuaded of this inadequacy when we have considered how he conceives of actual religion in the various forms in which it exists among us. He has but one distinct thing to say of them,—that they subdue the obvious faults of our animality. They form a sort of spiritual police: that is all. He says nothing of the emotional side of religion; of the infinite and infinitely varied vent which it gives, in its various forms, for the deepest fountains of feeling. He says nothing of its intellectual side: of the indefinite but inevitable questions about the world and human destiny into which the eternal metaphysical problems form themselves in minds of rudimentary development; questions needing confident answers, nay, imperatively demanding, it seems, from age to age, different answers: of the actual facts of psychological experience, so strangely mixed up with and expressed in the mere conventional 'jargon' of religion (which he characterizes with appropriate contempt)—how the moral growth of men and nations, while profoundly influenced and controlled by the formulæ of traditional religions, is yet obedient to laws of its own, and in its turn reacts upon and modifies these formulæ: of all this Mr Arnold does not give a hint. He may say that he is not treating of religions, but of culture. But it may be replied that he is treating of the relation of culture to religions; and that a man ought not to touch cursorily upon such a question, much less to dogmatize placidly upon it, without showing us that he has mastered the elements of the problem.

I may, perhaps, illustrate my meaning by referring to another essayist—one of the very few whom I consider superior to Mr Arnold—one who is as strongly attached to culture as Mr Arnold himself, and perhaps more passionately,—M. Renan. It will be seen that I am not going to quote a partisan. From 'my country-man's' judgment of our Protestant organizations I appeal boldly to a Frenchman and an infidel. Let any one turn to M. Renan's delicate, tender, sympathetic studies of religious phenomena—I do not refer to the *Vie de Jésus*, but to a much superior work, the *Essais d'Histoire religieuse*,—he will feel, I think, how coarse, shallow, unappreciative, is Mr Arnold's summing up, 'they conquer the more obvious faults of our animality.' To take one special point. When Mr Arnold is harping on the 'dissidence of Dissent,' I recall the little phrase which M. Renan throws at the magnificent fabric of Bossuet's attack upon Protestantism. 'En France,' he says, 'on ne comprend pas qu'on se divise pour si peu de chose.' M. Renan knows that ever since the reviving intellect of Europe was turned upon theology, religious dissidence and variation has meant religious life and force. Mr Arnold, of course, can find texts inculcating unity: how should unity not be included in the ideal of a religion claiming to be universal? But Mr Arnold, as a cultivated man, has read the New Testament records with the light of German erudition, and knows how much unity was attained by the Church in its fresh and fervent youth. Still, unity is a part of the ideal even of the religion that came not to send peace, but a sword: let us be grateful to any one who keeps that in view, who keeps reminding us of that. But it may be done without sneers. Mr Arnold might know (if he would only study them a little more closely and tenderly) the passionate longing for unity that may be cherished within small dissident organizations. I am not defending them. I am not saying a word for separatism against multitudinism. But those who feel that worship ought to be the true expression of the convictions on which it is based, and out of which it grows, and that in the present fragmentary state of truth it is supremely difficult to reconcile unity of worship with sincerity of conviction; those who know that the struggle to realize in combination the ideals of truth and peace in many minds reaches the pitch of agony; will hardly think that Mr Arnold's taunt is the less cruel because it is pointed with a text.

I wish it to be distinctly understood that it is as judged by his own rules and principles that I venture to condemn Mr Arnold's treatment of our actual religions. He has said that culture in its most limited phase is curiosity, and I quite sympathise in his effort to vindicate for this word the more exalted meaning that the French give to it. Even of the ideal culture he considers curiosity (if I understand him rightly) to be the most essential, though not the noblest, element. Well, then, I complain that in regard to some of the most important elements of social life he has so little curiosity; and therefore so thin and superficial an appreciation of them. I do not mean that every cultivated man ought to have formed for himself a theory of religion. 'Non omnia possumus omnes,' and a man must, to some extent, select the subjects that suit his special faculties. But every man of deep culture ought to have a conception of the importance and intricacy of the religious problem, a sense of the kind and amount of study that is required for it, a tact to discriminate worthy and unworthy treatment of it, an instinct which, if he has to touch on it, will guide him round the lacunæ of apprehension that the limits of his nature and leisure have rendered inevitable. Now this cultivated tact, sense, instinct (Mr Arnold could express my meaning for me much more felicitously than I can for myself) he seems to me altogether to want on this topic. He seems to me (if so humble a simile may be pardoned) to judge of religious organizations as a dog judges of human beings, chiefly by the scent. One admires in either case the exquisite development of the organ, but feels that the use of it for this particular object implies a curious, an almost ludicrous, limitation of sympathy. When these popular religions are brought before Mr Arnold, he is content to detect their strong odours of Philistinism and vulgarity; he will not stoop down and look into them; he is not sufficiently interested in their dynamical importance; he does not care to penetrate the secret of their fire and strength, and learn the sources and effects of these; much less does he consider how sweetness and light may be added without any loss of fire and strength.

This limitation of view in Mr Arnold seems to me the more extraordinary, when I compare it with the fervent language he uses with respect to what is called, *par excellence*, the Oxford movement. He even half associates himself with the movement—or rather he half associates the movement with himself.

It was directed, he rightly says, against 'Liberalism as Dr Newman* saw it.' What was this? 'It was,' he explains, 'the great middle class Liberalism, which had for the cardinal points of its belief the Reform Bill of 1832 and local self-government in politics; in the social sphere free trade, unrestricted competition, and the making of large industrial fortunes; in the religious sphere the dissidence of Dissent and the Protestantism of the Protestant religion.' Liberalism to Dr Newman may have meant something of all this; but what (as I infer from the *Apology*) it more especially meant to him was a much more intelligent force than all these, which Mr Arnold omits; and *pour cause*; for it was precisely that view of the functions of religion and its place in the social organism in which Mr Arnold seems at least complacently to acquiesce. Liberalism, Dr Newman thought (and it seems to me true of one phase or side of Liberalism), wished to extend just the languid patronage to religion that Mr Arnold does. What priesthoods were good for in the eyes of Liberalism were the functions, as I have said, of spiritual police; and that is all Mr. Arnold thinks they are good for at present; and even in the future (unless I misunderstand him), if we want more, he would have us come to culture. But Dr Newman knew that even the existing religions, far as they fell below his ideal, were good for much more than this; this view of them seemed to him not only shallow and untrue, but perilous, deadly, soul-destroying; and inasmuch as it commended itself to intellectual men, and was an intelligent force, he fought against it, not, I think, with much sweetness or light, but with a blind, eager, glowing asperity which, tempered always by humility and candour, was and is very impressive. Dr Newman fought for a point of view which it required culture to appreciate, and therefore he fought in some sense with culture; but he did not fight for culture, and to conceive him combating side by side with Mr Matthew Arnold is almost comical.

I think, then, that without saying more about religion, Mr Arnold might have said truer things about it; and I think also that without saying less about culture—we have a strong need of all he can say to recommend it—he might have shown that he was alive to one or two of its besetting faults. And some notice of these might have strengthened his case; for he might have shown that the faults of culture really arise from lack of culture; and that more culture, deeper and truer culture, removes them. I have ventured to hint this in speaking of Mr Arnold's tone about religion. What I dislike in it seems to me, when examined, to be exactly what he calls Philistinism; just as when he commences his last lecture before a great university by referring to his petty literary squabbles, he seems to me guilty of what he calls 'provincialism.'—And so, again, the attitude that culture often assumes towards enthusiasm in general seems to spring from narrowness, from imperfection of culture. The fostering care of culture, and a soft application of sweetness and light, might do so much for enthusiasm—enthusiasm does so much want it. Enthusiasm is often a turbid issue of smoke and sparks. Culture might refine this to a steady glow. It is melancholy when, instead, it takes to pouring cold water on it. The worst result is not the natural hissing and sputtering that ensues, though that cannot be pleasing to culture or to anything else, but the waste of power that is the inevitable consequence.

It is wrong to exaggerate the antagonism between enthusiasm and culture; because, in the first place, culture has an enthusiasm of its own, by virtue of which indeed, as Mr Arnold contemplates, it is presently to transcend and absorb religion. But at present this enthusiasm, so far from being adequate to this, is hardly sufficient— is often insufficient—to prevent culture degenerating into dilettant-ism. In the second place, culture has an appreciation of enthusiasm (with the source of which it has nothing to do), when that enthusi-asm is beautiful and picturesque, or thrilling and sublime, as it often is. But the enthusiasm must be very picturesque, very sublime; upon some completed excellence of form culture will rigorously insist. May it not be that culture is short-sighted and pedantic in the rigour of these demands, and thus really defeats its own ends, just as it is often liable to do by purely artistic pedantry and conventionality? If it had larger and healthier sympathies, it might see beauty in the stage of becoming (if I may use a German phrase), in much rough and violent work at which it now shudders. In pure art culture is always erring on the side of antiquity—much more in its sympathy with the actual life of men and society. In some of the most beautiful lines he has written, Owen Meredith* expresses a truth that deserves to be set in beautiful language:

> I know that all acted time
> By that which succeeds it is ever received
> As calmer, completer, and more sublime,
> Only because it is finished; because
> We only behold the thing it achieved,
> We behold not the thing that it was.
> For while it stands whole and immutable
> In the marble of memory, how can we tell
> What the men that have hewn at the block may have been?
> Their passion is merged in its passionlessness;
> Their strife in its stillness closed for ever;
> Their change upon change in its changelessness;
> In its final achievement their feverish endeavour.

Passion, strife, feverish endeavour—surely in the midst of these have been produced not only the rough blocks with which the common world builds, but the jewels with which culture is adorned. Culture the other day thought Mr Garrison* a very prosy and uninteresting person, and did not see why so much fuss should be made about him; but I should not be surprised if in a hundred years or so he were found to be poetical and picturesque.

And I will go farther, and plead for interests duller and vulgarer than any fanaticism.

If any culture really has what Mr Arnold in his finest mood calls its noblest element, the passion for propagating itself, for making itself prevail, then let it learn 'to call nothing common or unclean.' It can only propagate itself by shedding the light of its sympathy liberally; by learning to love common people and common things, to feel common interests. Make people feel that their own poor life is ever so little beautiful and poetical; then they will begin to turn and seek after the treasures of beauty and poetry outside and above it. Pictorial culture is a little vexed at the success of Mr Frith's* pictures, at the thousands of pounds he gets, and the thousands of people that crowd to see them. Now I do not myself admire Mr Frith's pictures; but I think he diffuses culture more than some of his acid critics, and I should like to think that he got twice as many pounds and spectators. If any one of these grows eagerly fond of a picture of Mr Frith's, then, it seems to me, the infinite path of culture is open to him; I do not see why he should not go on till he can conscientiously praise the works of Pietro Perugino.* But leaving Mr Frith (and other painters and novelists that might be ranked with him), let us consider a much greater man, Macaulay.* Culture has turned up its nose a little at our latest English classic, and would, I think, have done so more, but that it is touched and awed by his wonderful devotion to literature. But Macaulay, though he loved literature, loved also common people and common things, and therefore he can make the common people who live among common things love literature. How Philistinish it is of him to be stirred to eloquence by the thought of 'the opulent and enlightened states of Italy, the vast and magnificent cities, the ports, the arsenals, the villas, the museums, the libraries, the marts filled with every article of comfort and luxury, the factories swarming with artizans, the Apennines covered with rich cultivation up to their very summits, the Po wafting the harvest of Lombardy to the granaries of Venice, and carrying back the silks of Bengal and the furs of Siberia to the palaces of Milan.' But the Philistine's heart is opened by these images; through his heart a way is found to his taste; he learns how delightful a melodious current of stirring words may be; and then, when Macaulay asks him to mourn for 'the wit and the learning and the genius' of Florence, he does not refuse faintly to mourn; and so Philistinism and culture kiss each other.

Again, when our greatest living poet* 'dips into the future,' what does he see?

> The heavens fill with commerce, argosies of magic sails,
> Pilots of the purple twilight, dropping down with costly bales.

Why, it might be the vision of a young general merchant. I doubt whether anything similar could be found in a French or German poet (I might except Victor Hugo* to prove the rule): he would not feel the image poetical, and perhaps if he did, would not dare to say so. The Germans have in their way immense honesty and breadth of sympathy, and I like them for it. I like to be made to sympathize with their middle-class enthusiasm for domestic life and bread-and-butter. Let us be bold, and make them sympathize with our middle-class affection for commerce and bustle.

Ah, I wish I could believe that Mr Arnold was describing the ideal and not the actual, when he dwells on the educational, the missionary, function of culture, and says that its greatest passion is for making sweetness and light prevail. For I think we might soon be agreed as to how they may be made to prevail. Religions have been propagated by the sword: but culture cannot be propagated by the sword, nor by the pen sharpened and wielded like an offensive weapon. Culture, like all spiritual gifts, can only be propagated by enthusiasm: and by enthusiasm that has got rid of asperity, that has become sympathetic; that has got rid of Pharisaism, and become humble. I suppose Mr Arnold would hardly deny that in the attitude in which he shows himself, contemplating the wealthy Philistine through his eyeglass, he has at least a superficial resemblance to a Pharisee. Let us not be too hard on Pharisaism of any kind. It is better that religion should be self-asserting than that it should be crushed and stifled by rampant worldliness; and where the worship of wealth is predominant it is perhaps a necessary antagonism that intellect should be self-asserting. But I cannot see that intellectual Pharisaism is any less injurious to true culture than religious Pharisaism to true worship; and when a poet keeps congratulating himself that he is not a Philistine, and pointing out (even exaggerating) all the differences between himself and a Philistine, I ask myself, Where is the sweetness of culture. For the moment it seems to have turned sour.

Perhaps what is most disappointing in our culture is its want of appreciation of the 'sap of progress,' the creative and active element of things. We all remember the profound epigram of Agassiz,* that the world in dealing with a new truth passes through three stages: it first says that it is not true, then that it is contrary to religion, and finally, that we knew it before. Culture is raised above the first two stages, but it is apt to disport itself complacently in the third. 'Culture,' we are told, 'is always assigning to the system-maker and his system a smaller share in the bent of human destiny than their friends like.' Quite so: a most useful function: but culture does this with so much zest that it is continually over-doing it. The system-maker may be compared to a man who sees that mankind want a house built. He erects a scaffolding with much unassisted labour, and begins to build. The scaffolding is often unnecessarily large and clumsy, and the system-maker is apt to keep it up much longer than it is needed. Culture looks at the unsightly structure with contempt, and from time to time kicks over some useless piece of timber. The house however gets built, is seen to be serviceable, and culture is soon found benevolently diffusing sweetness and light through the apartments. For culture perceives the need of houses; and is even ready to say in its royal way, 'Let suitable mansions be prepared; only without this eternal hammering, these obtrusive stones and timber.' We must not forget, however, that construction and destruction are treated with equal impartiality. When a miserable fanatic has knocked down some social abuse with much peril of life and limb, culture is good enough to point out to him that he need not have taken so much trouble: culture had seen the thing was falling; it would soon have fallen of its own accord; the crash has been unpleasant, and raised a good deal of disagreeable dust.

All this criticism of action is very valuable; but it is usually given in excess, just because, I think, culture is a little sore in conscience, is uncomfortably eager to excuse its own evident incapacity for action. Culture is always hinting at a convenient season, that rarely seems to arrive. It is always suggesting one decisive blow that is to be grace-fully given; but it is so difficult to strike quite harmoniously, and without some derangement of attitude. Hence an instinctive, and, I think, irrational, discouragement of the action upon which less cultivated people are meanwhile spending themselves. For what does action, social action, really mean? It means losing oneself in a mass of disagreeable, hard, mechanical details, and trying to influence many dull or careless or bigoted people for the sake of ends that were at first of doubtful brilliancy, and are continually being dimmed and dwarfed by the clouds of conflict. Is this the kind of thing to which human nature is desperately prone, and into which it is continually rushing with perilous avidity? Mr Arnold may say that he does not discourage action, but only asks for delay, in order that we may act with sufficient knowledge. This is the eternal excuse of indolence—insufficient knowledge: still, taken cautiously, the warning is valuable, and we may thank Mr Arnold for it: we cannot be too much stimulated to study the laws of the social phenomena that we wish to modify, in order that 'reason the card' may be as complete and accurate as possible. But we remember that we have heard all this before at much length from a very different sort of prophet. It has been preached to us by a school small, but energetic (energetic to a degree that causes Mr Arnold to scream 'Jacobinism!'): and the preaching has been not in the name of culture, but in the name of religion and self-sacrifice.

I do not ask much sympathy for the people of action from the people of culture: I will show by an example how much. Paley* somewhere, in one of his optimistic expositions of the comfortableness of things, remarks, that if he is ever inclined to grumble at his taxes, when he gets his newspaper he feels repaid; he feels that he could not lay out the money better than in purchasing the spectacle of all this varied life and bustle. There are more taxes now, but there are more and bigger newspapers: let us hope that Paley would still consider the account balanced. Now, might not Mr Arnold imbibe a little of this pleasant spirit? As it is, no one who is doing anything can feel that Mr Arnold hearing of it is the least bit more content to pay his taxes—that is, unless he is doing it in some supremely graceful and harmonious way.

One cannot think on this subject without recalling the great man who recommended to philosophy a position very similar to that now claimed for culture. I wish to give Mr Arnold the full benefit of his resemblance to Plato. But when we look closer at the two positions, the dissimilarity comes out: they have a very different effect on our feelings and imagination; and I confess I feel more sympathy with the melancholy philosopher looking out with hopeless placidity 'from beneath the shelter of some wall' on the storms and dust-clouds of blind and selfish conflict, than with a cheerful modern liberal, tempered by renouncement, shuddering aloof from the rank exhalations of vulgar enthusiasm, and holding up the pouncet-box of culture betwixt the wind and his nobility.

To prolong this fault-finding would be neither pleasant nor profitable. But perhaps many who love culture much—and respect the enthusiasm of those who love it more—may be sorry when it is brought into antagonism with things that are more dear to them even than culture. I think Mr Arnold wishes for the reconciliation of antagonisms: I think that in many respects, with his subtle eloquence, his breadth of view, and above all his admirable temper, he is excellently fitted to reconcile antagonisms; and therefore I am vexed when I find him, in an access of dilettante humour, doing not a little to exasperate and exacerbate them, and dropping from the prophet of an ideal culture into a more or less prejudiced advocate of the actual.

EXPLANATORY NOTES

PREFACE

3 *Society for Promoting Christian Knowledge*: founded in 1699 to promote the erection of charity schools, and to distribute bibles and religious tracts. Much of the educational and missionary work was taken over by the Society for the Propagation of the Gospel (SPG) and the National Society, but the SPCK remained an important publisher of religious books.

Bishop Wilson: Thomas Wilson (1663–1755), Bishop of Sodor and Man for fifty-eight years, was renowned for his spiritual seriousness and for his pastoral dedication. He was open and welcoming to non-Anglicans, and both Dissenters and Roman Catholics attended his services. A great promoter of education in English on the Isle of Man, whilst sponsoring Manx translations, he embodied the tension which was to characterize Arnold's attitude to Celtic literature. His devotional works were promoted by the Oxford Movement. John Henry Newman introduced a small-format edition of the *Sacra Privata: The Private Meditations and Prayers of Thomas Wilson, D.D., Lord Bishop of Sodor and Man* (published by Parker in Oxford in 1841) by saying: 'No words are necessary to introduce the name of Bishop Wilson to the members of that Church of which he was in his day, and has been since, in sacred language, "a burning and shining light" '. John Keble, one of the leaders of the Oxford Movement (and Matthew Arnold's godfather), wrote Wilson's life and edited the *Works of the Right Reverend Father in God, Thomas Wilson, D.D., Lord Bishop of Sodor and Man* (in 8 volumes, published by Parker in Oxford in 1847–63). A shorter version, without notes, was produced by Parker in 1870. Arnold found a copy of Wilson's '*Manual*' (*Maxims*) in his father's study at Fox How in autumn 1866. In 1867–8 he noted seventy-four quotations from *Sacra Privata* and the *Maxims* in his diary. The SPCK first printed an edition of *Sacra Privata* in 1792. Frederic Relton edited the *Maxims* for Macmillan's 'English Theological Library' in 1898.

brilliant and distinguished votary of the natural sciences: Thomas Henry Huxley (1825–95) was a biologist (not physicist), science educationalist, and promoter of Darwin's theory of evolution. The attribution is supported by a letter from Arnold to his mother on 20 February 1869 about a speech given by Huxley, who 'brought in my *Culture and Anarchy*, and my having made game of him in the Preface', *Letters*, iii. 316; cf. Super, v. 447. Huxley was a self-proclaimed agnostic, and passionately anti-sectarian. He mixed in Liberal Anglican, as well as non-religious, circles. Arnold was pleased (1875) by Huxley's willingness to own 'the charm and salutariness of J.C. [Jesus Christ]', and found it all the more striking given the hostility to Christianity of many of his friends and allies. See *Letters*, iv. 290 and 292 (8 Dec. and ?11 Dec. 1875). He was to have more debate with him over the promotion of science education. In 1880 Huxley spoke at the opening of Mason's College in Birmingham, where the focus on science and lack of 'mere literary instruction' gave him a chance to attack Arnold's argument that only literature could provide an adequate criticism of life. Arnold replied in his Rede Lecture in Cambridge in July 1882 (published in August that year in the *Nineteenth Century*). See S. Coulling, *Matthew Arnold and his Critics: A Study of Arnold's Controversies* (Athens, Ohio, 1974), 283–4.

3 *recreative religion*: Huxley launched his 'Sunday evenings for the people' lectures in 1866, which attracted huge crowds. On 19 November 1868 the Court of Common Pleas ruled (in Baxter *v.* Langley) that these lectures in St Martin's Hall, Longacre, London, did not constitute a violation of an eighteenth-century statute prohibiting public entertainments or debates on Sundays. *The Times*, 20 Nov. 1868, 11.

4 *Meditations of Marcus Aurelius*: Marcus Aurelius (AD 121–80) was Roman emperor from 161. He was a professed Stoic, whose philosophical views were close to those of Epictetus (see note to p. 40). The *Meditations* was a private work intended to strengthen his own convictions. See Arnold's essay on him [1863], published in *Essays in Criticism, Series 1* (Super, iii. 133–57). In this essay Arnold commended a recent translation of the moral writings of Marcus Aurelius for treating them not just as dead learning, but as of immediate relevance as guides to living a good life. In accordance with his father's idea that certain periods of ancient history were modern in their characteristics and thus had an affinity with and were relevant to the present, Arnold drew out the instructive themes, whilst emphasizing that Marcus Aurelius lacked (and implying that he yearned for) the power of religion to 'light up' morality and provide inspiration for the cultivation of perfection.

Joubert: Joseph Joubert (1754–1824) was a religious philosopher, greatly esteemed by his contemporaries, whose *Pensées* were published post-humously (in 1838), and had twice been reprinted by the time Arnold wrote a lecture on him (delivered in November 1863 and first published in 1864; *Essays in Criticism, Series 1*, Super, iii. 183–211). Arnold compared him to Coleridge: 'both of them curious explorers of words, and of the latent significance hidden under the popular use of them; both of them, in a certain sense, conservative in religion and politics, by antipathy to the narrow and shallow foolishness of vulgar modern liberalism . . . they both had from nature an ardent impulse for seeking the genuine truth on all matters they thought about, and a gift for finding it and recognising it when it was found' (p. 189). For Arnold, though, Joubert was more intelligible, and more compelling because of his love of light and the degree to which he was irradiated by it. This quality marked him out as a natural critic of Philistinism. Joubert's injunction to read with a direct aim at practice was one followed by Arnold in his own notebooks.

Nicole: Pierre Nicole (1625–95) was a moralist and Jansenist theologian. He taught at Port-Royal, where he collaborated with Arnauld in writing the *Logique ou l'Art de Penser*, commonly known as the *Logique de Port-Royal* (1662), influenced by Augustine, Pascal, and Descartes. See 'Joubert', Super, iii. 203.

Monsieur Michelet: Jules Michelet (1798–1874) was a critic and historian, who translated Vico's *Scienza nuova*, and wrote an introduction to universal history, a history of the Roman republic, and a multi-volume history of France—a biography of the nation as a whole—which was published between 1833 and 1867. Seeing France as the highest embodiment of freedom, realized by the Revolution, he emphasized the creative combination of Celtic, Roman, Greek, and Germanic elements in French history and culture. He also wrote popular books on morality, including *L'Amour* (1858), extracts from which Arnold noted (*Note-Books*, 58, 79, 93). This reference comes from the *Histoire de France*, vol. v, bk. 10, ch. 4.

Imitation: the *Imitation of Christ* was a devotional work attributed to the Augustinian monk Thomas à Kempis (*c.*1380–1471), very widely read in England in the eighteenth and nineteenth centuries. It was designed to guide the Christian in the seeking of perfection through imitation of the life of Christ. From 1857 onwards Arnold repeatedly copied sentences from the *De Imitatione Christi* (in Latin) in his notebooks—in fact even more frequently (and over a longer period) than he noted passages from Bishop Wilson. See also his citation of his favourite moral precepts from the *Imitation* at the beginning of his essay on Marcus Aurelius (see note to p. 4 above), Super, iii. 133–4: e.g. 'Our improvement is proportionate to our purpose'; 'Always place a definite purpose before thee'.

5 *whether or no, having read something, he has read the newspapers only*: cf. Bishop Wilson, 'Maxims', *Works*, ed. Keble, v. 486 on the importance of not reading newspapers simply to satisfy curiosity or as a pastime. See also *A French Eton*, Super, ii. 314–15 on the declining cultural level of the upper class: 'If only, instead of reading Homer and Cicero, it now read Goethe and Montesquieu;—but it does not; it reads the *Times* and the *Agricultural Journal*. And it devotes itself to practical life'.

6 *French Academy*: this body was established in Paris in 1637 'to work with all the care and all the diligence possible at giving sure rules to the [French] language, and rendering it pure, eloquent and capable of treating the arts and sciences'. It was also to be a literary tribunal and to set standards for educated opinion. See Arnold's 'The Literary Influence of Academies', *Essays in Criticism, Series 1*, Super, iii. 232–57.

trusting to an arm of flesh: 2 Chronicles 32: 8. 'With him is an arm of flesh; but with us is the Lord our God to help us, and to fight our battles.'

Corinthian style, or the whimsies about the One Primeval Language: Arnold defined the Corinthian as the journalistic style, possessing 'glitter without warmth, rapidity without ease, effectiveness without charm. Its characteristic is, that it has no *soul*; all it exists for, is to get its ends, to make its points, to damage its adversaries, to be admired, to triumph' ('The Literary Influence of Academies', Super, iii. 255). In the same essay (p. 244) he refers to *The One Primeval Language* by Charles Forster (London, 1851–4), a work which could be ridiculed by the French critic Renan, yet which could be published in England in all seriousness.

6 *Lord Stanhope*: Philip, 5th Earl Stanhope (1805–75), historian and politician. He was a member of several Royal Commissions, including those on clerical subscription (1864), the Irish Church (1867), and ritual and rubrics (1868). He wrote histories of the eighteenth century and of his own time, using primary material extensively. From 1846 for thirty years he was president of the Society of Antiquaries; he was a trustee of the British Museum and proposed the establishment of the National Portrait Gallery, acting as the chair of trustees from 1857 until his death.

Bishop of Oxford: Samuel Wilberforce (1805–73) was bishop of Oxford from 1845 to 1869, when he became bishop of Winchester. In 1836 he had joined in the protest at the Liberal Anglican Renn Dickson Hampden's appointment as Regius Professor of Divinity in Oxford (a controversy in which Thomas Arnold played a prominent part on Hampden's behalf), and in 1847 he rashly got involved in querying Hampden's orthodoxy when he was nominated bishop of Hereford.

Mr Gladstone: William Ewart Gladstone (1809–98), Liberal prime minister at the time at which Arnold was writing the Preface. His political principles were shaped in the first instance by his religious and ecclesiological positions, and his ongoing reflection on the relationship between Church and State determined not only his move from Toryism to Liberalism but also his ideas about the Irish Church and about education. Arnold knew that in his references to the Liberal policy of disestablishing the Church in Ireland he was exaggerating the political opportunism of the Liberals. He wrote to Gladstone on 26 March 1869 about *Culture and Anarchy*, a copy of which he had sent him. Arnold said, 'I am afraid that you will find in the Preface one or two impertinences about the Liberal policy towards the Irish Church, but they were written while I was a daily witness of the confident hope of the Protestant Nonconformists to settle matters with the Irish Church all their own way. As you have settled them, on the other hand, the Irish Episcopalians have a status and a public character left to them which may well satisfy those who hate unjust ascendancy, but who value, as my father so much valued, that which is really Salutary in Establishment' (*Letters*, iii. 328; cf. 330).

Dean of Westminster: Arthur Penrhyn Stanley (1815–81), dean of Westminster from 1864 until his death. A Broad Churchman, he had been educated at Rugby under Thomas Arnold, and became his biographer. At Westminster he tried to give the Abbey an inclusive national religious focus, and aroused controversy (including the opposition of Samuel Wilberforce) in 1870 by inviting all the scholars who had worked on the Revised Version of the Bible (including a Unitarian) to receive communion. Although he was a close friend of Arnold, and they shared Thomas Arnold's influence, Arnold could be clear-sighted about his limitations. On 5 April 1869 he wrote to his mother about a service at Westminster Abbey the previous evening: 'a grand spectacle, and a long sermon from Stanley not at all equal to the spectacle. It is on these occasions one feels his want of deep religious power of any kind; the narrowest Evangelical, who had this, would have been a relief in his place' (*Letters*, iii. 330). Cf. Arnold's comment on latitudinarianism on p. 18.

Mr Froude: James Anthony Froude (1818–94), historian and essayist, whose main historical work was the *History of England from the Fall of Wolsey to the Defeat of the Spanish Armada*, which came out in eleven volumes from 1856 to 1870. Although he developed a very different idea of the national church from that of Arnold, coming closer to the anti-systematic position of F. D. Maurice, like Arnold he was stimulated to write by concerns about liberalism and party spirit, and was concerned to reinforce the Christian identity of the nation. He took a much more critical view of the Elizabethan religious settlement. In 1871 Froude offered Arnold the editorship of *Fraser's Magazine*, which he was giving up, but Arnold refused on the ground that it would take up all his spare time on work 'for which I have a great distaste', as he explained to his mother, 'and I think, too, my taking it would look greedy—and as if I could not refuse £400 a year, in whatever shape it came' (*Letters*, iv. 18).

Mr Henry Reeve: (1813–95), Liberal journalist and well-connected participant in London literary life. He translated his friend de Tocqueville's *De la démocratie en Amérique* (1835; 1840); from 1840 he was a leader writer and foreign correspondent on *The Times*, and from 1855 to his death editor of the *Edinburgh Review*.

Mr G. A. Sala: George Augustus Sala (1828–96), raffish and overblown popular journalist, especially for *Household Words*, *All the Year Round*, and the *Daily Telegraph*, for which he became a leader writer and special correspondent. See also ' "Life", as Mr G. A. Sala Says, "A Dream!" ', *Friendship's Garland*, Super, v. 346–50.

7 *the want of sensitiveness of intellectual conscience*: see 'The Literary Influence of Academies', 236–7: 'A Frenchman has, to a considerable degree, what one may call a conscience in intellectual matters; he has an active belief that there is a right and a wrong in them, that he is bound to honour and obey the right, that he is disgraced by cleaving to the wrong. All the world has, or professes to have, this conscience in moral matters . . . this lively susceptibility of feeling is, in the moral sphere, so far more common than in the intellectual sphere.' Arnold argued that in England there was a disinclination in intellectual matters to accept a higher ideal than one's own. Openness and flexibility of mind were lacking.

Mr Oscar Browning: (1837–1923), an under-master at Eton, who criticized Arnold's report on education on the Continent in the *Quarterly*

Review, 125 (Oct. 1868), 473–90. Browning argued that Arnold was unfair to English public schools, being ignorant of what had changed in the last twenty years and simply drawing on his own schoolboy recollections. See also Arnold, *Letters*, iii. 290 (24 Oct. 1868). Browning, who ran a somewhat aesthetic boarding house at Eton from 1862, with William Morris wallpaper and decent food, was a keen promoter of the study of history and modern languages, and of the appreciation of intellectual rather than sporting achievements. This reforming drive, combined with a touchy and pugnacious manner, did not win him favour at Eton. He was dismissed in 1875, ostensibly for administrative inefficiency, in fact because his homosexuality was felt to be threatening. He returned to Cambridge, where he was a life fellow of King's, and taught history. This section on Browning in *Culture and Anarchy*, which was gratuitously carping and touchy on Arnold's part, was cut from the second and subsequent editions. Browning's brother was a curate in Northamptonshire, who tutored him before he went to Eton as a schoolboy (in 1851).

7 *Dr William Smith*: (1813–93), classicist and biblical scholar, editor of the conservative *Quarterly Review* from 1867 to his death. A Congregationalist, he studied at University College London, and acted as classical examiner at London University from 1853 to 1869. He edited popular editions of classical texts and dictionaries on classical themes, and applied the same principles of historical criticism to the production of a *Dictionary of the Bible* (1860–3). Arnold reported (20 Feb. 1869) that Smith had come up to him to say that he 'forgave him all that he had said about him and the Quarterly—which, he added, was a great deal—for the sake of the truth and usefulness of what I had said about the Nonconformists' (*Letters*, iii. 316).

8 *Malvina's Oscar*: a reference to the 'Ossian' poems by James Macpherson (1736–96). Oscar, whose lover was Malvina, was the son of Ossian and the grandson of Fingal, Gaelic Irish heroes. The allusion serves no particular purpose, except perhaps to suggest Browning's snobbery and pretentiousness, which might lead to his creating an epic ancestry for himself. The quotation is taken from James Macpherson, 'The War of Inis-Thona', *The Poems of Ossian and Related Works*, ed. H. Gaskill (Edinburgh, 1996), 115–18, at p. 116.

disestablishing the Irish Church: in 1869, under Gladstone's first ministry, the Church of Ireland was disestablished and disendowed, after extensive debate (see pp. 121–3 and notes for the controversy about what was to be done with the surplus revenues). The Liberals had been returned in December 1868 with an increased majority, having pledged to introduce this legislation.

Nonconformists: originally (from the 1662 Act of Uniformity) those who, whilst not rejecting the doctrines of the Church of England, refused to conform to its discipline and practice. By the nineteenth century the term was used more generally to refer to all Protestant dissenters. The anniversary of the bicentenary of 1662 had aroused great controversy;

the Congregational Union had decided to celebrate it, as had other Nonconformists, whilst Anglican evangelicals opposed them.

9 *Puritans*: originally used to refer to those extreme Protestants who wanted to reform the Elizabethan Anglican settlement in a more Calvinist direction, some of whom came to attack the notion of episcopacy and to call for a Presbyterian order. The term was a fluid one, which came to have different significations in the seventeenth century, and subsequently. Arnold uses it to denote the literal adherence to Scripture as a mechanical set of rules.

staunchly walking by the best light they have: Bishop Wilson, 'Maxims', *Works*, ed. Keble, v. 429; see also pp. 28, 71, 95, 102 of this edition.

Hebraism and Hellenism: Arnold took this contrast from Heine, as he also took the term Philistine: see 'Heinrich Heine', Super, iii. 127–8; and p. 96 and note to p. 15 of this edition. The terms encompassed a range of meanings, which Arnold elaborated through *Culture and Anarchy*. The contrast was glossed as strictness of conscience vs. spontaneity of consciousness; as the privileging of action vs. the privileging of thought; and as stern and intense religious energy vs. the free play of the intellect. Christian Johann Heinrich Heine (1797–1856) was a German poet, whose work was set to music by many contemporary composers, including Mendelssohn, Schubert, and Schumann. He studied in Berlin with Hegel, who shared his admiration for Napoleon. In 1831 he went to Paris, where he mixed in left-liberal and socialist circles, and wrote critically about political, cultural, and socio-economic developments in France, the German states, and Europe as a whole.

sweetness and light: a phrase taken from the satirical tale written by Jonathan Swift in 1697—*The Battle of the Books*—in which the dispute between the Ancients and the Moderns in a library is focused in an encounter between a spider, who has made an elaborate web, following modern rules, boasting of not owing anything to anyone else, and the bee, who flies into the web and breaks it. Aesop, representing the Ancients, takes the part of the bee, and says: 'We are content with the Bee, to pretend to nothing of our own, beyond our Wings and our Voice. For the rest, whatever we have got, has been by infinite Labour, and search, and ranging through every Corner of Nature . . . instead of Dirt and Poison, we have rather chose to fill our Hives with the two Noblest of Things, which are Sweetness and Light' (J. Swift, *A Tale of a Tub with The Battle of the Books and The Mechanical Operation of the Spirit 1710* (Menston, Scolar Press, 1971), 271). Cf. Arnold, *Note-Books*, 41 (for the year 1866).

10 *Mr Baxter*: William Edward Baxter (1825–90), Liberal MP for Montrose Burghs from 1855 to 1885; reformer, retrencher, and promoter of the disestablishment of the Church of England.

Mr Charles Buxton: (1822–71), Liberal MP from 1857. Son and biographer of the famous philanthropist Thomas Fowell Buxton, on leaving university he became a partner in the firm of Hanbury, Buxton and Co.

In 1853 he bought an estate in Ireland, and in the same year wrote a pamphlet advocating denominational education in Ireland. He was a keen promoter of Church reform and disestablishment.

10 *Dean of Canterbury*: Henry Alford (1810–71). See 'The Church of the Future', *Contemporary Review*, 9 (Oct. 1868), 161–78. A scholar who produced an edition of the Greek New Testament as well as a translation of the *Odyssey* and an edition of the works of John Donne, he was also the first editor of the *Contemporary Review*. In the first year of the *Contemporary Review* he wrote an article, 'Recent Nonconformist Sermons', in which he stated: 'We do not hesitate to say, that the great phenomenon of Nonconformity is not fairly and truthfully dealt with by us Churchmen'. He castigated Anglican arrogance and pride in their social and ecclesiastical privileges, and asserted that the Nonconformists had already passed the Anglicans by in biblical scholarship and ministerial training. He argued that in place of either High Church hostility or liberal attempts at compromise, Nonconformist distinctiveness and influence should be acknowledged, so that Anglicans and Nonconformists could work together 'on all great matters of public utility and Christian benevolence', *Contemporary Review*, 2 (1866), 338–56, at 355–6. Compare the patronising tone of Arnold's remark about R. W. Dale (the noted Congregationalist whose sermons were among those discussed by Alford) in 'The Church of England' [1876], *Last Essays on Church and Religion* (London, 1877), Super, viii. 84: 'The chief Dissenting ministers are becoming quite the intellectual equals of the ablest of the clergy'. See also R. W. Dale, 'Mr Matthew Arnold and the Nonconformists', *Contemporary Review*, 14 (July 1870), 540–71, in which Dale had very effectively turned Arnold's irony (and arguments) back on him.

Rev. Edward White: (1819–98), for thirty years Congregationalist minister of St Paul's Chapel, Hawley Road, Camden Town, London, and later professor of homiletics at New College, London. On 24 February 1869 Arnold wrote a letter of thanks for two books which he had sent him. He commented: 'No one knows better than I do how considerable a movement of mind there is among the ministers of the Nonconformist Churches, among those of the Independents and Baptists particularly. All I could wish is that they should as little let their nonconformity bias this movement, as I, for my part, would let Churchism bias it' (*Letters*, iii. 318).

to abolish Church-rates: the Church rate was an annual rate, voted by parishioners in vestries and levied on all occupiers of land and houses in the parish for the upkeep of the Anglican parish church. The obligation to pay Church rates was a long-standing Nonconformist grievance, especially aggravated after the Church of England lost its constitutional monopoly following the repeal of the Test and Corporation Acts in 1828 and Catholic Emancipation in 1829. After a long period of debate and a series of orchestrated local campaigns of non-payment, the rates were abolished by the Compulsory Church-Rate Abolition Act in 1868.

to legalise marriage with a deceased wife's sister: the Bill was brought in on 25 February 1869, passed its second reading, but was then deferred and eventually withdrawn on 2 August. There had been an extensive public debate, and many pamphlets had been published from across the Anglican spectrum deploring the proposal. Many Nonconformists supported it, hence its rhetorical usefulness to Arnold in this section. Marriage with a deceased wife's sister was not legalized until 1907.

Dr Watts: Isaac Watts (1674–1748), Independent minister, poet, and hymn writer, who set out to transform congregational worship through turning passages of the Bible (especially the Psalms) into hymns. He was the author of 'O God our help in ages past', 'Jesus shall reign where'er the sun', and 'When I survey the wondrous cross'.

Hooker: Richard Hooker (*c.*1554–1600), Anglican Churchman, author of the treatise *Of the Laws of Ecclesiastical Polity* (preface and books 1–4 published 1593; book 5 in 1597; book 8 and surviving part of book 6 in 1648; book 7 in 1662), written to justify the Elizabethan Anglican settlement and to confound biblical literalism by setting the Bible and the Church in the context of systems of natural and human law. It included an elaboration of the role of public worship in developing spiritual depth, both at an individual and a corporate level. He developed an organic conception of the Church–State relationship, which supported his view that political communities did not simply deal with material concerns. Coleridge admired his idea of a national church, and built on aspects of his thinking, as did Thomas Arnold. For the dedication to Whitgift, see *The Works of that Learned and Judicious Divine Mr Richard Hooker: With an Account of his Life and Death by Isaac Walton*, ed. J. Keble, 5 vols. (Oxford, 1836), ii. 3.

Barrow: Isaac Barrow (1630–77), Anglican theologian, royalist, classical scholar, and mathematician (who taught Isaac Newton).

Butler: Joseph Butler (1692–1752), bishop of Durham from 1750 to his death. From 1718 to 1726 he preached a famous series of sermons at the Rolls Chapel, and in 1736 he published the *Analogy of Religion* which was very widely read in the nineteenth century. The *Fifteen Sermons* were prescribed as a set text to be read alongside Aristotle's *Ethics* in early nineteenth-century Oxford. Arnold gave two lectures on him to the Edinburgh Philosophical Institution, published as 'Bishop Butler and the Zeit-Geist', *Last Essays on Church and Religion* (1877), Super, viii. 11–62. He was keen to show that Butler was not as immune to criticism as he had been presented in Arnold's youth (his father had revered Butler). He saw his mode of argument—designed as it was to tackle mid-eighteenth-century deists—as dry and alienating in the very different religious context of a century later, and his definition of self-love as arbitrary. Yet he praised Butler for his religious seriousness, his reverence for 'the sacred light of reason', and his commitment to virtue as the law under which men are born. He noted a long passage from the *Analogy* on habits in his notebook for 1876 (*Note-Books*, 264–5). The Christian Socialist Henry

Scott Holland used Arnold's own terminology to contest his reading of Butler: Scott Holland praised Butler's combination of 'Hellenic width of outlook' with 'the practical securities of the concrete Hebraistic mind', *The Optimism of Butler's Analogy* (London, 1905), 8.

11 *Milton*: John Milton (1608–74), poet and religious and political controversialist. In 1641 he joined the Presbyterians, although he split from them when he published a treatise arguing for reform of the divorce laws. He then moved towards the Independents, believing that the existence of sects was a positive good.

Baxter: Richard Baxter (1615–91), Puritan minister and writer, famous for his pastoral qualities and moderation. In 1638 he was ordained by the bishop of Worcester, and from 1641 to 1660 he was curate to the incumbent of Kidderminster, so far as possible working ecumenically with Presbyterians, Episcopalians, and Independents. On Charles II's restoration, his hostility to episcopacy led him to turn down the bishopric of Hereford, and from then on he was debarred from ecclesiastical office.

Wesley: John Wesley (1703–91), founder of the Methodist movement. Son of an Anglican clergyman, he was strongly influenced both by High Church and Catholic devotional writings. In 1738, following contact with the Moravians, he had a conversion experience, which led him to spend the rest of his life promoting 'vital practical religion'. He wanted the Methodist movement to remain within the Church of England, and formally it did so until his death.

Scotland; but in an Establishment: the established Church of Scotland (continuously from 1690) was Presbyterian, not Episcopalian.

to Hebraise: cf. *St Paul and Protestantism*, Super, vi. 21, where it is used to denote an 'exclusive attention to the moral side of our nature, to conscience, and to doing rather than knowing'.

12 *a Church which is historical, as the State itself is historical*: Arnold here argued from the historical tradition of the Anglican Establishment, perspectives on which he drew on the one hand from Hooker, and on the other from Samuel Taylor Coleridge (whose *On the Constitution of the Church and State, According to the Idea of Each* was published in 1830) and his father, Thomas Arnold, who wrote *Principles of Church Reform* in 1834.

the Universities: i.e. the ancient English universities of Oxford and Cambridge.

The sectary's eigene grosse Erfindungen, as Goethe calls them: 'their own great discoveries'. Cf. Goethe's advice to Eckermann, 18 September 1823, about the writing of poetry. See J. P. Eckermann, *Gespräche mit Goethe* (Boston, 1839), cited by Super, v. 449. Johann Wolfgang von Goethe (1749–1832) was a poet, dramatist, novelist, painter, scientific and philosophical writer and (for ten years) minister of state at Weimar. See 'A French Critic on Goethe' [1878], *Mixed Essays* (1879), Super, viii. 252–76, at 274–5. Arnold said that it was not as the greatest of poets that

Goethe merited the pride of his countrymen, but as the 'clearest, largest, most helpful critic of modern times . . . by far our greatest modern critic'. Cf. Thomas Carlyle, 'Goethe' [1828], *Critical and Miscellaneous Essays* (London, 1899), i. 198–257. Carlyle had described Goethe as 'a clear and universal *Man* . . . the Teacher and exemplar of his age' (p. 208). For Carlyle, see notes to pp. 37, 61; for Goethe, see notes to pp. 29, 153.

for in affirming them he affirms himself, and that is what we all like: cf. *A French Eton* [1863–4], Super, ii. 316 on the extent to which the middle class had the power to transform itself: 'So far this class has only shown power and disposition to *affirm* itself'.

13 *example of religious equality in our colonies*: *The Times*, 12 Aug. 1868, 6. Cf. 'The Church of England' [1876], *Last Essays on Church and Religion* (1877), Super, viii. 63–86, at 68.

Mr Bright: John Bright (1811–89), Radical Quaker politician. He began his career as a temperance advocate, then becoming a founder member of the Rochdale Reform Association. Active in the Anti-Corn Law League, he linked free trade to franchise reform, of which he was to become a powerful advocate in the 1850s and 1860s. He was also a keen promoter of land reform. From 1843 he was MP for Durham City, from 1847 to 1856 for Manchester (elected alongside Thomas Milner Gibson), and from 1858 for Birmingham. A lifelong spokesman for religious dissent and opponent of the privileges of Church establishment, he promoted the abolition of Church rates and the ending of religious tests at the ancient universities. He defended the right of the Reform League to hold its meeting in Hyde Park in 1866. Arnold refers to *The Times* report (6 Feb. 1868, 10) of Bright's speech at a breakfast in Birmingham on 5 February for delegates from the Society of Arts to the Paris Exhibition. In the edition of Bright's *Public Addresses*, ed. Thorold Rogers (London, 1879) the passage quoted by Arnold reads 'more valuable inventions', rather than 'more valuable information' (see M. M. Bevington, cited in Super, v. 450).

Monsieur Renan: Joseph Ernest Renan (1823–92) was a French philosopher, Hebrew scholar, and theologian. His *Vie de Jésus* (1863) was hugely controversial, because of its repudiation of the supernatural and moral aspects of Christ and his portrayal of him merely as an attractive Galilean preacher. In 1869 he published his *St Paul*, depicting Paul as a gloomy fanatic whose teaching was increasingly irrelevant, an interpretation to which Arnold was in part responding in his *St Paul and Protestantism* (1870). Arnold copied in his notebooks passages from his articles in the *Revue des deux mondes* (reprinted in *Questions contemporaines*), as well as from his *Études d'histoire religieuse* and other works. This particular reference about America was noted on p. 115 of the *Note-Books*, and was printed in *Questions contemporaines* (2nd edn., Paris, 1868), p. vii.

14 *Mr Bright . . . calls 'a commendable interest' in politics and political*

agitations: this speech in Birmingham was on 9 November 1868, and reported in *The Times*, 11 Nov., 12.

14 *Liberals*: here used by Arnold to denote the political party developing at a national level in the 1860s out of a coalition of Whigs, Radicals, and Nonconformists.

15 *Tories*: the other main political party in Britain in the mid-nineteenth century, also by this point known as the Conservatives.

Barbarians, Philistines, and Populace: terms used to describe the three main social classes—the aristocracy, middle classes, and working classes respectively. See Ch. 3. Arnold took the term Philistine from Heine, whom he depicted as conducting a life and death battle with Philistinism. See his lecture on Heine, delivered in Oxford on 13 June 1863 and published in the *Cornhill* that August (Super, iii. 107–32, at 111–14). The term Philistine carried biblical allusions, whereas Barbarian and Populace were classical terms. The term 'Barbarian' carried the further connotation of referring to the peoples who invaded the late Roman Empire—which 'reinvigorated and renewed our worn-out Europe'—as Arnold puts it (p. 76), and from some of whom the English were descended.

all America Hebraises: at this point Arnold saw America as an extreme case of Hebraism in the sense of rampant individualism and commercialism. He was somewhat to soften his tone in later years, although he persisted in feeling that as a culture it was raw and lacked interest.

16 *Mr Hammond, the American revivalist*: Edward Payson Hammond (1831–1910), an American Presbyterian revivalist, who in November 1868 conducted a series of controversial meetings for children at Spurgeon's Tabernacle in London.

Spurgeon's Tabernacle: the Metropolitan Tabernacle in Newington Causeway, which could hold 5,500 people, built especially in 1861 to accommodate the crowds who flocked to hear Spurgeon preach. Charles Haddon Spurgeon (1834–92) was a Baptist and fervent Calvinist.

our first crude notions of the one thing needful: a reference to the text from Luke 10: 42—the story of Mary, who sat at Jesus's feet and listened to him when he visited their house, and Martha, who busied herself with preparing food. When Martha complained, Jesus said: 'But one thing is needful: and Mary hath chosen that good part, which shall not be taken away from her'. This was a text associated with Puritan readings. The Vulgate version ('Porro unum est necessarium') was used as the title for the fifth chapter of *Culture and Anarchy* from the second edition onwards.

making a solitude, they call it heavenly peace: Tacitus, *Agricola*, 30: 'ubi solitudinem faciunt, pacem appellant'.

17 *Mr Beecher*: Henry Ward Beecher (1813–87), American Congregationalist minister, from 1847 at Plymouth Congregational church in Brooklyn, New York. An advocate of liberal Christianity, temperance, women's

suffrage, the abolition of slavery, and enhanced commercial morality, he
was the brother of Harriet Beecher Stowe, the famous anti-slavery writer.
See also Arnold, *A French Eton*, Super, ii. 262–325, at 319. Commenting
on the old American republic, full of rawness, hardness, and imperfection, Arnold wrote: 'Even if they had overrun the whole earth, their old
national style would have still been detestable, and Mr Beecher would
have still been a heated barbarian'. Beecher had come to England on a
lecture tour in 1863, and had passionately attacked English attitudes to
the federal government (Super, ii. 381).

Brother Noyes: John Humphrey Noyes (1811–86), radical American
religious reformer and founder of Bible communism and of the Oneida
community. See William Hepworth Dixon's *New America*, 2 vols.
(London, 1867), vol. ii., chs. 20–4; cf. his *Spiritual Wives*, 2 vols. (London,
1868), vol. ii, chs. 4–6, 13–14, 17, 20. The preface to the sixth edition
(1867) noted that Noyes had complained about Dixon's account of the
community. Arnold's linkage of Noyes and Beecher, who came from very
different religious, social, and intellectual contexts, was provocative.

Ezra Cornell: (1807–74), a self-made man, who made a fortune in the
telegraphic industry, and founded Cornell University, which first admitted students in 1868. Its founding purpose (set out in 1865) was to teach
areas of study related to 'agriculture and the mechanic arts, including
military tactics'. But the trustees were left free to authorize teaching and
research in any area.

disinterestedness: Arnold's criterion for good criticism. See 'The Function
of Criticism at the Present Time', Super, iii. 258–83, at 270–5, 283.
Arnold argued that criticism needed to keep aloof from the 'practical
view of things' by resolutely following its own nature, which was to be
the free play of mind on all subjects. He focused this by contrast with
what he saw as the current situation, in which criticism was too polemical
and controversial, involving itself in partisan activities. The critic needed
to focus rather on 'what is excellent in itself, and the absolute beauty and
fitness of things'. Criticism was to be a disinterested endeavour to learn
and propagate the best that is known and thought in the world. At the
same time this was not to be a narrowly aesthetic or detached literary
criticism, but a broader social and moral principle.

18 *he and we were trained in the same school to mark the narrowness of Puritanism*: both Stanley and Matthew Arnold were strongly influenced by
Thomas Arnold in this respect (and both had been to Rugby School,
which was the context within which Thomas Arnold tried to foster a
broad-based Christian ethic).

latitudinarianism of our Broad Churchmen: as Thomas Arnold had also
denied in response to critics of his *Principles of Church Reform*, Matthew
Arnold was keen to distinguish his position from that of Broad Church
Anglicans like Stanley, whose conception of the Church of England as a
whole was neither High nor Low, but Broad, and who (cf. Arnold's

comments on Stanley cited in the note to p. 6) risked losing religious power and energy. This comment was also framed by Arnold in response to those critics of his articles who had challenged his approach to Nonconformity.

18 *'in truth . . . in serious manner'*: Hooker, *Works*, ed. Keble, ii. 3.

19 *Isaac Walton's*: Izaak Walton (1593–1683) was a writer and biographer, who, apart from the life of Hooker, cited in the note to p. 10, was most famous as the author of *The Compleat Angler* (1653), which Arnold as a keen fisherman would have known.

Whitgift: John Whitgift (1532–1604), archbishop of Canterbury from 1583 and strong proponent of a unified Church of England, free from both papal and Puritan influences. He worked hard to repress Puritanism.

Mr Walter Travers: Walter Travers (*c.*1548–1635), Presbyterian theologian, whose controversy with Richard Hooker, the new Master of the Temple, was stopped by Whitgift, the archbishop of Canterbury, in 1586. Travers's defence of the Presbyterian form of church government was very influential on the Puritan movement.

a Presbyterian, a partisan of the Geneva church-discipline: adherent to a form of church government by presbyters, held to be derived from the apostolic model of the New Testament. This form of church was associated with the Calvinism of Geneva.

Cartwright: Thomas Cartwright (1535–1603) was a Presbyterian scholar who was one of the most learned of the sixteenth-century Puritans. Villers has not been identified.

'had taken orders . . . for the discipline': Hooker, *Works*, ed. Keble, ii. 3.

Mr Binney: Thomas Binney (1798–1874), Congregationalist minister, from 1829 at King's Weigh House Chapel in London, where he built up a formidable reputation. Samuel Morley (see note to p. 153) was a member of his congregation, as was George Williams, founder of the inter-denominational evangelical organization the Young Men's Christian Association (YMCA), to which Binney gave many popular lectures. Keeping out of the campaigns of political dissent, he focused his ministry on setting out an integrated economic ethic for Christians in business to follow. His *Is it Possible to Make the Best of Both Worlds?* (1853) sold 31,000 copies in its first year and went into ten editions by 1856. Firmly opposed to the State establishment of religion, he nonetheless promoted cooperative activity between Nonconformists and Anglicans, and in *Dissent not Schism* (1834) argued that disagreement on church government was a secondary rather than primary matter.

20 *Cecils*: William Cecil, 1st Baron Burghley (1520/1–1598), was minister to Elizabeth I and consistent promoter of the new religious settlement. His son Robert, 1st Earl of Salisbury (1563–1612), succeeded him, working both for Elizabeth and for James I.

Lord Bolingbroke: Henry St John, 1st Viscount Bolingbroke (1678–1751), was a politician and writer, who turned to history while in political exile in France from 1715 to 1725. He believed that history taught moral lessons and developed social virtue. Back in England, he contributed regularly to *The Craftsman*, the powerful vehicle of opposition to Walpole. In his *Remarks on the History of England from the Minutes of Humphrey Oldcastle Esq.* [i.e. Henry St John] (London, 1743) he developed the theme of corrupt ministers threatening the liberty and constitution of the nation, and of the iniquities of party. See letter 18, pp. 214–16, where Bolingbroke cites the preface to Hooker's *Ecclesiastical Polity*, also a point of reference for Arnold (see note to p. 10 for Hooker).

Clarendon: Edward Hyde, 1st Earl of Clarendon (1609–74), politician and historian. As part of the Great Tew circle, he debated the role of reason in religion. His *History of the Rebellion and Civil Wars in England* supported a monarchy founded in law, including Church government as a key part of the constitution. At Charles II's restoration, he helped to shape the Act of Uniformity of 1662, although he tried (unsuccessfully) to provide temporary respite for Presbyterians. Here Arnold cites his praise for Bancroft for almost having 'rescued' the Church from the 'Calvinian' party and for having 'very much subdued the unruly spirit of the nonconformists' (*History*, 7 vols. (Oxford, 1839), i. 145–6).

Bishop Andrewes: Lancelot Andrewes (1555–1626), bishop of Winchester from 1619. He was a scholar who was one of the translators of the Authorized Version of the Bible. Theologically he was opposed to Puritanism and promoted an ideal of Anglicanism which was reasonable and moderately Catholic in tone.

Bancroft: Richard Bancroft (1544–1610), archbishop of Canterbury from 1604. Noted as a strong opponent of Puritanism.

Presbyterianism . . . itself in Charles the Second's reign . . . was finally cast out from the Church of England: by the Act of Uniformity of 1662.

21 *'the principles of the Nonconformists . . . perilous consequences of it'*: Hooker, *Works*, ed. Keble, i. 36.

22 *Church since Constantine*: the Roman emperor Constantine (d. 337), founder of Constantinople, aimed at the closest possible unity of the Church and State. On 29 February 1869 Arnold reported to his mother that Stanley had complimented him on the Preface to *Culture and Anarchy*, saying that the 'ideas of it—particularly those of a passage about Constantine—were exactly what Papa would have approved' (*Letters*, iii. 316).

23 *Augustine*: St Augustine (354–430), bishop of Hippo and Doctor of the Church. Author of the *Confessions*, written to refute his Manichaean past, and *The City of God*. Arnold absorbed Augustine's emphasis on the fundamental ethical distinction between ends and means, and was attracted by his Neoplatonism.

Dante: Dante Alighieri (1265–1321), Italian poet and author of the *Divina Commedia*. In 1861 Arnold made a note to himself to read one

canto of the *Divina Commedia* daily (*Note-Books*, 13), and his reading
lists regularly included sections of Dante.

23 *Monsieur Albert Réville*: (1826–1906), French Protestant theologian and
historian of religion, whom Arnold read much from 1867. On 1 August
1867 he wrote to his mother that he had just been reading two excellent
articles by Réville on Isaiah—'one of the best French writers going
which have made me think of Papa—he would so have liked them—
though they could not have been written in his time' (*Letters*, iii. 166).

Socinians: a term used to denote anti-Trinitarianism (or Unitarianism),
derived from Lelio and Fausto Socinus (1525–62 and 1539–1604).

Luther . . . Commentary on the Book of Daniel: [Martin Luther] *D. Martin
Luthers Werke, Kritische Gesamtausgabe* (i.e. Weimarer Lutherausgabe),
Abteilung 3: Die Deutsche Bibel, vol. xi/2: Deutsche Bibel: Daniel—
Maleach 1530–2/45; Anhang: Widmungsbrief zur Danielübersetzung an
Kurprinz Johann Friedrich 1530; Handschrift der Erstübersetzung von
Hos. 7, 9–8, 12 (Weimar, 1960). This quotation came from the commen-
tary on verse 38. Martin Luther (1483–1546) was the most important
leader of the German Reformation. Arnold had called him a 'Philistine
of genius' in *On the Study of Celtic Literature*, Super, iii. 364.

Mr Greg: William Rathbone Greg (1809–81), industrialist, essayist, social
and political commentator. Unitarian by background, he became a member of the Plinian Society, which challenged orthodox religious belief,
and expressed his religious scepticism in the *Creed of Christendom* (1851).
Greg had responded to Arnold's essay 'The Bishop and the Philosopher'
[1863], Super, iii. 40–55, in 'Truth vs. Edification', reprinted in *Literary
and Social Judgements* (London, 1868).

24 *Benthamism*: utilitarianism, following the principles of Jeremy Bentham
(see note to p. 50).

Mialism: a term coined by Arnold to denote the philosophy of Edward
Miall. Miall (1809–81) was a Congregationalist minister, journalist, and
politician. Having become involved in the campaign against the payment
of Church rates, in 1840 he resigned his ministry and committed himself
to political and journalistic campaigning. In April 1841 the *Nonconformist*
(see note to p. 42) was launched. In 1844 he became one of the three
secretaries of the British Anti-State Church Association (which from
1853 became the Society for the Liberation of Religion from State Control or Patronage, or Liberation Society). He also promoted extension of
the franchise and the peace movement. From 1852 to 1857 he was MP for
Rochdale, and from 1869 to 1874 for Bradford. On 18 April 1870 Arnold
wrote to his publisher George Smith to say how pleased he was with 'the
two sub-forms of Hebraism and Hellenism—*Mialism and Millism* (with
further degeneration below each),—which I have established' (*Letters*, iii.
408). Given Arnold's views on the corrupting effects of popular under-
standings of Mill, Millism was hardly given the complimentary connotations which the analogy with Hellenism suggested here, although Mill

did belong in the camp of spontaneity rather than strictness. Cf. a letter from Arnold to his mother on 17 October 1871 referring to the Millite and Mialite coalition (*Letters*, iv. 55).

Sir Henry Wotton: (1568–1639), a diplomat and writer, who travelled widely in the course of his career. Izaak Walton wrote his life (1651), and then an idealized portrait of him in the *Compleat Angler* (1653). The Latin epitaph on his tomb in Eton Chapel translates as: 'Here lies the first author of this sentence: "The Itch of Disputation will prove the Scab of the Church." Inquire his name elsewhere.'

Father Jackson: Thomas Jackson (1783–1873), Methodist minister, biographer of Charles Wesley, and editor of the works of John Wesley.

Whitfield: George Whitefield (1714–70), Methodist evangelist, who split from the Wesleys over his adherence to Calvinism.

St Francis: St Francis of Assisi (1181/2–1226), founder of the Franciscan Order. Brought up in a rich merchant family, he renounced worldly goods and devoted his life to God. He was a very popular saint in the nineteenth century. In 1863 Arnold made fourteen entries in his notebook on St Francis and his renunciation of the things of the world. He also commented on the success of the Third Order Franciscans with the thirteenth-century middle class. In 1864 he was reading about mystic Franciscan poets. The comparison of Wesley to Francis was an apposite one, given Wesley's preaching of radical poverty and renunciation.

Lacordaire: Henry-Dominique Lacordaire (1802–61), French Dominican, who in 1843 established the first Dominican House in France since the suppression of the Order in 1790. In the early 1830s he contributed to de Lammenais's periodical *L'Avenir*, and in the mid-1830s gave famous conferences at Notre-Dame, which attracted large numbers of intellectuals. A political liberal (although theologically ultramontane), in 1848 he was elected deputy for Marseilles in the National Assembly. He was headmaster of the famous school at Sorèze (Tarn) which Arnold visited in 1859 (*A French Eton*, Super, ii. 271–8). Arnold criticized Lacordaire's emphasis on reaffirming absolute devotion to the Church and on reviving medieval religious orders. But he commended his concerns about the weakness of a state of anarchy, and his making the formation of character the most important aspect of education: 'for want of character our age is the age of miscarriages. Let us form Christians in our schools, but, first of all, let us form Christians in our own hearts; the one great thing is *to have a life of one's own*'. He also praised his 'passion, in an age which seems to think that progress can be achieved only by our herding together and making a noise, for the antique discipline of retirement and silence . . . A man is formed from within, and not from without' (ibid. 274). Cf. note to p. 36.

25 *machinery*: cf. Thomas Carlyle, 'Signs of the Times' [1829], *Critical and Miscellaneous Essays*, 5 vols. (London, 1899), ii. 56–82, at 59: 'Were we required to characterise this age of ours by any single epithet, we should

be tempted to call it, not an Heroical, Devotional, Philosophical, or Moral Age, but, above all others, the Mechanical Age. It is the Age of Machinery, in every outward and inward sense of that word.' For Carlyle, see notes to pp. 37, 61.

25 *as Mr Spurgeon says, 'a setting up of the Roman image'*: see note to p. 123 for discussion of Spurgeon's hostility to any suggestion of endowing the Roman Catholic Church in Ireland.

26 *to make reason and the will of God prevail*: see note to p. 34.

   like Ephraim, 'a wild ass alone by himself': Hosea 8: 9.

27 *culture . . . insists that men should not mistake . . . their natural taste for the bathos for a relish for the sublime*: see note to p. 82.

28 *They . . . call the new Parliament a Philistine Parliament*: the first Parliament under the Second Reform Act, returned in the autumn of 1868, had produced a large Liberal majority.

   Valley of Jehoshaphat: Joel 3: 1–14: a reference to God's threat of judgement against the enemies of Israel.

   the days of Israel are innumerable: Ecclesiasticus 37: 25. Arnold read Ecclesiasticus a lot, and copied several passages in his notebooks, including on the day of his death.

   To walk staunchly . . . one has: see note to p. 9.

29 *'without holiness no man shall see God'*: Hebrews 12: 14.

   the substance of things hoped for, the evidence of things not seen: Hebrews 11: 1. Cf. *Note-Books*, 56 (for 1867).

   'If ye know these things, happy are ye if ye do them!': John 13: 17. Cf. *Note-Books*, 266 (for 1876). This text comes from a passage in which Jesus washed his disciples' feet as an example of humility and charity, also making the point that 'the servant is not greater than his lord; neither is he that is sent greater than he that sent him'.

   the Bible . . . will forever remain, as Goethe called it, not only a national book, but the Book of the Nations: 'Jene grosse Verehrung, welche der Bibel von vielen Völkern und Geschlechtern der Erde gewidmet worden, verdankt sie ihrem innern Wert. Sie ist nicht etwa nur ein Volksbuch, sondern das Buch der Völker, weil sie die Schicksale eines Volks zum Symbol aller übrigen aufstellt, die Geschichte desselben an die Entstehung der Welt anknüpft und durch eine Stufenreihe irdischer und geistiger Entwickelungen, notwendiger und zufälliger Ereignisse bis in die entferntesten Regionen der äussersten Ewigkeiten hinausführt.' Johann Wolfgang von Goethe, *Geschichte der Farbenlehre*, in Goethe, *Werke*, Hamburger edn. in 14 vols., xiv. *Naturwissenschaftliche Schriften II* (Munich, 1988), 52. (Every great cult which many peoples and races of the earth have dedicated to the Bible, owes to this book its fundamental worth. It is perhaps not merely a people's book, but a book of peoples: for it sets up the destiny of a people as a supreme symbol; it binds the people's history to the formation of the world; and through a succession of earthly and spiritual narratives, it conducts both inevitable and chance events to the furthest regions of uttermost eternity.) It is interesting that Goethe speaks of a book of peoples, not a book of nations, as Arnold reads it. There was a real difference, especially given the importance of *Volk* in late eighteenth-century German intellectual circles (cf. Lessing and Herder). Goethe develops similar ideas about the Bible in *West-östlicher Divan, Noten und Abhandlungen, Werke*, ii. *Gedichte und Epen II*, 128; and *Aus meinem Leben. Dichtung und Wahrheit*, Zweiter Teil, 7, *Werke*, ix: *Autobiographische Schriften I*, 274. He compared the Bible with the Qur'an and other eastern religious writings, underlining the universality of these texts in responding to fundamental metaphysical questions in the West and the East.

Lo, thy sons come . . . remembrance of God: Baruch 4: 37. The Book of Baruch is a book of the Apocrypha, forming an appendix to the Book of Jeremiah.

INTRODUCTION

('Estote ergo vos perfecti', 'Be ye therefore perfect' (Matthew 5: 48), was the motto given to this introductory chapter from the second edition onwards.)

31 *In one of his speeches a year or two ago*: Arnold quotes John Bright speaking in the parliamentary debate on the Franchise Bill, 30 May 1866. The Bill proposed an education test for the franchise. In this second reading debate, Bright instead urged householding as the basis of the franchise, and made frequent references to the 'ancient constitution' to support this position. Hansard, 3rd ser., 183, 30 May 1866, cols. 1511–20, at 1518.

Mr Frederic Harrison: 'Our Venetian Constitution', *Fortnightly Review*, 7. 276–7 (Mar. 1867). When Harrison reprinted this essay, as 'Parliament before Reform' in *Order and Progress* (London, 1875), he added a footnote: 'It seems necessary to say that these words were not directed against mental cultivation or literary grace, much less against a poet and writer whom to speak of these qualities is to name. My complaint was of a *political* faction, who brought to the great national struggle nothing but the bitterest reaction and trivial criticism of the academic sort.' Cited Super, v. 417. Frederic Harrison (1831–1923) was an essayist and famous positivist. As a scholar at Wadham (matriculating in 1849) he read John Stuart Mill and was taught by Richard Congreve, who had just returned from meeting Comte in Paris in 1848. He was to succeed to Congreve's tutorship and fellowship. Harrison studied law and was called to the Bar in 1858, whilst becoming a campaigning journalist. He supported the Liberation Society, and also deplored latitudinarianism in the Anglican Church, which he saw as hypocritical. For Comte and Congreve, see notes to p. 49.

31 *Know Thyself!*: motto inscribed (alongside 'Avoid extremes') on the tem-
    ple of Apollo at Delphi. Discussed by Socrates in Plato, *Charmides*,
    164D–167A and *Protagoras*, 343B.

32 *Daily Telegraph . . . 'an elegant Jeremiah'*: 8 Sept. 1866, 4–5. The phrase
    'elegant Jeremiah' was used to attack Arnold's remarks on the English,
    by comparison with the French and Germans, in his discussion of Celtic
    literature.

    simple, unsystematic way: Arnold made repeated rhetorical play with the
    presentation of himself as simple and unphilosophical—partly as a
    defence against criticisms of his intellectual detachment. Cf. notes to
    pp. 73 and 121.

CHAPTER I

(Entitled 'Sweetness and Light' from the second edition onwards.)

32 *The disparagers of culture make its motive curiosity*: see 'The Function of
    Criticism at the Present Time', Super, iii. 268, where Arnold began the
    process of rescuing criticism from its negative and dilettantish connota-
    tions. Cf. his use of Bishop Wilson in the 'Culture and its Enemies'
    lecture, which became this first chapter of *Culture and Anarchy* (see
    Introduction, p. xvii).

33 *I have before now pointed out*: 'The Function of Criticism at the Present
    Time', Super, iii. 268.

    Monsieur Sainte-Beuve: [F. T. Marzials], 'M. Sainte-Beuve', *Quarterly
    Review*, 119 (Jan. 1866), 80–108. Arnold cut a sentence on Sainte-Beuve
    from 'Culture and its Enemies', whether before or after delivering the
    lecture is not clear: his praise was qualified by saying that Sainte-Beuve's
    'critical activity belongs chiefly to a time of no great faith and ardour',
    and was therefore 'founded mainly in curiosity', rather than 'in a
    study of perfection' (S. Coulling, 'The Manuscript of "Culture and its
    Enemies" ', *Nineteenth-Century Prose*, 21 (1994), 8–16 at 9; cf. 'Culture
    and its Enemies', MS, Balliol College, Oxford). When Sainte-Beuve
    died, Arnold commented that George Sand and Newman were the only
    remaining living writers by whom he had been strongly influenced as he
    had been by Sainte-Beuve (*Letters*, iii. 370: 16 Oct. 1869). In writing to
    Newman two and a half years later, Arnold varied the mixture, mention-
    ing as key influences Goethe, Wordsworth, Newman, and Sainte-Beuve
    (*Letters*, iv. 123: 28 May 1872).

    pleasure of seeing them as they are: 'The Function of Criticism at the
    Present Time', Super, iii. 258; cf. 'On Translating Homer', Super, i. 140.

    Montesquieu: Charles-Louis de Secondat, Baron de la Brède et de
    Montesquieu (1689–1755), 'Discours sur les motifs qui doivent nous
    encourager aux sciences', *Œuvres complètes*, ed. E. Laboulaye (Paris,
    1879), vii. 78. Montesquieu's most famous works were the *Lettres*

persanes (1721)—a witty and savage satire on European culture as seen by two fictional Persians; and *L'Esprit des lois* (1748), a treatise on the ways in which laws should be adapted to the people for whom they are framed.

34 *Bishop Wilson: 'To make reason and the will of God prevail!'*: 'Sacra Privata', *Works*, ed. Keble, v. 152, 153: Wilson actually says that we should resolve to sacrifice our will to reason, and reason to the word of God, which gives a slightly different emphasis. See *Note-Books*, 48 (entry for 3 Feb. 1867). Cf. *Note-Books*, 40 (for 1866). Arnold had even more references to Wilson's maxims in the original draft of 'Culture and its Enemies', which were cut at some stage. Arnold noted some passages from an anonymous article by J. C. Shairp on Coleridge in the *North British Review* (43/86 (Dec. 1865), 251–322, at 304): 'Faith is allegiance of the moral nature to Universal Reason, or the will of God'; 'An approving conscience is the sense of harmony of the personal will of man with that impersonal light which is in him, representative of the will of God'. These were followed by a quotation from an article on Plato in the same issue of the periodical: 'We must sacrifice, says Plato, all individual will to reason, to that higher nature which is incapable of being the object of selfish impulse. N.B. on Plato.' Both Coleridge quotations were repeated in his notebook for 1867 (*Note-Books*, 50), and the second one in 1868 (p. 72), where it was immediately followed by John 6: 38: 'I came, not to do mine own will, but the will of him that sent me'.

times of faith and ardour: cf. 'The Function of Criticism at the Present Day', 260–4, in which Arnold argues that creation is not possible in all epochs, but criticism is needed to prepare the ground.

35 *people who had a routine which they had christened reason and the will of God*: see also [J. C. Shairp], 'Samuel Taylor Coleridge', *North British Review*, 43/86 (Dec. 1865), 251–322, at 251–3, on the degree to which a mechanical philosophy had saturated the eighteenth century, resulting in utilitarianism, individualism, and lack of spiritual insight; this was the context against which Coleridge had reacted.

36 *Religion says: The kingdom of God is within you*: Luke 17: 21. Cf. *Note-Books*, 268 (for 1876), alongside John 18: 36. Most of the entries in Arnold's *Note-Books* on this point are in fact from religious authorities: e.g. Lacordaire: 'Un homme se fait en dedans de lui, et non en dehors' (p. 18); *Imitation* (p. 50); Wilson (p. 61). He also notes J. Barthélemy St-Hilaire, *Morale d'Aristote*, 3 vols. (Paris, 1856), i. 51, citing Plato on right reason which is the voice of God speaking within us (*Note-Books*, p. 65).

As I have said on a former occasion: *A French Eton*, Super, ii. 318.

the individual is obliged . . . to carry others along with him in his march towards perfection: see also Arnold's poem 'Rugby Chapel' (1857), which follows through the imagery of Thomas Arnold moving through the ranks and keeping the Israelites together, not looking for individual salvation but carrying others along with him. See *The Poems of Matthew*

Arnold, ed. K. Allott (London, 1965), 444–52, and a letter from Arnold to his mother (27 Feb. 1855, *Letters*, i. 304), saying the same thing about his father; see also Ezekiel 14: 14, 20.

36 *Bishop Wilson ... 'to promote the kingdom of God is to increase and hasten one's own happiness'*: 'Sacra Privata', *Works*, ed. Keble, v. 93; 366. Arnold, *Note-Books*, 48, 50 (entries for 4 Feb. and 1 Mar. 1867).

harmonious expansion: cf. Coleridge, *On the Constitution of the Church and State* (1830; London, 1972 edn.), 33–4: 'civilization is itself but a mixed good, if ... [it] is not grounded in *cultivation*, in the harmonious development of those qualities and faculties that characterise our *humanity*. We must be men in order to be citizens'.

Here it goes beyond religion, as religion is generally conceived by us: here Arnold is attempting to distinguish between ideal religion and some aspects of actual religion, especially in its narrow (dissenting) form.

37 *our maxim of 'every man for himself'*: a reference to the hegemonic classical political economy of laissez-faire, derived in a simplified form from Adam Smith's *Wealth of Nations* (1776) and reinforced by utilitarian principles of individualism.

Faith in machinery is, I said, our besetting danger: the next few lines are taken directly from Carlyle's 'Signs of the Times' (see note to p. 25).

38 *Mr Roebuck's stock argument*: John Roebuck (1801–79) was a Radical politician, greatly influenced by the utilitarian ideas of Bentham and James Mill and a doctrinaire believer in free trade; MP for Bath 1832–7 and 1841–7; and for Sheffield 1849–68 and 1874–9. In 1864, under the heading 'An Unfettered Press', Arnold copied this extract from Roebuck's speech in Sheffield: 'I look around me and ask What is the state of England. Is not property safe? Is not every man able to say what he likes? ... I pray that our unrivalled happiness may last' (*The Times*, 19 Aug. 1864, 4). In the notebook, this immediately followed another extract from *The Times* (9 Aug. 1864, 6), which Arnold set down and then commented on himself: 'The Times says: "A sure instinct may warn France that there is more danger from the excesses of revolution than from those of power." The converse—A sure instinct may warn England that there is more danger from the excesses of Philistinism than from those of power' (*Note-Books*, 25–6).

The Times: Super (v. 419) refers to 18 September 1867, when *The Times* reported an article in *Figaro* commenting on the slovenly habits of the English abroad.

late discussions as to the possible failure of our supplies of coal: W. S. Jevons (1835–82), mathematical economist and philosopher of science, published *The Coal Question* in 1865. His argument was that because both industry and population were increasing so fast, the demand for and therefore the costs of producing coal would increase (as mining had to be extended to less productive seams). Within fifty years Britain's competitive industrial advantage would be threatened, in so far as this was built on cheap coal. In a speech in the House of Commons in April 1866 John Stuart Mill commended Jevons's argument, and his proposal that this challenge should be prepared for by an attempt to reduce the national debt. Gladstone, then Chancellor of the Exchequer, took up the idea. Ironically Jevons's own concluding remarks set up a paradox which raised similar questions to the ones which Arnold develops in this paragraph, and he, too, emphasized that commerce was but a means to an end. However he drew a different conclusion in linking economic progress to philosophical progress, and citing the Elizabethan age as an example: 'The resplendent genius of our Elizabethan age might never have been manifest but in a period equally conspicuous for good order, industrial progress and general enterprise . . . A clear and vigorous mind is to be looked for in a wholesome state of the body' (W. S. Jevons, *The Coal Question: An Inquiry Concerning the Progress of the Nation, and the Probable Exhaustion of our Coal-mines* (London, 1865), 345–6). See also Sidgwick's comments in 'The Prophet of Culture', *Macmillan's Magazine*, 16 (1867), 271–80, at 278 (see Appendix, pp. 168–9).

the England of Elizabeth: Arnold believed that the Elizabethan age had represented a high point in English culture, before Puritanism had set in. See 'Equality' [1878], Super, viii. 277–305, at 294 on the middle class having entered 'the prison of Puritanism, and had the key turned upon its spirit there two hundred years ago'. Cf. also p. 105.

40 *The Times on the Registrar-General's returns of marriages and births*: 3 Feb. 1866, 9: 'When Marriages are many and Deaths are few it is certain that the people are doing well.'

'Bodily exercise profiteth little; but godliness is profitable unto all things': 1 Timothy 4: 8. Cf. discussion of *'muscular Christianity'*, note to p. 45.

the utilitarian Franklin: *Poor Richard, An Almanack for 1742*. Arnold recorded the maxim in his diary 30 June 1867 (*Note-Books*, 56). On 20 June Arnold had entered an injunction to himself *'not to sleep after dinner'* (ibid.). Benjamin Franklin (1706–90) was a natural philosopher, writer, and politician, who was one of the philosophical shapers of the American Revolution.

Epictetus: *Encheiridion*, xli. Epictetus (*c.* 50–*c.* 130) was a Stoic philosopher whose principles were valued by Christian ascetics. He emphasized the obligation of moral perfection, to be achieved by resignation and renunciation. He wrote nothing himself, but the *Encheiridion* was a collection of his philosophical discourses compiled by his pupil Flavius Arrianus. His work was rediscovered in the Renaissance.

Swift . . . in his Battle of the Books: see note to p. 9.

42 *to resist the Devil, to overcome the Wicked One*: James 4: 7; 1 John 2: 13, 14.

Independents: another name for the Congregationalists, who believed in the independence and autonomy of each local church.

the Nonconformist: a weekly newspaper, started in 1841 and edited by

Edward Miall. Miall reviewed (anonymously) 'Culture and its Enemies' in the *Nonconformist*, 28, 10 July 1867, 557–8. He stressed indignantly that the paper was not the organ of the Independents, or of any other religious group, but was independent in the sense of free-standing. He pointed out that the motto with which Arnold took issue was taken from Burke, and observed that it ill-became an Oxford professor to tax Nonconformists with lack of culture or poetry when for two hundred years they had been excluded from the University.

42 *'Finally, be of one mind, united in feeling'*: 1 Peter 3: 8.

43 *Pilgrim Fathers*: English Puritans who emigrated to America to escape Elizabethan persecution. They sailed on the *Mayflower* in 1620, and founded the colony of Plymouth, Massachusetts.

 Virgil: (70 BC–19 BC), after Homer, the greatest epic poet of antiquity; author of the *Aeneid*.

44 *Epsom on the Derby day*: the Derby, the annual popular horse-race run in June at Epsom Race Course. The occasion had become a point of reference for a real mixture of social classes, and was used as such in cartoons of the period. In Sidgwick's review, 'The Prophet of Culture' (see Appendix, p. 168), the reference to Frith's famous painting *Derby Day* (1858) is hardly coincidental. *Derby Day* (exh. 1858) had been praised as a microcosm, a whole world on canvas. It set out to depict as wide as possible a range of 'types' of human nature. See M. Cowling, *The Artist as Anthropologist: The Representation of Type and Character in Victorian Art* (Cambridge, 1989), 319–33. Sidgwick used Frith's popularity to challenge Arnold's loftiness about the culture of the commercial middle classes.

 children of God: Galatians 3: 26. 'For ye are all the children of God by faith in Christ Jesus' (a famous passage about living by faith rather than by law, which goes on in v. 28: 'There is neither Jew nor Greek, there is neither bond nor free, there is neither male nor female: for ye are all one in Christ Jesus'). See *Note-Books* (1874), 212 (and again (1875), 236, when Arnold was thinking about 'God and the Bible').

 our city which we have builded for us to dwell in: the phrase carries an echo of Genesis 4: 17 ('And Cain . . . builded a city'), where the city comes out of sin. There is also an echo here of a speech by Bright (reported in the *Morning Star*, 9 Oct. 1866, 2) which Arnold noted in 1866, and which he quoted three times in *Culture and Anarchy* (see pp. 48–9, 77, and 136): '*You* are the great nation excluded. See what you have done—I look over this country and see the cities you have built, the railroads you have made, the manufactures you have produced . . . I see that you have converted by your labour what was once a wilderness, these islands, into a fruitful garden' (*Note-Books*, 36–7). The desirable ideal is of course the City of God.

 publicé egestas, privatim opulentia: Sallust, *De Conjuratione Catilinae Historia*, 52. 22. See *Note-Books*, 53 (entry for 16 Apr. 1867).

45 *muscular Christianity*: a phrase used by various reviewers to refer to the novelist and Christian Socialist Charles Kingsley and his followers, and also to Thomas Hughes, author of *Tom Brown's Schooldays* (1858), a fictionalized account of Rugby School. See e.g. [T. C. Sandars], reviewing Kingsley in *Saturday Review*, 3 (Feb. 1857), 176; [Fitzjames Stephen], reviewing *Tom Brown's Schooldays*, *Edinburgh Review*, 107 (Jan. 1858), 190; 'Tangled Talk: Muscular Christianity', *Tait's Edinburgh Magazine*, 25 (Feb. 1858), 100–2. See N. Vance, *The Sinews of the Spirit: The Ideal of Christian Manliness in Victorian Literature and Religious Thought* (Cambridge, 1985), 2. Thomas Arnold had been opposed to too great an emphasis on games at Rugby (drawing for justification on Aristotle's criticism of the Spartans). Matthew Arnold felt that *Tom Brown's Schooldays* gave a very one-sided view of Rugby. Arnold's protégé, the school inspector and educationalist Sir Joshua Fitch, observed that the book would be held to illustrate the 'low standard of civilization, false ideal of manliness and deep-seated indifference to learning for its own sake which characterised the upper classes in the first half of the nineteenth century'; it would justify the epithet of 'Barbarians'. See J. Fitch, *Thomas and Matthew Arnold and their Influence on English Education* (London, 1897), 103–6.

Mr Gladstone well pointed out, in a speech at Paris: at a dinner of the Society of Political Economy in Paris, 31 January 1867; reported in *The Times*, 1 Feb. 1867, 10.

46 *young lions of the Daily Telegraph*: in his memoirs G. A. Sala commented on Arnold's fixation with the hostility of the *Daily Telegraph*, even after its attitude had in fact softened. Sala, *Life and Adventures*, 2 vols. (London, 1895), i. 18–19.

Mr Beales: Edmond Beales (1803–81), radical campaigner on behalf of European nationalists and American slaves. He founded the Reform League in 1865, and organized the huge meeting in Hyde Park of 23 July 1866.

Mr Bradlaugh: Charles Bradlaugh (1833–91) was a freethinker, who was brought up in the Church of England but who became an atheist. He was president of the London Secular Society from 1858 to 1890, and from 1860 ran the *National Reformer*; he was a prominent member of the Reform League and helped to organize the Hyde Park meeting in 1866. He stood for parliament, and, when he was finally elected in 1880, he refused to take the oath, and was several times excluded and re-elected. In 1886 he was finally allowed to make the oath required under the Parliamentary Oaths Act of 1866 and to take his seat.

the Oxford of the past: i.e. before the reforms of the University, especially the Oxford University Act of 1854, which amended the constitution of the University to abolish religious tests at the stage of the first degree, and opened up the curriculum. Dissenters were still excluded from fellowships, until the University Tests Act of 1871 which opened up all degrees and offices to men of any religion or none.

47 *the great movement which shook Oxford to its centre*: the Oxford Movement, traditionally dated from John Keble's *Assize Sermon* of 1833, aimed at the revival of High Church spiritual and devotional principles in the Church of England and at the defence of the authority of the Church as a divine institution. Its chief leaders were Keble, John Henry Newman, and Edward Bouverie Pusey, who organized the publication of *Tracts for the Times* to promote their cause. Huge controversy was aroused in Oxford, where Thomas Arnold led the liberal attack.

Liberalism prevailed: in Newman's *Apologia pro vita sua* (1864), he was in fact much more concerned with philosophical and religious liberalism, although the nostrums of political and economic liberalism were also seen as challenging to religious energy. In the short term, liberalism of different sorts could seem to have prevailed—within the University, where the reformers consolidated their position, and intellectually, as Mill's philosophy established a hegemonic position. But, as Arnold suggests in his praise for the Oxford Movement, it did maintain its position and its principles, despite high-profile conversions to Catholicism such as Newman's. By the 1870s it was stronger again in Oxford, and a revival of idealist philosophy to challenge Mill helped to underpin the Anglo-Catholic movement of the last quarter of the century. See Sidgwick, 'The Prophet of Culture' (Appendix, pp. 165–6), for a cogent discussion of the limitations of Arnold's depiction of Newman.

Quæ regio in terris nostri non plena laboris?: Virgil, *Aeneid*, i. 460. 'What land on earth is not full of our sorrow?'

Mr Lowe: Robert Lowe (1811–92), Liberal politician. From 1851 he was a leader writer for *The Times*, and in 1852 was elected MP for Kidderminster. In Palmerston's ministry of 1859 he was given responsibility for education, and in 1861 introduced the 'revised code' which laid down that government grants to voluntary schools should be given on the basis of the number of children who passed an examination in reading, writing, and arithmetic—the infamous 'payment by results' which Arnold so deplored. In 1862 this code was implemented, in a slightly modified form. He opposed the reform bills of 1866 and 1867; as a believer in rule by intelligence he was very nervous about a more popular franchise. As Chancellor of the Exchequer in Gladstone's first ministry, he introduced competitive examination for the civil service, and played a key role in the Education Act of 1870. Here Arnold refers to his speech in the parliamentary debate on the Borough Franchise Extension Bill, 3 May 1866.

A new power: the Conservatives came into power in 1866, and put forward the Reform Act of 1867.

49 *Mr Bright . . . throughout all the world*: *Morning Star*, 9 Oct. 1866, 4; 2. *Note-Books*, 36–7 (entry for 12 Oct.).

Tabernacle: a reference both to Spurgeon's Metropolitan Tabernacle and to the Bible.

Only the middle classes are told they have done it all with their energy: a reference to the misplaced self-confidence of the spider in Swift's fable. See note to p. 9.

without having on a wedding garment: Matthew 22: 11–14. The parable compares entry to the kingdom of heaven to being bidden to attend a king's wedding party. The man who was unprepared and turned up without a wedding garment was cast into outer darkness, 'For many are called, but few are chosen'.

Journeyman Engineer: [Thomas Wright], *Some Habits and Customs of the Working Classes, by a Journeyman Engineer* (1867).

the ways of Jacobinism: a reference to the extreme radicals of the French Revolution, who were adherents to an abstract revolutionary model.

Comte: Auguste Comte (1798–1857), founder of French Positivism. The Positivist system rested on three phases—the theological, the metaphysical, and the positive. Under the positive phase in which scientific law was to be the key explanatory principle, a new kind of religion, that of humanity, was to provide the context for the necessary triumph of altruism over egoism.

Mr Congreve: Richard Congreve (1818–99), Positivist. Educated at Rugby under Thomas Arnold in the 1830s, and then at Wadham College, Oxford. He was ordained and became a Fellow of Wadham (where he taught Frederic Harrison), but he resigned in 1854, having been converted to Comte's philosophy. He published translations of Comte's *Catéchisme positiviste* and of the *Système de politique positive*.

50 *Bentham*: Jeremy Bentham (1748–1832), philosopher, jurist, and reformer, founder of modern utilitarianism, who worked to extend economic concepts to the understanding of law and politics. He was a fierce opponent of religion and of the role of the Church in education.

The excellent German historian of the mythology of Rome, Preller: Ludwig Preller, *Römische Mythologie* (Berlin, 1858; 2nd edn, 1865). This book was on Arnold's reading list for 1866 and 1867 (*Note-Books*, 579, 582).

Benjamin Franklin: 'Bagatelles', *Works*, ed. Jared Sparks (Boston, 1839), ii. 167. As Super observes (Super, v. 421–2), Arnold misread the tone here. Franklin, influenced by satirical writers like Addison, Rabelais, and Swift, produced his bagatelles as literary jokes which could also make moral points. His 'modernization' of part of the Book of Job was to be seen in this context. He enjoyed inserting his invented Bible passages as if they were part of the real text when he read the Bible aloud to friends.

51 *Deontology*: J. Bentham, *Deontology; or, the Science of Morality*, ed. J. Bowring, 2 vols. (London, 1834), i. 39–44.

Mr Buckle: Henry William Buckle (1821–62), historian, greatly influenced by John Stuart Mill and by Scottish Enlightenment philosophers, especially the conjectural historians who believed in universal laws of human society and progress. His *History of Civilization in England*

(London, 1857–61) compared England favourably to other countries, and emphasized the role of the development of national intellect in driving progress.

51 *Mr Mill*: John Stuart Mill (1806–73), philosopher, political economist, reformer. His *System of Logic* (1843) and *Principles of Political Economy* (1848) crystallized his reputation as the central philosopher of the mid-century, and his modified utilitarianism was extremely influential, as were simplified popularizations of his ideas.

'Be not ye called Rabbi!': Matthew 23: 8. 'But be ye not called Rabbi: for one is your master, even Christ; and all ye are brethren.' Bishop Wilson meditated on this text in the Supplement to his 'Maxims' (*Works*, ed. Keble, v. 509–10). Commenting that it was a text abused by the Quakers, he observed: 'words have a very Instructive meaning; and for want of observing this Rule Religion suffers very much. People are apt to believe that those they esteem are always in the Right; they espouse their Principles in the Bulk, without examining which are sound, or which otherwise . . . Men are so zealous for their Party that they forget the Words of Christ & . . . the Concernes of a good life are forgot'.

52 *Again and again*: see Arnold's Inaugural Lecture as Professor of Poetry, 'On the Modern Element in Literature', Super, i. 23–9.

culture . . . seeks to do away with classes: this was an important part of the integrative role of culture. In 1866 Arnold jotted in his notebook without any reference: ' "The feeling between classes" but the distinction of classes should die away and we should be one people' (*Note-Books*, 37).

53 *Abelard*: Peter Abelard (1079–1142/3) was a French philosopher and theologian. Particularly influential on liberal theologians in the late nineteenth century was his *Sic et Non*—the setting side by side of apparently contradictory texts from the Bible, the Fathers, and occasional pagan philosophers, not to undermine the credibility of the tradition but to demonstrate and explore the significance of the different contexts in which words were used. He was very concerned with practical social and moral problems, and stressed the persuasive role of reason in religious understanding.

Lessing: Gotthold Ephraim Lessing (1729–81), German critic and playwright, who turned to theological writing later in life. He distinguished between uniformity and unity, arguing that the former (a principle of Jacobinism) was fatal to real unity. The unity of history in the sense of a Christian teleology was an overarching process, of which epochs of civilization formed a part. Coleridge annotated his writings, and derived from him arguments against the literal reading of the Bible.

Herder: Johann Gottfried Herder (1744–1833), German Romantic philosopher of mind, language, history, and religion; poet; critic; and biblical scholar. He believed passionately in the need for his philosophy to reach out and have a wide social and moral impact, and in the moral influence of literature: art was to be judged by its capacity to form character. The study of the literature and art of different historical periods would reveal people at their best, and would focus self-development by the judicious comparison of one's own perspective with that of others.

Saint Augustine: Confessions, 13. 18.

CHAPTER II

(Entitled 'Doing as One Likes' from the second edition onwards.)

54 *'religion of culture'*: see 'Mr Arnold on Culture', *Saturday Review*, 24 (20 July 1867), 78–9, and 'Culture and Action', *Saturday Review*, 24 (9 Nov. 1867), 591–3. The reference to 'parmaceti' was to a speech of Hotspur in Shakespeare's *The First Part of Henry IV*, Act I, scene 3, lines which Frederic Harrison used as an epigraph for his article 'Culture; A Dialogue', *Fortnightly Review*, 11 (Nov. 1867), 614: 'And telling me the sovereign'st thing on earth | Was parmaceti for an inward bruise'. Harrison was picking up on a reference which had been used by the *Saturday Review*, 18 (3 Dec. 1864), 685 to signify what they saw as Arnold's effeteness and detachment from action. The motif was also used by the *Daily Telegraph*, 2 July 1867, 6, and by Henry Sidgwick, 'The Prophet of Culture' (Appendix, pp. 157–72); further in [Henry Allon], 'Mr Arnold and Culture', *British Quarterly Review*, 52 (1870), 170–99, at 180–1.

Alcibiades: fifth-century Athenian, known as a self-willed and capricious man, who became notorious for his debauchery and contempt for temperance, holiness, and patriotism. He played a prominent and somewhat equivocal part in the Peloponnesian War. Plutarch compared him to Coriolanus, who represented the Roman aristocracy, arguing against the democratic claims of the plebeians, and who was banished permanently from Rome for misappropriation of public funds.

Morning Star: 28 June 1867, 4. The paper attacked Arnold's reading of Bright's comments about culture: 'To be a man of culture . . . in the modern and slangy sense . . . is to be a small, pedantic Tory prig who, knowing very little Latin and less Greek, is proud of declaring that he knows and wants to know nothing else' (Super, v. 423, citing Coulling).

editor of the Daily Telegraph: 2 July 1867, 6.

Nation: [E. L. Godkin], 'Sweetness and Light', *Nation*, 5 (12 Sept. 1867), 212–13.

Arminius: Arminius von Thunder-Ten-Tronkh, the imaginary author of a series of letters written by Arnold for the *Pall Mall Gazette* from 1866 to 1870, republished as *Friendship's Garland* (1871). Arminius/Hermann was a German national hero who defeated the Romans in AD 9. The surname was taken from Voltaire's *Candide* (1759), a satire on the philosophical principle that 'all is for the best in the best of all possible worlds'. Frederic Harrison's 'Culture: A Dialogue' was an imaginary conversation between him (masquerading as an admirer of Arnoldian Culture) and Arnold's Arminius. *Fortnightly Review*, 8 (Nov. 1867). On 30 October 1867 Arnold wrote to Louisa, Lady de Rothschild about Harrison's article: 'It is scarcely the least vicious, and in parts so amusing that I laughed till I cried' (*Letters*, iii. 181). After the next paragraph Arnold cut from the *Cornhill* article a long defence of himself against the charge of having misrepresented the Comtists.

55 *Our familiar praise of the British Constitution*: a reference to Walter Bagehot's *The English Constitution*, which was published serially in the *Fortnightly Review* between 1865 and 1867, throughout the reform debates. The eighth part was called 'Its Supposed Checks and Balances'. *Fortnightly Review*, 6 (Dec. 1866), 807–26.

Mr Bright . . . in one of his great speeches: in his speech on the Franchise Bill on 30 May 1866. See note to p. 31.

56 *notion . . . of the State—the nation, in its collective and corporate character*: Arnold alludes here to the Athenian city state (cf. his father's reverence for the Greek polis) and to the stronger model of the state in France and Germany. His idea of the State as a moral entity seems very Hegelian, although it is not clear whether he actually read him (Sidgwick's review implies that it was imagined that he had done so). The principal theoretical influences on his thinking on the State were Burke, his father, and Coleridge.

lord-lieutenancy, deputy-lieutenancy, and the posse comitatûs: the lord lieutenants and their deputies were county officers appointed by the Crown.

vestrymanship and guardianship: vestries were Anglican parochial bodies made up of the Anglican incumbent, the people rated for relief of the poor, and the occupiers of rated property, which, until the Local Government Act of 1894 which restricted their power to the administration of the Church, had a more extensive local government role.

Monsieur Michelet . . . of the people of France: see 'The Popular Education of France', Super, ii. 162.

57 *his right to march where he likes*: a reference to the Hyde Park riots in London in 1866. On 23 July 1866 the Reform League organized a massive meeting in Hyde Park, flouting a government prohibition.

majestic repose: two companies of Guards were called out to deal with the demonstration, but were not used.

man who gives an inflammatory lecture: on 16 June 1867 William Murphy began a series of anti-Catholic lectures in Birmingham. Since there was a threat of violence, the police and armed forces were alerted, but the lectures continued, Murphy defending his right to freedom of speech. *The Times*, 19–21 June 1867.

breaks down the Park railings: when the Reform League crowd was refused entry to Hyde Park, they broke down the railings along Bayswater Road and Park Lane in order to get in. The next day there were renewed disturbances, and windows were broken. Arnold wrote to his mother on 27 July 1866 about the crowd which had broken into their square and had thrown stones (*Letters*, iii. 58–9).

invades a Secretary of State's office: on 18 November 1867 a group of English Fenian sympathizers broke into the outer office of the Home Secretary to demand pardon for a group of Fenians sentenced to death for killing a policeman in Manchester. For Fenianism, see note to p. 59.

58 *Mr Hardy*: Gathorne Gathorne-Hardy, later 1st Earl of Cranbrook (1814–1906), became Home Secretary after the resignation in May 1867 of Spencer Walpole, following what was seen as his weakness in dealing with the Hyde Park demonstration. Coming in with a reputation for toughness, Gathorne-Hardy introduced a bill to make it illegal to use the royal parks for political meetings, but he was forced to withdraw it because of Liberal opposition. He stood firm in response to the pressure to commute the death sentence passed on the Fenians convicted of murdering a policeman in Manchester in November 1867 (see previous note).

Mr Murphy: see note to p. 57: 'man who gives an inflammatory lecture'.

Chancery Judge: see James Kay Shuttleworth, *A Scheme for General and Local Administration of Endowments* (London, 1866), 16.

59 *Fenianism*: Irish-American republican secret society (known as the Irish Republican Brotherhood in Ireland) formed in 1858.

it never was any part of our creed that the great right and blessedness of an Irishman, or, indeed, of anybody on earth except an Englishman, is to do as he likes: Arnold here uses strong irony to point up the inconsistency between Liberalism in England and in Ireland, and the self-serving way in which Liberal definitions worked solely for the English, whilst rhetorically purporting to have a universal currency.

Truss manufactory on the finest site in Europe: Coles's Truss Manufactory was on the edge of Trafalgar Square; cf. 'I Introduce Arminius and "Geist" to the British Public', *Friendship's Garland*, Super, v. 41: 'A Coles's Truss Manufactory standing where it ought not, a glorious monument of individualism and industrialisation, to adorn the finest site in Europe'.

60 *Sir Daniel Gooch*: (1816–89), railway engineer with the Great Western Railway; Conservative MP for Cricklade 1865–85. For his mother's advice, see his *Diaries* (London, 1892), 25–6.

he says he is being butchered by the aristocracy: cf. p. 70. In his 'Introduction' to *On the Study of Celtic Literature*, Super, iii. 393–4, Arnold contrasted the situation in France.

61 *Mr Carlyle*: Thomas Carlyle, 'Shooting Niagara: and After?', *Macmillan's Magazine*, 16 (Aug. 1867), 124, repr. in *Critical and Miscellaneous Essays* (London, 1899), v. 1–48. Arnold rather distorts what Carlyle had said. In fact, in this essay Carlyle expresses the hope that there is still good in the

aristocracy by title, but if that should fail, he looks to the 'still unclassed Aristocracy by nature'. This category he divides into two: the Speculative and the Practical or Industrial. He comments that the Industrial Hero is already almost an aristocrat by class, and that it falls to him to recivilize the world of industry (pp. 21–32). Here he reiterates his plea to the 'Captains of Industry' in *Past and Present* (1848). Thomas Carlyle (1795–1881) was a historian and social critic whose lectures and writings were enormously influential in challenging liberal nostrums and the complacency which could result from unreflective following of the laws of political economy or utilitarianism. Particularly popular were his *Past and Present* (1843), *On Heroes, Hero-Worship and the Heroic in History* (1841), and *The French Revolution*, 3 vols. (1837).

62 *epochs of concentration . . . epochs of expansion*: cf. 'The Function of Criticism at the Present Time' (Super, i. 266 f.); Thomas Arnold thought in terms of epochs with different characteristics: Greece, Rome, and modern Europe were three epochs of civilization, each of which had a childhood and a manhood—its own ancient and modern history. Matthew Arnold tried to develop this idea in his 'On the Modern Element in Literature' [delivered 1857], Super, i. 18–37. Cf., for the concept of epoch-forming revolutions, S. T. Coleridge, *The Statesman's Manual* (1816).

Now is the judgment of this world: John 12: 31. Christ has just ridden into Jerusalem and is foretelling his death. This passage comes just before that about walking in the light: 'While ye have light, believe in the light, that ye may be the children of light'.

Mrs Lincoln: widow of Abraham Lincoln, left in straitened circumstances after her husband's assassination.

63 *young Dives*: the rich man in Luke 16: 19, who feasted every day, whilst Lazarus begged for crumbs from his table.

64 *as one of my many critics says*: Frederic Harrison in 'Culture: A Dialogue', *Fortnightly Review*, 11 (Nov. 1867), 603–14, at 608.

Lowe's great speech at Edinburgh: 1 November 1867 on the need to reform higher education; reported in *The Times*, 4 Nov. 1867, 8.

Aristotle's machinery of the mean: *Nicomachean Ethics*, II. vi. 15–16. Arnold studied Aristotle's *Ethics* in Oxford. Cf. Thomas Arnold's devotion to Aristotle as a guide to studying life, society, and polity in a true perspective. Matthew Arnold here plays on the double sense of machinery. He wittily defends the study of Greek, and proceeds immediately to put it into practice.

Lord Elcho: Francis Wemyss-Charteris-Douglas, 8th earl of Wemyss and 6th earl of March (1818–1914), styled Lord Elcho after the death of his grandfather in 1853, Whig aristocrat and paternalist. He was MP for East Lothian until his father's death in 1883, when he went to the House of Lords. He joined Lowe in the 'Cave of Adullam' to resist the Reform

Bill in 1866, and the meetings of the 'Cave' took place in his house, whose windows Reform League supporters stoned. He was to vote for Disraeli's Reform Bill. Cf. Letter 3 of *Friendship's Garland*, Super, v. 50: 'Everybody knows Lord Elcho's appearance, and how admirably he looks the part of our governing classes; to my mind, indeed, the mere cock of his lordship's hat is one of the finest and most aristocratic things we have'.

Sir Thomas Bateson: MP for Devizes in 1865.

grand merit of our race being really our honesty: see 'The Literary Influence of Academies', Super, iii. 237; *On the Study of Celtic Literature*, ibid. 341; 'My Countrymen', ibid., v. 13.

65 *'The principles which will obtain recognition in the future,' says Mr Miall*: the precise source has not been located, but see e.g. 'Mr Miall on the Union of Church and State', a speech at a meeting of the Liberation Society reported in *The Times*, 19 Nov. 1858, 10; 'Springtime', *An Editor off the Line; or, Wayside Musings and Reminiscences* (London, 1865), 175–87.

'If we would really know . . . our actions': 'Maxims', *Works*, ed. Keble, v. 483.

66 *An American friend of the English liberals*: E. L. Godkin. See *Nation*, 5 (12 Sept. 1867), 213.

Another American defender of theirs: 'A Plea for the Uncultivated', signed 'A Philistine', *Nation*, 5 (12 Sept. 1867), 215.

Mr Jacob Bright: Jacob Bright (1821–99) was a Radical politician like his brother. He was elected MP for Manchester in November 1867. He focused in his career on promoting women's rights, introduced the first Women's Suffrage Bill in 1870, and moved the amendment to the Municipal Corporations Act of 1869, giving women householders the vote in borough elections. On 9 October 1867, the poet Swinburne wrote a playful and ironic letter to Arnold, whose apparent faith in the French Academy, and the idea of academies in general, he thought mistaken: 'The Academy, meantime, was irresistibly provocative of attack to me in passing after its ultra-Philistine election and doctrine of this year, choosing before Théophile Gautier, "le poëte impeccable", some M. Chose or other—bourgeois politicians & babes-of-letters—not men. Here I am convinced they would elect Mr John (or say Jacob) Bright & Mr Coventry Patmore rather than you, were you a candidate' (*Letters*, iii. 177). For Swinburne, see note to p. 79.

67 *Mr Bazley*: (1797–1885), cotton spinner and politician. An Evangelical Anglican, who, with his partner Robert Gardner, established a model community for their workforce, including a non-denominational educational institute. He played an important part in the National (Lancashire) Public Schools Association, a group pressing for the extension of non-denominational education. He was also president of the Manchester School of Art, and played a leading role in organizing the Manchester Art Treasures exhibition in 1857. His commitment to

the enhancement of the cultural life of the working classes was strong. He became MP for Manchester in 1858, and held his seat until 1880. In his notebook for 1864 Arnold copied an extract from the report of Bazley's speech at Manchester about middle-class education (*The Times*, 1 Dec. 1864, 7; *Note-Books*, 28). He copied it out again in 1865. Given Bazley's cultural breadth and educational activities, as well as his Anglicanism, he was an ironic example of Philistinism for Arnold to have chosen.

68 *Rev. W. Cattle*: on 18 June 1867 Revd William Cattle, a Wesleyan minister from Walsall, chaired the anti-Catholic meeting in Birmingham at which Murphy in fact made the comments quoted by Arnold. *The Times*, 20 June, 7. In subsequent editions of *Culture and Anarchy* Cattle's name was dropped.

Melancthon: Philipp Melancthon (1497–1560), one of the leaders of the German Reformation.

Alderman Wilson: Alderman Samuel Wilson was the 75-year-old colonel of the City of London Militia which marched into the West End on 3 June 1867, and, when the attendant crowd was set upon by 'roughs', did not act.

69 *Colonel Dickson or Mr Beales*: cf. 'I Take up the Cudgels for Our Beloved Country', *Friendship's Garland*, Super, v. 343.

70 *Julius Cæsar and Mirabeau*: Julius Caesar (102/100 BC–44 BC) was born of a patrician family, although he achieved success through his talents; the Comte de Mirabeau (1749–91) was a moderate constitutional monarchist in the French Revolution.

Mr Odger: George Odger (1820–77), trade union leader.

'Intemperance in talk makes a dreadful havoc in the heart': 'Maxims', *Works*, ed. Keble, v. 478.

71 *Firstly, never go against the best light . . . light be not darkness*: 'Maxims', ibid. 429.

72 *Duke of Wellington . . . 'a revolution by due course of law'*: referring to the Reform Bill of 1832.

CHAPTER III

(Entitled 'Barbarians, Philistines, Populace' from the second edition onwards.)

73 *a plain, unsystematic writer*: again, Arnold plays on this theme of his critical detachment and flexibility, on the one hand, and of his down-to-earth nature, on the other. His reference to the completion of his Aristotelian analysis points to his capacity to be systematic, whilst he rejects the mechanistic systems by which his contemporaries are inclined to live.

74 *to 'refuse to lend a hand . . . definite evils'*: a reference to [Fitzjames Stephen], 'Culture and Action', *Saturday Review*, 24 (9 Nov. 1867), 593.

Canning's 'Needy Knife-Grinder': 'The Friend of Humanity and the Knife-Grinder' by George Canning and John Hookham Frere in the *Anti-Jacobin*, 27 Nov. 1797. George Canning (1770–1827) founded the satirical *Anti-Jacobin* to combat the principles of the French Revolution. This article was a parody of Southey and his sympathy for the Revolution.

Zephaniah Diggs: an imaginary poacher, who, Arnold envisages, had lots of children by a second wife, none of whom would be sent to school. See *Friendship's Garland*, Super, v. 66 ff.

75 *a kind of image or shadow of sweetness*: an allusion to Plato's simile of the cave; see *Republic*, 514–21. The 'image' or 'shadow' of sweetness is illusory. See also pp. 78 (and note) and 99.

76 *The chivalry of the Barbarians*: this passage alludes to Carlyle, 'Shooting Niagara: And After?', *Critical and Miscellaneous Essays* (1899), v. 19. Cf. note to p. 61.

77 *'the cities it has built . . . has ever seen'*: see notes to pp. 44 and 49.

78 *Plato's subtle expression*: a reference to Plato's theory of forms (see *Republic*, 475–80), according to which the unchanging forms, which are the object of philosophical knowledge, are what is real, whereas the everyday world of appearance is changeable and susceptible only to belief or opinion. The 'things of itself' here correspond to the world of appearance, whereas what is needed is a focus on trying (through rational argument) to 'see as they are' the forms which represent the higher potentialities (cf. the distinction which Arnold makes between the ordinary self and the best self). There is a strong echo here of Plato's *Apology*, 36, where Socrates defends his pursuit of genuine knowledge against the attacks of the Sophists. An allusion to Socrates' defence of his philosophical and educational (rather than practical, political or material) preoccupations served to reinforce the critical position which Arnold was developing for himself. See also pp. 33, 71, 75, 99, 104, and 108.

79 *Mr Swinburne would add, the son of a Philistine*: 'Mr Arnold's New Poems', *Fortnightly Review*, NS 2 (Oct. 1867), 425. Algernon Charles Swinburne (1837–1909), poet and critic, said that 'A profane alien in my hearing once defined [Matthew Arnold] as "David, the son of Goliath" '. When rebuked, he had said that he could not understand how Matthew could have been the son of the head of the school which was the main producer of 'Philistine saplings'. Swinburne went on, 'Son of Goliath, or son of Jesse, this David or Samson or Jephthah of our day'.

80 *Of another kind of Philistine, the graver self likes trades' unions*: in the second edition Arnold substituted 'rattening' for 'trades' unions', which gave more negative force to his point.

82 *Martinus Scriblerus*: *The Memoirs of Martinus Scriblerus*, a satire directed against pedantry, which emerged from the Scriblerus Club founded in 1714 by Pope, Swift, Gay, and Arbuthnot. *The Memoirs* were published in the second volume of Pope's prose works (1741), although most of the satire was probably written by Arbuthnot. Pope was the first to use the

term 'bathos' in its modern sense, in a parody of Longinus' *On the Sublime*, in his *On Bathos*, in which he satirized his contemporary poets for their artificiality. See note to p. 27.

82 *Saturday Review*: this periodical was founded in 1855, and quickly established itself as the leading weekly. Its stance was robust and middle-of-the-road. In its critiques of both Matthew Arnold and John Ruskin gendered terminology was used to undercut their challenges to the language and dogmas of political economy.

British Banner: this was a populist Nonconformist weekly which closed in 1858.

Mr Hepworth Dixon: William Hepworth Dixon (1821–79), journalist and popular writer. In 1853 he became editor of the *Athenaeum* (until 1869, when he resigned). Amongst other books of travel, he wrote *New America*, 2 vols. (London, 1867), which went through eight editions in the first year and was translated into other languages, and *Spiritual Wives* (London, 1868), which caused him to be sued for indecency. These quotations come from *New America*, 168, 351, 358, and 353–4. In 'New America in its Religious Aspect' (*Fraser's Magazine*, 75 (1867), 640–56) a much more sympathetic assessment of *New America* was given. Picking up Hepworth Dixon's rhetorical question: 'Has Convocation ever given up a day to the Book of Mormon?', the reviewer commented (p. 648): 'if the dignitaries who are so fond of baiting the Bishop of Natal and the authors of *Essays and Reviews* really want to get at the truth or right meaning of inspiration and revelation, they must investigate what is popularly deemed false as well as what is conventionally deemed true— mark well the signs common to all religions that gain ground, true or false,—and so learn to avoid propping up their cause, however sound and orthodox, by arguments that cut both ways'.

83 *Judge Edmonds, Dr Hare, Elder Frederick, and Professor Bush*: Judge John Worth Edmonds (1816–74) was an influential early American spiritualist, who had to resign his position as judge of the Supreme Court of New York because of his views. Elder Frederick (Frederick W. Evans) was a leading member of the Shaker community at Mount Lebanon, New York (see *New America*, vol. ii, chs. 9–14; *Spiritual Wives*, vol. ii, ch. 21). Professor Bush was a Presbyterian minister who became a Swedenborgian; he was a professor of Hebrew and Oriental Literature and an Old Testament scholar (see *Spiritual Wives*, ii. 243).

Newman Weeks, Sarah Horton, Deborah Butler: Newman Weeks was president and Sarah Horton and Deborah Butler two of the vice-presidents of the 3rd National Convention of Spiritualism held at Pratt's Hall (*not* Rolt's Hall), Providence, Rhode Island (*New America*, vol. ii, ch. 15).

Elderess Polly, and Elderess Antoinette: Elderess Antoinette (Mary Antoinette Dolittle) was the co-head with Elder Frederick of one of the large Shaker houses in the community at Mount Lebanon. Elderess Polly was co-head of another (*New America*, vol. ii, chs. 9–14).

Shakerism: a communistic religious group which began as 'Shaking Quakers' in Bolton, Lancashire, in 1747; the original leaders, Jane and James Wardley, were succeeded by Ann Lee—'Mother Ann', who, as 'the female principle in Christ', was held to embody the Second Coming. She led a small group to America in 1774, and settled near Albany, New York. Their numbers swelled through the addition of other revivalist groups, and further communities were founded. The term 'Shaker' came from the shaking which was the effect of spiritual excitement at their meetings; this was later ritualized into formal dances.

84 *Joe Smiths and Deborah Butlers*: Joseph Smith (1805–44) was the founder (in 1830 in Manchester, New York) of the 'Church of Jesus Christ of Latter-Day Saints' (the Mormons). He claimed to have been given in a revelation *The Book of Mormon*; another revelation in 1843 sanctioned polygamy. Dixon focused on Mormonism in volume i of *New America*.

85 *'he that trusteth in his own heart,' says the Wise Man, 'is a fool'*: Proverbs 28: 26. There is a huge quantity of references to Proverbs in Arnold's *Note-Books*—the largest category of biblical entries.

   Bishop Wilson . . . 'The number of those who need to be awakened . . . those who need comfort': 'Maxims', *Works*, ed. Keble, v. 423.

   With Mr Tennyson, they celebrate 'the great broad-shouldered genial Englishman': *The Princess*, conclusion.

   when Sir Thomas Bateson describes: in the Commons debate on the Reform Bill, 4 June 1866.

   when Mr Lowe calls the Populace drunken and venal: in a speech in the Commons as part of the Reform Bill debate on 13 March 1866, Lowe characterized the working classes as drunken and venal by reference to the crowd which had attacked and injured him when he won the election at Kidderminster in 1857, angered because he had not provided the customary beer. A. P. Martin, *Life and Letters of . . . Robert Lowe, Viscount Sherbrooke*, 2 vols. (London, 1893), ii. 153–5, 173–4.

86 *excellence dwells among high and steep rocks*: Simonides of Chios.

   Qui est-ce qu'on trompe ici?: Who is one tricking here? (aside of Don Bazile in Beaumarchais's *Le Barbier de Séville* (1775), Act 3).

87 *Sir James Graham's useful Education Clauses*: Sir James Graham (1792–1861), brought up a devout Evangelical Anglican, was Sir Robert Peel's Home Secretary in the early 1840s. In the wake of Chartist disorder and social unrest in a period of economic depression, one scheme for reinforcing social control was to attach education clauses to a factory bill in 1843 which would have given children in textile factories three hours of education daily. However, the framework of the scheme was Anglican, and—not least because textile factories were predominantly in northern areas where Nonconformity was strong—there was fierce Nonconformist opposition. Amendments made to save the clauses alienated sectors of Anglican opinion, and the education proposals had to be dropped.

Arnold's tone in referring to 'a transport of blind zeal' was excessive. Thomas Milner Gibson, who is quoted (Hansard, 3rd ser., 70, col. 95: debate of 19 June 1843), in fact spoke judiciously and to the point. Graham had underestimated how controversial these clauses were going to be, and how much reasonable objection there would be amongst Nonconformists.

87 *Frederic Harrison . . . 'shriek of superstition'*: 'Our Venetian Constitution', *Fortnightly Review*, 7 (Mar. 1867), 271, 277.

In Prussia, the best schools are Crown patronage schools: *Schools and Universities on the Continent*, Super, iv. 197–8.

88 *Licensed Victuallers or the Commercial Travellers*: possibly an oblique reference to the opening by the Prince of Wales of a Warehousemen's and Clerks' School near Caterham on 18 June 1866 (*The Times*, 19 June, 14). Both the Licensed Victuallers' Society and the Commercial Travellers' Society had set up schools for children of their members. Arnold's choice of these two societies connected with drink and commercialism makes his point more vivid by association. Cf. 'Porro Unum est Necessarium' [1878], Super, viii. 348–69, at 368, where Arnold refers to 'schools for licensed victuallers, commercial travellers, Wesleyans, Quakers' (extending the association of prejudice), whereas the 'one thing needful' was a homogenous intelligent middle class brought up in good public schools and at the highest level.

Wilhelm von Humboldt: (1767–1835), philosopher, poet, naturalist, and politician; reformer of the Prussian educational system and founder of the University of Berlin.

Schleiermacher: Friedrich Daniel Ernst Schleiermacher (1768–1834), German Protestant theologian and philosopher. His emphasis on feeling as the basis of religion, independent of dogma, was attractive to Arnold, as it had been to his father. See also note to p. 104.

89 *Quietism*: see note to p. 91: 'the milder doctrine'.

90 *Atheism . . . preached in The Times*: 3 Jan. 1868, 7: leading article on an appeal from American Fenians to the English and Irish to establish a republic.

Mr Roebuck's celebrated definition of happiness: quoted by Arnold on p. 38, and in 'The Function of Criticism at the Present Time'.
The Times: 2 Dec. 1867, 9.

91 *the milder doctrine of our other philosophical teacher, the Daily News*: 30 Dec. 1867, 4.

92 *Providence*: this is not so much a divine providence as a belief in John Stuart Mill's 'infinite variety of experiments', coupled with an optimism that 'common reason', if left to its natural operation, could act as a check on eccentricity.

93 *a recent number of the Westminster Review*: [S. Amos], 'Dangers of Democracy', *Westminster Review* NS 33 (1868), 1–37.

95 *Monsieur Renan, on State action*: 'L'instruction supérieure en France', *Revue des deux mondes*, 51 (1 May 1864), repr. in *Questions contemporaines* (Paris, 1868), 73; cf. Arnold's *Note-Books*, 29 (entry for 1864).

CHAPTER IV

(Entitled 'Hebraism and Hellenism' from the second edition onwards.)

95 *Bishop Wilson:—'First, never go against the best light ... light be not darkness'*: See notes to pp. 9, 28, 71, and 102.

96 *'that we might be partakers of the divine nature'*: 2 Peter 1: 4. 'Whereby are given unto us exceeding great and precious promises: that by these ye might be partakers of the divine nature, having escaped the corruption that is in the world through lust.'

  Frederick Robertson: 'Notes of Advent Lectures no. 1: The Grecian' [preached 6 Dec. 1849], *Sermons Preached at Brighton*, 1st ser. (London, 1872), 162–73. This was the first of a series of Advent Lectures, focusing on what Christianity had superseded; the next two were on 'The Roman' and 'The Barbarian'. Robertson identified four characteristics of Greek life and religion, which had caused degeneration: 'Restlessness—Worldliness—The Worship of the Beautiful—The Worship of the Human'. Whereas in Greece religion ended in taste or mere intellectual refinement, in Rome a religion which started with an emphasis on duty and obedience to the law, degenerated into worship of the State. The Barbarian virtues (identified with reference to Paul's encounter with the Miletans) were those of sympathy and hospitality, which Christianity purged of selfishness, just as love replaced the worship of the marvellous. See W. F. Stevenson, 'Frederick William Robertson', *Contemporary Review*, 1 (1866), 220–49, on Robertson's passage away from evangelicalism, under the influence of Carlyle and German metaphysics. See also S. A. Brooke, *Life and Letters of Fredk. W. Robertson M.A.* (new edn., 1868).

  Heine: see notes to pp. 9 and 15.

97 *'He that keepeth the law, happy is he'*: Proverbs 29: 18. 'Where there is no vision, the people perish: but he that keepeth the law, happy is he.'

  'There is nothing sweeter than to take heed unto the commandments of the Lord': Psalms 112: 1.

  when they abhor that which is evil: Romans 12: 9.

  when they exercise themselves in the law of the Lord day and night: Psalms 1: 2.

  when they die daily: 1 Corinthians 15: 31.

  when they walk about the New Jerusalem with palms in their hands: Revelation 7: 9.

  C'est le bonheur des hommes ... quand ils pensent juste: men are happy when they think aright. Frederick the Great, quoted by Sainte-Beuve, and noted by Arnold in a diary entry for 20 January 1867 (see *Note-Books*, 48).

97 *spontaneity of consciousness . . . strictness of conscience*: on 16 April 1869 Arnold wrote to the lawyer William Erle to thank him for his compliments on *Culture and Anarchy*. He commented: 'I quite agree that the expression *strictness of conscience* does not quite go on four legs, and this has been on my mind continually ever since I used it; but I do not yet quite see my way to mending it. Many of the notions in these Essays are notions for which our time is so ripe that they lodge in people's minds even when they are controverting them, and will produce their effect sooner or later, when nobody will care to ask who uttered them' (*Letters*, iii. 331).

Self-conquest, self-devotion: this seems to respond to a review of 'Culture and its Enemies' in the *Aberdeen Free Press* (12 July 1867), which had referred to the lack of attention in that article to the need for self-conquest. Arnold thought this review the best critique of his article from the 'Puritan' point of view.

98 *Christianity, as St Paul truly says, 'establishes the law'*: Romans 3: 31.

prophet Zechariah: Zechariah 9: 13.

Solomon will praise knowing: Proverbs 16: 22. 'Understanding is a well-spring of life unto him that hath it: but the instruction of fools is folly.'

And in the New Testament, again, Christ is a 'light,' and 'truth makes us free': Luke 2: 32; John 8: 32.

Aristotle . . . 'In what concerns . . . little importance': Ethics II. iv. 3.

St James enjoins a man to be not a forgetful hearer, but a doer of the work: James 1: 22. Arnold wrote this text in his notebook for 1867 (*Note-Books*, 60).

Epictetus exhorts us to do what we have demonstrated to ourselves we ought to do: Encheiridion, 35: 52. This was a repeated theme in Arnold's notebooks.

99 *Plato, in words which are almost the words of the New Testament or the Imitation, calls life a learning to die*: Phaedo, 64A.

The understanding of Solomon: 1 Kings 3: 11–14; Proverbs 3: 13–17.

New Testament: Philippians 4: 7; John 8: 32; Galatians 5: 24; Romans 3: 31.

The moral virtues . . . are with Aristotle but the porch and access to the intellectual: Ethics X. viii.

That partaking of the divine life . . . Plato expressly denies to the man of practical virtue merely: Republic, end of book 5, 478–80; cf. *Phaedo*, 82D–83E. See also pp. 33, 70, 75, 78 (and note), 104, and 108.

the true Socrates of the Memorabilia: Xenophon, IV. viii. 6.

Carlyle about Socrates: the reference was in fact to Plato being at his ease in Zion (Tillotson, cited by Super, v. 437).

100 *Dr Pusey*: Edward Bouverie Pusey (1800–82), one of the original promoters of the Oxford Movement, was left as its leader in Oxford after Newman's conversion to the Catholic Church in 1845.

unhappy chained captive: Romans 8: 26, 7: 24; cf. Isaiah 52: 2.

101 *Zechariah*: 8: 23.

'my Saviour banished joy!' says George Herbert: (1593–1633), poet and Anglican clergyman. Izaak Walton's life of him (1670) emphasized his personal holiness and commitment to the Anglican Church; the second half of the biography was a celebration of the Book of Common Prayer. Herbert was greatly admired by Coleridge. This reference comes from 'The Size', the beginning of the fifth verse—'Thy Saviour sentenc'd joy'.

alma Venus: invoked by Lucretius (*c.*99–*c.*55 BC) to inspire his work *De Rerum Natura* (On the Nature of Things), a famous work of philosophical naturalism much discussed by Victorian naturalists. As Arnold hints here, the use of the figure of Venus to represent the creative power of nature, whilst clearly of a different order to the redemptive self-sacrifice of Christ, none the less qualified Lucretius's materialism.

'Let no man deceive you . . . children of disobedience': Ephesians 5: 6–8. 'Let no man deceive you with vain words . . . walk as children of light.'

102 *Jewish people . . . 'entrusted with the oracles of God'*: Acts 7: 38, a reference to Moses.

104 *the attitude of mind of Protestantism towards the Bible in no respect differs from the attitude of mind of Catholicism towards the Church*: a deliberately provocative claim to a predominantly Protestant readership, and one which is crucial to the establishment of the underlying principle which Arnold is setting out here.

genius and history of an Indo-European people: see *Letters*, iii. 207 (to his mother, Christmas Day 1867): 'I have been reading this year in connection with the New Testament a good deal of Aristotle and Plato: and this has brought Papa very much to my mind again. Bunsen used to say that our great business was to get rid of all that was purely semitic in Christianity, and to make it Indo-germanic; and Schleiermacher, that in the Christianity of us western nations there was really much more of Plato and Aristotle than of the wild Bedouins with Joshua and David—and on the whole, Papa worked in the direction of these ideas of Bunsen and Schleiermacher, and was, perhaps, the only Englishman of his day who did so. In fact he was the only deeply religious man who had the necessary culture for it.' Arnold seems to have taken this directly from Renan's 'De l'avenir religieuse des sociétés modernes', *Revue des deux mondes* (15 Oct. 1860), 761–97, at 766–7 (repr. in *Questions contemporaines*, 1868), copied in Arnold's general notebooks, *Note-Books*, 465.

CHAPTER V

(Entitled 'Porro unum est necessarium' (But one thing is needful)—Luke 10: 42—from the second edition onwards.)

107 *The book which contains this invaluable law they call the Word of God*: this point was central to Arnold's argument in this essay, and was to be developed further in 'St Paul and Protestantism'. See *Letters*, iii. 412 (10 May 1870 to T. H. Huxley): 'Protestant Dissenters imagine themselves in possession of an instrument called *the gospel* which enables them to regard de haut en bas poetry, philosophy, science and spiritual effort of all kind other than in the gospel'. Cf. below (p. 113), '*No man who knows nothing else, knows even his Bible*'.

109 *an acute, though somewhat rigid critic, Mr Sidgwick*: H. Sidgwick, 'The Prophet of Culture' (Appendix, p. 161). Henry Sidgwick (1838–1900) was a philosopher and educational reformer, like Arnold the son of a clergyman. He regarded as his true vocation 'thought exercised on central problems of human life', and his moral philosophy made a serious contribution to the development of a modified utilitarianism. He wrestled with the challenges of faith, and reflected deeply on the relationship of religious and moral feeling.

the late Mr Buckle: see note to p. 51.

110 *The Puritan's great danger is that he imagines himself in possession of a rule telling him the unum necessarium, or one thing needful*: cf. note to p. 16.

111 *St Paul, in the very Epistle of which we are speaking*: Romans 11: 34.

112 *not in the connected and fluid way . . . but in an isolated, fixed, mechanical way*: Arnold's critical principle, which is here counterposed to scholastic and Calvinist readings of St Paul (lumped under the label 'Puritan'), from which Arnold wanted to rescue him. In this section is the germ of what became *St Paul and Protestantism*.

113 *one of the noblest collects of the Prayer-Book*: the collect for Easter evening in the Anglican Book of Common Prayer: 'Grant, O Lord, that as we are baptized into the death of thy blessed Son our Saviour Jesus Christ, so by continual mortifying our corrupt affections we may be buried with him; and that through the grave, and gate of death, we may pass to our joyful resurrection; for his merits, who died, and was buried, and rose again for us, thy Son Jesus Christ our Lord.'

'No man, who knows nothing else, knows even his Bible': cf. *St Paul and Protestantism*, Super, vi, 7 ff.; and *Literature and Dogma*, ibid. 152: 'A man of no range in his reading, must almost inevitably misunderstand the Bible'.

114 *Faraday*: Michael Faraday (1791–1867), the famous natural philosopher, who was a Sandemanian. The Sandemanians (also known as Glasites) were followers of John Glas (1695–1773) and Robert Sandeman (1718–71), who were opposed to the principle of a State Church, and formed

independent communities led by non-ordained elders, members of which pledged themselves to live in Christian brotherhood on strict scriptural principles. Faraday, who was an elder, saw his scientific activity as uncovering the theistic laws of the universe. In 1832, at the second meeting of the British Association for the Advancement of Science in Oxford, the University conferred the DCL on Faraday, David Brewster, John Dalton, and Robert Brown; since they were all dissenters, there were protests from members of the group who were to form the Oxford Movement, including Newman.

Archimedes: (287–212 BC), mathematician and inventor of engines of war, born in Syracuse, Sicily.

115 *the desire which, as Plato says, 'for ever through all the universe tends towards that which is lovely'*: *Symposium*, 197B.

'Not slothful in business,' or 'Whatsoever thy hand findeth to do, do it with all thy might': Romans 12: 11; Ecclesiastes 9: 10.

Mr Smith: on 29 February 1868 Frederick G. Smith, secretary to the London Board of the Scottish Union Fire and Life Insurance Company, shot himself in his office. *The Times*, 4 Mar., 10. Super, v. 439.

117 *Christianity . . . transformed and renewed Hebraism*: here Arnold uses Hebraism in the sense of Judaism.

St Paul used the contradiction between the Jew's profession and practice: Romans 2: 21–2.

we hear so much said of the growth of commercial immorality in our serious middle-class: the 1860s had seen a proliferation of high-profile cases of bankruptcy and/or fraud at a time of intense competitive pressure, so there had been extensive press and periodical debate. However the decade also saw the continued growth of serious engagement with the moral context of commerce on the part of both Anglicans and Nonconformists, which Arnold does not notice.

CHAPTER VI

(Entitled 'Our Liberal Practitioners' from the second edition onwards.)

121 *But an unpretending writer*: the rhetorical strategy noted before reaches its apogee in Arnold's starting the whole article with a 'But'. The paragraph was originally in the middle of the first part of the final section of 'Anarchy and Authority', *Cornhill Magazine*, 18 (1868), 91–107, at p. 97.

122 *The State is of the religion of all its citizens, without the fanaticism of any of them*: see also 'Popular Education of France' (1861), Super, ii, 198.

the national mind, as it is called, is grown averse to endowments for religion: William Edward Baxter (1825–90), Liberal MP, in a speech to his Montrose constituents on 3 October 1867, argued that the separation of Church and State in every case was merely a matter of time. He

contended that the examples of the United States and the British colonies, the Free Church of Scotland, the Dissenters, 'and of the church of
England itself' were gradually convincing politicians and churchmen that
the future lay with free churches supported by voluntary contributions.
The immediate proposal for the disestablishment of the Irish Church
should be supported, and its revenues appropriated to secular purposes.
He strongly opposed the endowment of the Roman Catholic Church (an
earlier Liberal proposal). *Daily News*, 5 Oct. 1867, 3; cited by Super, v.
440. Charles Buxton (1823–71) was Liberal MP from 1857 to his death.

122 *'My kingdom is not of this world'*: John 18: 36.

123 *Mr Spurgeon, in his eloquent and memorable letter*: Spurgeon, laid up by
gout, and unable to attend a huge meeting in the Metropolitan Tabernacle
addressed by John Bright in support of the Liberal proposals for the
disestablishment of the Irish Church, wrote a letter, in which he said:
'Our Lord's Kingdom is not of this world. This truth is the corner-stone
of our dissent . . . The one point about which the Dissenters of England
have any fear is . . . lest any share of the Church property should be
given to the Papists.' *The Times*, 23 Apr. 1868, 5; Super, v. 441. Cf. 'A
Recantation and an Apology', *Friendship's Garland*, Super, v. 323–4.

124 *No Popery!*: popular anti-Catholicism, which flourished particularly in
areas of Irish immigration.

Liberation Society: a society dedicated to the removal of the privileges of
the Established Church, and to disestablishment. It was founded in 1853
out of the previous Anti-State-Church Society (established 1844).

125 *Miss Cobbe, and the British College of Health in the New Road*: cf. 'The
Function of Criticism at the Present Time', Super, iii. 278–80. Frances
Power Cobbe (1822–1904) was a journalist, feminist campaigner, and
anti-vivisectionist; brought up in a devoutly Evangelical family, she
became a deist.

as Joubert says again: *Pensées*, ed. P. de Raynal (7th edn., Paris, 1877), 2,
29, 28, 24. For Joubert, see note to p. 4.

126 *that Nonconformity does not at all differ from the Established Church by
having worthier or more philosophical ideas about God*: [H. Allon], 'Mr
Matthew Arnold and Puritanism', *British Quarterly Review*, 52 (1870),
170–99, at 194–7, challenged Arnold by drawing attention to the 'educational power of freely-expressed thought and life'—i.e. in Independent
chapels.

127 *effeminate horror*: Arnold again picks up on this type of critique of his
alleged detachment from practical action. Cf. p. 208 on the sort of critical
language used by the *Saturday Review*.

128 *Real Estate Intestacy Bill*: John Bright spoke in the debate on the second reading of this bill on 6 June 1866. The bill, which was defeated,
proposed a change in the law whereby fixed property passed to the eldest
son, in order that widows and younger children could benefit. Arnold

thought that it was a feeble proposal, and advocated a more thorough-going reform of the laws of inheritance and entail. Cf. *Friendship's Garland*, Super, v. 45; 'Equality' [1878], *Mixed Essays*, Super, viii. 277–305, esp. 280–2. His father had also been keen to promote a reform of the system of entail.

130 *as Bishop Wilson excellently says, 'Riches are almost always abused without a very extraordinary grace'*: 'Maxims', *Works*, ed. Keble, v. 465.

Pouvoir sans savoir est fort dangereux: power without knowledge is extremely dangerous.

what Solomon meant when he said: 'As he who putteth a stone in a sling, so is he that giveth honour to a fool': Proverbs 26: 8.

132 *Mr Lowe when he called, or was supposed to call, the working-class drunken and venal*: see note to p. 85.

the speech which Mr Chambers then made in support of his bill: on 2 May 1866, Thomas Chambers, MP for Marylebone, moved the second reading of the bill to allow a man to marry his deceased wife's sister. The bill was defeated.

Mr Hepworth Dixon . . . the Colenso of love and marriage: Colenso, bishop of Natal, had been ridiculed by Arnold for his pedantic approach to the Bible in 'The Bishop and the Philosopher', Super, iii. 40–55. Colenso had also argued (on missionary grounds) that polygamy should not be seen as incompatible with Christian morality. Hepworth Dixon's earlier book on America included discussion of the Mormons; *Spiritual Wives* (1868) wrote of the 'slackening and unwinding of the old-fashioned nuptial ties . . . due to a sudden quickening of the Gothic blood'. Super, v. 442. The newspaper to which Arnold refers was the *Daily Telegraph*, 30 Jan. 1868, 7.

133 *crowned Philistine, Henry the Eighth*: here Arnold by synecdoche associates the English Reformation (initiated by Henry VIII's desire for a divorce—the dissolution of the marriage tie) with the triumph of fervent Protestantism, the rise of capitalism, and the development of a narrowly commercially minded middle class.

we no more allow absolute validity . . . than we allow it to the opposite maxim: in Arnold's notebooks for 1867 and 1868 respectively, Arnold copied out the following passages from Bishop Wilson: 'God's service is not only safer but easier than that liberty we are naturally fond of. It makes the practice of virtue pleasant; frees us from the violence of corruption, and from being ruined by false pleasures'; 'he that will not obey the will of God must obey his own passions, which are the worst tyrants; he must obey the world, and the humours of others; all else is mere slavery, let the world call it what they please' (*Note-Books*, 53 and 69; cf. Wilson, 'Sacra Privata', *Works*, ed. Keble, v. 150, and 'Maxims', ibid. 402).

For we know that the only perfect freedom is, as our religion says, a service: second collect for peace in the Order for Morning Prayer, Book of Common Prayer.

134 *Bishop Wilson gives an admirable lesson to rigid Hebraisers*: 'Maxims', *Works*, ed. Keble, v. 459–60.

135 *the feminine nature, the feminine ideal*: cf. above, pp. 104–5, on Indo-Germanic characteristics.

whose wisest king had seven hundred wives and three hundred concubines: 1 Kings 11: 3.

136 *the cities it has built . . . the manufactures it has produced*: see notes to pp. 44 and 49.

137 *outrunning the constable*: i.e. spending more than one's income.

'Art is long,' says The Times, 'and life is short': 7 July 1868, 9. Compare: 'vita, si scias uti, longa est' (Seneca, quoted by Bishop Wilson, 'Sacra Privata', *Works*, ed. Keble, v. 264; which Arnold copied into his notebook in 1866: *Note-Books*, 53). See also the quotation from Goethe in the note to p. 153.

138 *Bastiat's favourite image*: in his notebook for 1868 Arnold copied part of a letter from the French political economist Bastiat to Richard Cobden: ' "Le capital est le signe caractéristique et la mesure du progrès. Il en est le véhicule nécessaire et unique; sa mission spéciale est de servir de transition de la valeur à la gratuité. Par consequent, au lieu de peser [the word was in fact 'presser'] sur le prix naturel, son role constant est de l'abaisser sans cesse." Bastiat said of the above: "Cette phrase renferme et résume le plus fécond des phénomènes économiques" ' (letter to Cobden, 9 Sept. 1850, quoting from an *Essai sur le capital* which had recently been sent to him. Bastiat took this to be encouraging evidence that he had not wasted his life because his theories had been taken up by others: *Œuvres complètes*, 6 vols. (Paris, 1855), i. 189). ('Capital is the characteristic sign and measure of progress. It is the sole necessary vehicle of progress, achieving the transition from value to free gift. As a result, instead of increasing the natural price, it constantly reduces it.' Bastiat said of the above, 'This phrase reinforces and summarizes the most productive of economic phenomena.') Frédéric Bastiat (1801–50) was a passionate promoter of the benefits of the free market economy and limited government.

139 *The East End*: in *The Times*, 11 Dec. 1867, 8 there was a discussion of the likelihood of greater than usual charitable appeals for the East End, to which, in the view of *The Times*, it would be bad to respond, because it would simply encourage labour to stay where there was no demand. The phrases given by Arnold evidently refer to this, but they are not direct quotations.

Mr Robert Buchanan: R. Buchanan, *David Gray and Other Essays, Chiefly on Poetry* (London, 1868), ii. 198–9. The line of poetry which follows served as a epigraph to the book. Buchanan (1841–1901) was a Scottish poet, novelist, journalist, and self-promoter, described by Arnold in 1868 as a 'clever but raw and temperate Scottish youth' who 'has been running rather a tilt against me and others' (*Letters*, iii. 233: 22 Feb. 1868).

Buchanan had referred to Arnold as a 'thin egotist, faintly inflated with intellectuality' (*Spectator*, 15 Feb. 1868, 197–8; see *Letters*, iii. 234). The *Spectator* for 8 February had already suggested that Arnold showed an intellectual's scorn for the unintellectual, and Super (v. 444–5) interprets this whole passage about the East End as an attempt to meet this charge.

141 *we are indeed, as our religion says, members of one body*: 1 Corinthians 12: 12–27.

'The multitude of the wise is the welfare of the world': Wisdom 6: 15. Cf. *Note-Books*, 57 (entry for 1867).

Bishop Wilson . . . striking words . . . that of others: 'Maxims', *Works*, ed. Keble, v. 481, 452. See *Note-Books*, 64 and 517 (entries for 12 Oct. 1867 and 'General' Notebook).

Imitation . . . the harder that way is to find: iii. 18.

142 *And though Hebraism . . . to prevent their accumulating still more*: this long sentence was omitted in the second and subsequent editions, which had the effect of making the powerlessness of Hebraism starker. The sentence as it stands here reaffirms the identity of the ultimate aim of both Hebraism and Hellenism (perfection), and underlines the positive connotations of Hebraism by reference to Bishop Wilson and the *Imitation of Christ*.

Be fruitful and multiply: Genesis 1: 28.

God's word in the Psalms: 127: 3–5.

The poor shall never cease out of the land: Genesis 8: 17; Deuteronomy 15: 11.

a good man: it has been suggested (Super, v. 446) that the reference is to Revd William Tyler (1812–90), Congregational minister in Spitalfields, to whom Arnold also referred in his sonnet 'East London', first published in 1867.

144 *psalm-verse*: see note to p. 142.

146 *Archdeacon Denison*: George Anthony Denison (1805–96), archdeacon of Taunton from 1851, was throughout his life a pugnacious defender of High Church orthodoxy. From 1839 to 1870 he strongly supported education under the auspices of the Anglican Church, and was opposed to the movement which was to lead to Forster's Education Act of 1870.

ritualism: the controversial movement to revive High Church ritual in the Church of England, which was the subject of investigation by the Royal Commission on Ritual set up in 1867. Four reports were produced between 1867 and 1870, which showed great diversity of opinion. In 1874 the Public Worship Regulation Act was passed with the intention of suppressing ritualism, but the Act soon became a dead letter.

148 *Sir Henry Hoare*: elected MP for Chelsea in 1868.

CONCLUSION

149 *without order there can be no society, and without society there can be no*
    human perfection: see also 'Equality' [1879], Super, viii. 277–305, at 286,
    where Arnold quoted Burke (in his *Reflections on the French Revolution*)
    defining civilization as the making of progress in civil society.

    'As for rioting, the old Roman way of dealing with that is always the right one
    ... Tarpeian Rock!': on 25 July 1868 Arnold wrote to his mother that he
    had finished the *Cornhill* series. 'In the passage quoted from Papa,
    Stanley's impression is that Papa's words were "Crucify the slave" instead
    of "Flog the rank & file"—but as the latter expression is the milder, and
    I have certainly got it in my memory, as what he said, I have retained
    it' (*Letters*, iii. 273). The passage was not mild enough, and was cut from
    the second and subsequent editions.

150 *the lovers of culture may prize and employ fire and strength*: cf. Sidgwick,
    'The Prophet of Culture' (Appendix, pp. 162 ff.).

151 *Aristotle says*: *Ethics* x. ix. 3–5.

152 *abolition of church-rates*: changed to 'abolition of establishments' in the
    second edition, by which time the abolition of Church rates was no
    longer a topical issue. Fewer Nonconformists, however, were opposed to
    the very existence of the Established Church in England than had been
    opposed to what had been seen as inequities in the way in which it
    operated (such as the continuance of Church rates). There were ongoing
    demands for the disestablishment of the Church in Wales (eventually
    disestablished by an Act of 1914).

153 *Mr Sidgwick says that social usefulness really means 'losing oneself ...*
    details': Sidgwick, 'The Prophet of Culture' (Appendix, p. 171).

    Goethe's maxim 'to act is easy, to think is hard': 'Die Kunst ist lang, das
    Leben kurz, das Urteil schwierig, die Gelegenheit flüchtig. Handeln ist
    leicht, Denken schwer; nach dem Gedanken handeln, unbequem. Aller
    Anfang ist heiter, die Schwelle ist der Platz der Erwartung.' Johann
    Wolfgang von Goethe, *Wilhelm Meisters Lehrjahre*, Siebentes Buch,
    Neuntes Kapitel [so-called Lehrbrief], in: Goethe, *Werke*, Hamburger
    edn. in 14 vols., vii. *Romane und Novellen II* (Munich, 1988), 496 (Art is
    long, life short; judgement is hard, opportunity transient. Action is easy,
    thought difficult, and to act in accordance with thought is irksome. Every
    beginning is glad; the threshold is the place of anticipation); cf. 'The
    Function of Criticism at the Present Time', Super, iii. 276.

    Mr Samuel Morley: (1809–86), Congregationalist businessman (and
    paternalistic employer), politician, and philanthropist. He attended
    King's Weigh House Chapel, whose minister was Thomas Binney. He
    contributed to the Home Missionary Society and to the building of
    eleven Congregational Training Colleges. He acquired a major holding in
    the *Daily News*, and reduced its price to 1*d*. in 1868 so that it could be

more influential. From 1868 to 1885 he was MP for Bristol. He started out as a fierce opponent of state involvement in education in the 1840s and 1850s, but later supported the 1870 Act, and served on the London School Board. He also resigned his role on the executive committee of the Liberation Society in 1868, and from then on worked for pan-evangelical Nonconformist/Anglican campaigns against popery and atheism.

154 *Thyesteän banquet*: a grotesque occasion (Thyestes ate his own son at a feast prepared out of revenge by his brother Atreus). Cf. 'Friendship's Garland', Super, vol. v, p. xiv.

155 *Pericles: Symposium*, 215–16.

Mr Disraeli educates: in a speech at Edinburgh on 29 October 1867 Disraeli said: 'I had to prepare the mind of the country and to educate— if it not be too arrogant to use such a phrase—to educate our party . . . on this question of Reform'. *The Times*, 30 Oct. 1867, 5.

APPENDIX

161 *Hegel*: Georg Wilhelm Friedrich Hegel (1770–1831), German idealist philosopher.

165 *Dr Newman*: John Henry Newman (1801–90), one of the founders of the Oxford Movement; he converted to Catholicism in 1845, and his *Apologia pro vita sua* was published in 1864.

167 *Owen Meredith*: pseudonym of Edward Robert Bulwer-Lytton, later 1st Earl of Lytton (1831–91), poet, diplomat and from 1876 to 1880 viceroy of India.

168 *Mr Garrison*: William Lloyd Garrison (1805–79), American anti-slavery activist, who in 1831 founded *The Liberator*, an influential newspaper dedicated to the cause.

Mr Frith's: William Powell Frith (1819–1909), painter of genre and modern life scenes, including *Derby Day* and *The Railway Station*.

Pietro Perugino: (1446–1524), Renaissance painter.

Macaulay: Thomas Babington Macaulay (1800–59), historian, essayist, and Whig politician. The quotation which follows is from his essay on Machiavelli (1827), *Critical and Historical Essays*, 3 vols. (8th edn., London, 1854), i. 62–112, at p. 73.

169 *our greatest living poet*: Alfred Tennyson (1809–92), 1st Baron Tennyson. The quotation is from *Locksley Hall*, lines 122–3.

Victor Hugo: (1802–85), French writer, author of *Les Misérables* and *Notre-Dame de Paris*.

170 *Agassiz*: Jean Louis Rodolphe Agassiz (1807–73), Swiss/American zoologist, palaeontologist, geologist, and glaciologist.

171 *Paley*: William Paley (1743–1805), philosopher and natural theologian.

ANTHONY TROLLOPE

The American Senator

An Autobiography

Barchester Towers

Can You Forgive Her?

The Claverings

Cousin Henry

The Duke's Children

The Eustace Diamonds

Framley Parsonage

He Knew He Was Right

Lady Anna

Orley Farm

Phineas Finn

Phineas Redux

The Prime Minister

Rachel Ray

The Small House at Allington

The Warden

The Way We Live Now

Six French Poets of the Nineteenth
Century

HONORÉ DE BALZAC   Cousin Bette
Eugénie Grandet
Père Goriot

CHARLES BAUDELAIRE   The Flowers of Evil
The Prose Poems and Fanfarlo

BENJAMIN CONSTANT   Adolphe

DENIS DIDEROT   Jacques the Fatalist
The Nun

ALEXANDRE DUMAS (PÈRE)   The Black Tulip
The Count of Monte Cristo
Louise de la Vallière
The Man in the Iron Mask
La Reine Margot
The Three Musketeers
Twenty Years After
The Vicomte de Bragelonne

ALEXANDRE DUMAS (FILS)   La Dame aux Camélias

GUSTAVE FLAUBERT   Madame Bovary
A Sentimental Education
Three Tales

VICTOR HUGO   The Essential Victor Hugo
Notre-Dame de Paris

J.-K. HUYSMANS   Against Nature

PIERRE CHODERLOS   Les Liaisons dangereuses
DE LACLOS

MME DE LAFAYETTE   The Princesse de Clèves

GUILLAUME DU LORRIS   The Romance of the Rose
and JEAN DE MEUN

A SELECTION OF **OXFORD WORLD'S CLASSICS**

The Oxford World's Classics Website

www.oup.com/uk/worldsclassics

- Information about new titles
- Explore the full range of Oxford World's Classics
- Links to other literary sites and the main OUP webpage
- Imaginative competitions, with bookish prizes
- Articles by editors
- Extracts from Introductions
- Special information for teachers and lecturers

www.oup.com/uk/worldsclassics

American Literature

Authors in Context

British and Irish Literature

Children's Literature

Classics and Ancient Literature

Colonial Literature

Eastern Literature

European Literature

History

Medieval Literature

Oxford English Drama

Poetry

Philosophy

Politics

Religion

The Oxford Shakespeare

A complete list of Oxford World's Classics, including Authors in Context, Oxford English Drama, and the Oxford Shakespeare, is available in the UK from the Marketing Services Department, Oxford University Press, Great Clarendon Street, Oxford OX2 6DP, or visit the website at www.oup.com/uk/worldsclassics.

In the USA, visit www.oup.com/us/owc for a complete title list.

Oxford World's Classics are available from all good bookshops. In case of difficulty, customers in the UK should contact Oxford University Press Bookshop, 116 High Street, Oxford OX1 4BR.